Oracle SQL and Introductory PL/SQL

Oracle SQL and Introductory PL/SQL

Linda L. Preece

Southern Illinois University Carbondale

Boston   Burr Ridge, IL   Dubuque, IA   Madison, WI   New York   San Francisco   St. Louis
Bangkok   Bogotá   Caracas   Kuala Lumpur   Lisbon   London   Madrid   Mexico City
Milan   Montreal   New Delhi   Santiago   Seoul   Singapore   Sydney   Taipei   Toronto

The McGraw·Hill Companies

McGraw Hill **Irwin**

ORACLE SQL AND INTRODUCTORY PL/SQL

Published by McGraw-Hill/Irwin, a business unit of The McGraw-Hill Companies, Inc.,
1221 Avenue of the Americas, New York, NY, 10020. Copyright © 2004 by The
McGraw-Hill Companies, Inc. All rights reserved. No part of this publication may be
reproduced or distributed in any form or by any means, or stored in a database or retrieval
system, without the prior written consent of The McGraw-Hill Companies, Inc.,
including, but not limited to, in any network or other electronic storage or transmission,
or broadcast for distance learning.

Some ancillaries, including electronic and print components, may not be available to
customers outside the United States.

This book is printed on acid-free paper.

1 2 3 4 5 6 7 8 9 0 QPD/QPD 0 9 8 7 6 5 4 3

ISBN   0-07-286046-4

Publisher: *Brent Gordon*
Senior sponsoring editor: *Paul Ducham*
Developmental editor: *Kelly L. Delso*
Marketing manager: *Greta Kleinert*
Media producer: *Greg Bates*
Project manager: *Natalie J. Ruffatto*
Production supervisor: *Debra R. Sylvester*
Designer: *Adam Rooke*
Supplement producer: *Matthew Perry*
Senior digital content specialist: *Brian Nacik*
Cover design: *Adam Rooke*
Typeface: *10/12 Times New Roman*
Compositor: *Interactive Composition Corporation*
Printer: *Quebecor World Dubuque Inc.*

Library of Congress Cataloging-in-Publication Data

Preece, Linda L.
      Oracle SQL and introductory PL/SQL / Linda L. Preece.—1st ed.
         p.   cm.
      ISBN 0-07-286046-4 (alk. paper)
       1. SQL (Computer program language) 2. PL/SQL (Computer program language) 3.
Oracle (Computer file) I. Title.
QA76.73.S67P75 2004
005.13'3—dc21
                                                                                              2003051040

www.mhhe.com

Dedication

To my parents, John and Charlotte Brune, for inspiring a passion for learning within me. To my husband, John, for his unconditional love and understanding. To my daughter, Jessica, for providing me with regular reminders that life is about far more than just work. With love, I dedicate this book to all of you.

Brief Contents

Contents

Preface

Intended Audience

This book provides basic coverage of Oracle's SQL and an introduction to Oracle's PL/SQL. It is intended for use in a second or third database course. Students are expected to be familiar with the fundamentals of database design and general usage prior to the beginning of the course.

The Method

The focus of the book is on the most commonly used SQL statements. The format is similar to that used for teaching math in that for each new statement, a concept is explained, general syntax is presented, and examples are solved. By this point in their college careers, there is usually no need for students to type examples verbatim out of a book, so that is not the intent here. Instead, students should read each chapter and then practice on their own by writing solutions to the exercises at the end of the chapter. Finally (and most importantly), computer work should be completed as assigned by the instructor.

Key Features

Overview of Example Database Creation

Two small databases are used in the examples. One is for a fictitious medical clinic, and the other is for a fictitious movie rental business. Specific entity-relationship (E-R) diagrams, table structures, and table contents are listed later in this preface and again in Appendix B.

The SQL* Plus tool for Oracle 9i was used for all examples. SQL* Plus is a command-line tool used to interact with the Oracle server. The user types a command at the prompt (there is no GUI) and presses Enter. Then the command is executed by the server, and the results are returned to the user's screen.

Typed commands may be saved to files with SQL extensions (called script files) for modification or for later use. A text editor (such as Notepad) is used to create or modify these scripts.

The SQL* Plus tool was also used for the initial creation of the tables, and an overview of that process is included here.

First, the user ID *lpreece* was created by the author's departmental database administrator, allowing the author to access the department's Oracle 9i server. The SQL* Plus tool was then used to connect to the server with that user ID. Tables were created by typing CREATE TABLE commands at the SQL* Plus prompt. Data values were placed in the tables by using INSERT commands. All additions were made permanent by using the COMMIT command. Specific script files for creating and filling the tables used in the example databases are included at the book's website.

The Example Databases

The first database represents a small medical clinic where each patient has one doctor, and each doctor may see many patients. Due to the large number of attributes associated with the patient entity, the original entity has been divided into two tables: PATIENT, which includes data needed for making appointments, and BILLING, which includes data needed for customer billing. All doctor-related information is maintained in one table, DOCTOR. The specific E-R diagram and table contents are shown here.

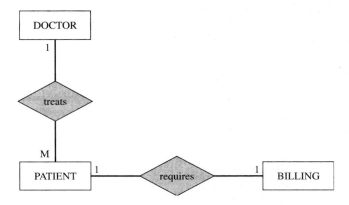

Note: A system date of July 1, 2003, was used for testing each example, and therefore, all data stored in the tables revolves around that particular date.

The DOCTOR Table

DOC_ID	DOC_NAME	DATEHIRED	SALPERMON	AREA	SUPERVISOR_ID	CHGPERAPPT	ANNUAL_BONUS
432	Harrison	05-DEC-94	12000	Pediatrics	100	75	4500
509	Vester	09-JAN-02	8100	Pediatrics	432	40	
389	Lewis	21-JAN-96	10000	Pediatrics	432	40	2250
504	Cotner	16-JUN-98	11500	Neurology	289	85	7500
235	Smith	22-JUN-98	4550	Family Practice	100	25	2250
356	James	01-AUG-98	7950	Neurology	289	80	6500
558	James	02-MAY-95	9800	Orthopedics	876	85	7700
876	Robertson	02-MAR-95	10500	Orthopedics	100	90	8900
889	Thompson	18-MAR-97	6500	Rehab	100	65	3200
239	Pronger	18-DEC-99	3500	Rehab	889	40	
289	Borque	30-JUN-89	16500	Neurology	100	95	6500
100	Stevenson	30-JUN-79	23500	Director			

The PATIENT Table

PT_ID	PT_LNAME	PT_FNAME	PTDOB	DOC_ID	NEXTAPPTD	LASTAPPTD
168	James	Paul	14-MAR-97	432	01-JUL-03	01-JUN-03
331	Anderson	Brian	31-MAR-48	235	01-JUL-03	01-JUN-03
313	James	Scott	26-MAR-33	235	20-JUL-03	20-JUN-03
816	Smith	Jason	12-DEC-99	509	15-NOV-03	15-MAY-03
314	Porter	Susan	14-NOV-67	235	01-OCT-03	01-MAR-03
315	Saillez	Debbie	09-SEP-55	235	01-JUL-03	01-JUN-03
719	Rogers	Anthony	01-JAN-42	504	01-NOV-03	01-JAN-03
264	Walters	Stephanie	26-JAN-45	504	12-DEC-03	12-DEC-02
267	Westra	Lynn	12-JUL-57	235	02-FEB-04	02-FEB-03
103	Poole	Jennifer	13-MAY-02	389	01-DEC-03	01-JUN-03
108	Baily	Ryan	25-DEC-77	235	06-JUN-05	06-JUN-03
943	Crow	Lewis	10-NOV-49	235	01-JUL-05	01-MAR-02
847	Cochran	John	28-MAR-48	356	02-DEC-05	01-JAN-02
163	Roach	Becky	08-SEP-75	235	01-DEC-05	01-JAN-02
504	Jackson	John	08-NOV-43	235	21-JUL-03	10-NOV-02

```
809 Kowalczyk      Paul        12-NOV-51     558 29-JUL-03 19-JUN-03
703 Davis          Linda       17-JUL-02     509 21-JUL-03 22-MAY-03
307 Jones          J.C.        17-JUL-02     509 21-JUL-03 22-MAY-03
439 Wright         Chasity     23-APR-73     235
696 Vanderchuck    Keith       08-AUG-68     504           15-JUN-03
966 Mcginnis       Allen       03-MAY-59     504           15-JUN-03
669 Sakic          Joe         16-SEP-76     504           15-JUN-03
```

The BILLING Table

PT_ID	BALANCE	DUEDATE	PHONE	ADDR	CITY	ST	ZIP	PT_INS
168	15650	21-AUG-03	833-9569	128 W. Apple #4	Jonesboro	IL	62952	SIH
331	300	09-SEP-03	833-5587	3434 Mulberry St.	Anna	IL	62906	BCBS
313	0	01-JAN-04	893-9987	334 Tailgate Ln	COBDEN	IL	62920	Military
816	0	01-JAN-04	833-6654	8814 W. Apple	JONESBORO	IL	62952	SIH
314	100	31-MAR-03	457-6658	445 Oak St.	Carbondale	IL	62901	BCBS
264	35000	11-JAN-03	942-8065	8898 Bighill Drive	HERRIN	IL	62948	MediSupplA
103	4500	01-JUL-03	833-5547	298 Murphy School Rd	Anna	IL	62906	HealthCare
108	0	01-JAN-05	833-5542	334 Pansie Hill Rd.	JONESBORO	IL	62952	HealthCare
943	0	01-JAN-07	529-9963	456 E. Grand #14	Carbondale	IL	62901	Military
847	98000	31-JAN-02	549-8854	6543 W. Parkview Ln.	Carbondale	IL	62901	BCBS
504	0	01-JAN-03	549-6139	6657 N. Allen	Carbondale	IL	62901	QualityCare
809	450	19-JUL-03	687-8852	3345 Hwy 127 N.	Murphysboro	IL	62966	QualityCare
703	225	31-AUG-03	529-8332	909 N. Brown St.	Carbondale	IL	62901	HealthCare
696	79850	15-JUL-03	549-7231	5546 W. James	Carbondale	IL	62901	BCBS
966	98700	15-JUL-03	833-5375	9009 Taylor Ave.	Anna	IL	62906	BCBS
267	0	01-JAN-05	942-3321	6755 US Route 148	HERRIN	IL	62948	QualityCare
307	450	31-AUG-03	457-6967	234 N. Allen	Carbondale	IL	62901	HealthCare
719	0	01-JAN-04	549-7848	867 Henderson St.	Carbondale	IL	62901	HealthCare
439	500	31-AUG-03	833-5541	4456 N. Springer	Anna	IL	62906	QualityCare
315	1500	14-SEP-03	833-6272	404 Williford Rd.	JONESBORO	IL	62952	HealthCare
163	0	01-JAN-04	833-2133	129 Fountain St.	Anna	IL	62906	HealthCare
669	128450	15-JUL-03	833-6654	353 Tin Bender Rd.	Jonesboro	IL	62952	BCBS

The second database could be used for a movie rental business, where each movie may be rented by many customers, and each customer may rent many movies. Movie data is stored in the MOVIE table, and customer data is stored in the CUSTOMER table. The RENTAL table is used as a bridge (also called bridging table, linking table, or intersection table) between the movie and customer entities.

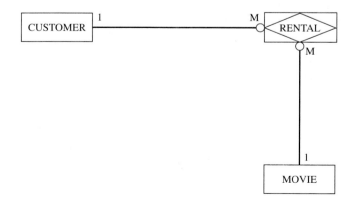

The CUSTOMER Table

C_ID	PHONE	LNAME	FNAME	CURR_BAL	DUEDATE
388	549-6730	Woolard	Jessica		
402	529-8420	St. James	Ellen	4.99	03-JUL-03
673	549-8400	Akers	Janet	9.97	23-JUN-03
579	549-1234	Poston	Blaine		
799	549-6711	Ackers	John	1.99	01-JUL-03
767	453-8228	Ralston	Cheri	14.9	30-JUN-03
133	453-2271	Akers	Leita	20.18	02-JUL-03
239	549-1235	Macke	Greg		
400	549-8440	Salyers	Loretta	5	06-JUL-03
701	549-8840	Williams	Tisha	20	28-JUN-03

The MOVIE Table

M_ID	FEE	TITLE	CATEGORY
204	1.99	City of Angels	Drama
216	2.99	Ocean's Eleven	Action
233	2.99	Gone in 60 Seconds	Action
236	.99	Monsters, Inc.	Kids
237	.99	E.T.	Kids
249	1.99	U-571	Action
254	2.99	Road to Perdition	Drama
255	2.99	Amelie	Foreign
278	1.99	Monster's Ball	Drama
287	2.99	A Knight's Tale	
289	1.99	The Royal Tenenbaums	Comedy
304	2.99	Wild, Wild West	Comedy
315	2.99	Himalaya	Foreign
316	.99	Horse Whisperer	Drama
320	1.99	A Beautiful Mind	Drama
324	2.99	Field of Dreams	Family
325	2.99	Beautiful Life	Foreign
337	1.99	Grease	
349	1.99	Cast Away	Drama
354	2.99	O Brother	
355	1.99	Spiderman	Kids

The RENTAL Table

C_ID	M_ID	DATE_OUT	DUE_DATE
673	216	30-JUN-03	02-JUL-03
673	249	30-JUN-03	01-JUL-03
388	320	01-JUL-03	04-JUL-03
400	354	29-JUN-03	30-JUN-03
579	354	01-JUL-03	04-JUL-03
673	304	29-JUN-03	01-JUL-03
673	337	01-JUL-03	04-JUL-03
388	216	30-JUN-03	02-JUL-03

```
388         316  01-JUL-03  04-JUL-03
388         236  01-JUL-03  04-JUL-03
400         320  01-JUL-03  04-JUL-03
400         255  29-JUN-03  01-JUL-03
701         216  30-JUN-03  02-JUL-03
701         278  29-JUN-03  01-JUL-03
579         320  01-JUL-03  03-JUL-03
```

General Syntax Standards

The following syntax standards are used throughout this book whenever general syntax is presented:

- Words that are entirely uppercase represent keywords and should be used as is.
- Words that are entirely lowercase represent items that should be replaced with the appropriate item for the application.
- Items and/or phrases enclosed in square brackets [ ] are optional; the brackets are not typed and are not part of the syntax.
- Items enclosed in curly braces { } and separated by a vertical bar | indicate choices available; choose one. The braces are not typed, and are not part of the syntax.

Again, those standards will be used when general statement syntax is given. When specific rather than general syntax is given (as is the case for each example), then similar standards will be used. Uppercase will be used for keywords only, and lowercase will be used for all other identifiers. The only exceptions are items contained in quotes, as those are always case-sensitive.

The case standards are only for the purpose of improving readability. As far as the software is concerned, the case makes no difference (unless the character string is enclosed within quotes). Also, be aware that when the commands typed are echoed to the screen by the Oracle software, they will be entirely uppercase; there is no facility for avoiding that conversion.

The bottom line here is that you will see a variety of cases used throughout your work with this software, and the only time it makes a difference in execution results is when the item is within quotes.

Using SQL* Plus

Specifics of connecting to the appropriate Oracle server should be provided by your instructor. Open the SQL* Plus tool to connect to the database. You will be prompted for the user ID, password, and host string. Use those provided by your instructor. Once connected and logged on, your session begins with the SQL> prompt displayed on the screen.

If you are using the software included with the book as a stand-alone system rather than using a client/server system, follow the steps listed in the documentation included with the software to mount and open a sample database. Once connected, you should see the prompt SQL> on the screen.

The list of commonly used SQL* Plus commands is fairly short and is presented here. In general, you will type each command at the prompt and press Enter. The syntax error messages that could be generated are usually self-explanatory, or can be looked up in the documentation that accompanies the software. As with SQL statements, SQL* Plus commands are not case-sensitive with the exception of values enclosed in quotes.

You should usually begin each session with these two commands:

1. **SET ECHO ON**   This causes commands executed from a file to be echoed to the screen. This is quite helpful when debugging code and trying to locate syntax errors, as an asterisk (*) is usually displayed directly below the location of the syntax error. If you forget to use this command, then you will not see a copy of the commands on the screen during execution and debugging is more difficult.

2. **SPOOL path:*filename*.txt**   This opens a spool file named *filename*.txt, and sends a copy of all screen output to the file. This spool file will contain a copy of everything you do in SQL* Plus (including your mistakes). Your instructor may require that you turn in a copy of your spool file for each lab assignment or session.

    Spool files are *not* executable by the Oracle software; they are merely a record of your work. They are text-only files, and can be edited in NotePad (or whichever text processor is defined in your installation). Depending on your instructor's preferences, you may or may not edit out your mistakes before submitting your spool file for grading.

You should end each session with these two commands:

1. **SPOOL OFF**   This closes the spool file, emptying out any text left in the spool buffer. If you open the spool file without closing it with this command, then the file may not contain a copy of the last portion of your session, as it may still be in the spool buffer. Therefore, avoid looking at an open spool file, and there really should be no need to do so.

    Again, a common misconception is that the commands in the spool file are executable, so those new to SQL* Plus sometimes try to open and execute the spool file. Unfortunately, that doesn't work. Just consider the spool file to be a record of your work and that's all.

2. **EXIT**   This ends the Oracle session and logs you off.

Other commonly used commands are as follows:

1. **DESCRIBE tablename (Example: DESCRIBE patient)**   This will list the column definitions (names and types) for the specified table.

2. **SAVE filename (with NO extension) (Example: SAVE step1)**   This will create a new script file named *filename* with an sql extension, and the file will contain a copy of the SQL statement currently in the SQL buffer. The SQL buffer will always contain the most recently executed SQL statement. SQL Plus commands are not stored in the buffer, and therefore, cannot be saved with this command.

    The default storage location for this script file is implementation dependent, but is usually C:\oracle\ora90\Bin\filename.sql. If you prefer, you can instead save the file to a location of your choice by including a path, as in SAVE path:\filename.

    If the script file already exists and you want to replace it, add the REPLACE option at the end by typing SAVE path:\filename REPLACE.

3. **EDIT filename (with NO extension) (Example: EDIT step1)**   This will open NotePad (or other text processor, depending on your installation). If the file does not exist, then a new script file will be created (with an automatic sql extension). If the script file already exists, then it will be opened so that changes can be made. As with the SAVE command, a path may be included in front of the filename.

    Be sure to save your changes and exit NotePad before returning to SQL Plus. If you leave NotePad open and just return to SQL Plus, the computer may lock up.

4. **@path:\filename (Example: @step1)**   This command executes the SQL statements and/or SQL Plus commands in the script file named filename.sql. As with the SAVE and EDIT commands, a path may be included in front of the filename.

In general, you will type an SQL statement (such as SELECT or UPDATE) at the SQL> prompt. If there are no syntax errors, the results will be displayed on the screen. However, if syntax errors are present, an asterisk (*) will be displayed directly beneath the likely source of the error. At that point, you should use the SAVE command to save the SQL statement to a script file. Then EDIT the script file, correcting the source of the syntax error. Then at the SQL> prompt, execute the script file with the @ command. Repeat as needed until all syntax errors are removed.

Clarifications

Script files are files with an **sql** extension that contain SQL statements and perhaps also SQL Plus commands. Script files are executable by the Oracle software. They are text-only files, and can be edited in NotePad (or other text processor depending on your installation).

Spool files will have a **txt** extension, and will contain a copy of everything you do in SQL Plus (including your mistakes). Spool files are *not* executable by the Oracle software. They are text-only files and can be edited in NotePad (or other text processor depending on your installation). Depending on your instructor's preferences, you may or may not edit out your mistakes before submitting your spool file for grading.

Teaching and Learning Resources

Website. The book's website at www.mhhe.com/preece provides instructors with SQL templates and solutions to end of chapter material.

Videos. The McGraw-Hill/Irwin Information Systems Video Library contains 2002 and 2003 video updates features various companies demonstrating the use of a multitude of IT areas such as intranets, multimedia, or computer-based training systems and concepts like client/server computing and business process reengineering. This Library is available free to adopters. For further information visit www.mhhe.com/business/mis/videos or www.mhhe.com/catalogs/irwin/mis/cio_index.mhtml or contact your local McGraw-Hill/Irwin sales representative.

Video Guide. A video guide for all updates is available on the Preece website.

Acknowledgments

I would like to acknowledge the following professors whose constructive criticism and suggestions helped in shaping this edition:

Mohammad Dadashzadeh
Wichita State University

Richard Holowczak
City University of New York

Shin-jeng Lin
Lemoyne College

Barbara Nicolai
Purdue University—Calumet

Emmanuel Udoh
Indiana—Purdue University

My sincere thanks go to Nelson Ferry for his contributions during the initial preparation of this book. His assistance in building tables and testing examples was extremely helpful. I also want to thank the following former IST370 students for taking the time to give me their suggestions as I began this project:

Dave Schwartz

Tom Whittington

Lee Barringer

Lois Dohmen

Amy Skerly

Kim Travelstead

Misty Whittington

Sue Zamora

Loren Cook

Melissa Kublick

Marcus Reid

Tim Bogard

Daniel Stover

My thanks also go out to the book team at McGraw-Hill/Irwin: Brent Gordon, publisher, Paul Ducham, senior sponsoring editor; Kelly Delso, developmental editor; Greta Kleinert, marketing manager; Natalie Ruffatto, project manager; Debra R. Sylvester, production supervisor; Adam Rooke, designer; and Greg Bates, media producer.

Linda L. Preece

1

Basic SELECT Statements

The SELECT statement is used to display table contents. All rows and columns or just selected columns and/or selected rows may be displayed. Column aliases can be used to improve the readability of the output. Column values may be calculated as the result of an expression, and rows may be displayed in a specific order. At any point, the user can supply values to be used within the SELECT through substitution parameters.

Section A: Fundamentals

Part 1: Column Selections and Aliases

General syntax of the basic SELECT statement is as follows:

SELECT column-list
FROM table-name;

where 1) column-list consists of one or more column names separated by commas. If all columns are to be included, then an asterisk (*) may be used for the column-list.

and 2) table-name is the name of the table.

Example 1.A.1

Display the contents of the DOCTOR table. (Use a small font to avoid wraparound.)

```
SQL: SELECT  *
     FROM doctor;
```

Execution Results

DOC_ID	DOC_NAME	DATEHIRED	SALPERMON	AREA	SUPERVISOR_ID	CHGPERAPPT	ANNUAL_BONUS
432	Harrison	05-DEC-94	12000	Pediatrics	100	75	4500
509	Vester	09-JAN-02	8100	Pediatrics	432	40	
389	Lewis	21-JAN-96	10000	Pediatrics	432	40	2250
504	Cotner	16-JUN-98	11500	Neurology	289	85	7500
235	Smith	22-JUN-98	4550	Family Practice	100	25	2250
356	James	01-AUG-98	7950	Neurology	289	80	6500
558	James	02-MAY-95	9800	Orthopedics	876	85	7700
876	Robertson	02-MAR-95	10500	Orthopedics	100	90	8000

```
889 Thompson  18-MAR-97    6500 Rehab              100       65      3200
239 Pronger   18-DEC-99    3500 Rehab              889       40
289 Borque    30-JUN-89   16500 Neurology          100       95      6500
100 Stevenson 30-JUN-79   23500 Director
```
12 rows selected.

Note: Variations in case are used only as an aid to the user in differentiating between key-words and other types of identifiers. As far as the software is concerned, the case makes no difference (unless the character string is enclosed within quotes). Hence, SELECT* FROM doctor, select* from DOCTOR, and Select* fROM dOcToR will each give the same execution results. Again, the conventions used in this book are uppercase for keywords only, and lowercase for all other identifiers.

Example 1.A.2

Display the contents of the CUSTOMER table.

```
SQL: SELECT    *
     FROM customer;
```

Execution Results

```
     C_ID PHONE     LNAME      FNAME        CURR_BAL DUEDATE
---------- --------  ---------- ------------ -------- ---------
      388 549-6730 Woolard    Jessica
      402 529-8420 St. James  Ellen            4.99 03-JUL-03
      673 549-8400 Akers      Janet            9.97 23-JUN-03
      579 549-1234 Poston     Blaine
      799 549-6711 Ackers     John             1.99 01-JUL-03
      767 453-8228 Ralston    Cheri            14.9 30-JUN-03
      133 453-2271 Akers      Leita           20.18 02-JUL-03
      239 549-1235 Macke      Greg
      400 549-8440 Salyers    Loretta             5 06-JUL-03
      701 549-8840 Williams   Tisha              20 28-JUN-03
```

10 rows selected.

Identical results could be produced by replacing the * with a list of the attribute names, separated by commas, as shown in the next statement.

```
SQL: SELECT c_id, phone, lname, fname, curr_bal, duedate
     FROM customer;
```

Execution Results

```
     C_ID PHONE     LNAME      FNAME        CURR_BAL DUEDATE
---------- --------  ---------- ------------ -------- ---------
      388 549-6730 Woolard    Jessica
      402 529-8420 St. James  Ellen            4.99 03-JUL-03
      673 549-8400 Akers      Janet            9.97 23-JUN-03
      579 549-1234 Poston     Blaine
      799 549-6711 Ackers     John             1.99 01-JUL-03
      767 453-8228 Ralston    Cheri            14.9 30-JUN-03
      133 453-2271 Akers      Leita           20.18 02-JUL-03
      239 549-1235 Macke      Greg
      400 549-8440 Salyers    Loretta             5 06-JUL-03
      701 549-8840 Williams   Tisha              20 28-JUN-03
```

10 rows selected.

Common Error: Including a comma after the last column in the list (the comma works as a separator, not a terminator).

Note: An advantage of using an attribute list rather than an * is that the order in which the columns are displayed may be changed.

Example 1.A.3

Display the ID, category, title, and fee for each movie.

```
SQL: SELECT m_id, category, title, fee
     FROM movie;
```

Execution Results

```
    M_ID CATEGORY    TITLE                     FEE
---------- ---------- -------------------- ----------
       204 Drama      City of Angels           1.99
       216 Action     Ocean's Eleven           2.99
       233 Action     Gone in 60 Seconds       2.99
       236 Kids       Monsters, Inc.            .99
       237 Kids       E.T.                      .99
       249 Action     U-571                    1.99
       254 Drama      Road to Perdition        2.99
       255 Foreign    Amelie                   2.99
       278 Drama      Monster's Ball           1.99
       287            A Knight's Tale          2.99
       289 Comedy     The Royal Tenenbaums     1.99
       304 Comedy     Wild, Wild West          2.99
       315 Foreign    Himalaya                 2.99
       316 Drama      Horse Whisperer           .99
       320 Drama      A Beautiful Mind         1.99
       324 Family     Field of Dreams          2.99
       325 Foreign    Beautiful Life           2.99
       337            Grease                   1.99
       349 Drama      Cast Away                1.99
       354            O Brother                2.99
       355 Kids       Spiderman                1.99

21 rows selected.
```

Example 1.A.4

Display each patient's name and their next appointment date.

```
SQL: SELECT pt_fname, pt_lname, nextapptdate
     FROM patient;
```

Execution Results

```
PT_FNAME          PT_LNAME          NEXTAPPTD
---------------- ---------------- ---------
Paul              James             01-JUL-03
Brian             Anderson          01-JUL-03
Scott             James             20-JUL-03
Jason             Smith             15-NOV-03
Susan             Porter            01-OCT-03
Debbie            Saillez           01-JUL-03
Anthony           Rogers            01-NOV-03
Stephanie         Walters           12-DEC-03
Lynn              Westra            02-FEB-04
```

```
Jennifer        Poole            01-DEC-03
Ryan            Baily            06-JUN-05
Lewis           Crow             01-JUL-05
John            Cochran          02-DEC-05
Becky           Roach            01-DEC-05
John            Jackson          21-JUL-03
Paul            Kowalczyk        29-JUL-03
Linda           Davis            21-JUL-03
J.C.            Jones            21-JUL-03
Chasity         Wright
Keith           Vanderchuck
Allen           Mcginnis
Joe             Sakic
```

```
22 rows selected.
```

Note: The column name of NEXTAPPTDATE is truncated to NEXTAPPTD in the results due to the usage of the default date display format. The command needed to enlarge the displayed column, COLUMN, is covered in Chapter 4.

Column Aliases

Column aliases may be used for various reasons. Their main purpose is to display improved column headings, especially when column names are overly abbreviated, or when calculated columns are displayed. Column aliases can also be referred to by other clauses of the SELECT statement, thus shortening the amount of code needed. For purposes of this book, they will be used whenever a column involves a calculation or a function in order to improve the appearance of the displayed output.

Each alias is listed immediately after the column name. If the alias is case-sensitive or includes spaces, it must be enclosed in double quotes. If the alias is not enclosed in double quotes, then it will be displayed in all capitals regardless of the case in which it is typed. When enclosed in double quotes, any characters may be used within the alias. Please be aware that throughout the rest of this book, when double quotes are not used around a column alias, it is *not* an error. It is just an indication that the alias is not case-sensitive, does not contain spaces, and therefore, does not need quotes.

Example 1.A.5

Display each patient's name and date of birth.

```
SQL: SELECT pt_fname "FIRST NAME", pt_lname "Last Name",
            ptdob BirthDate
     FROM patient;
```

Execution Results

```
FIRST NAME       Last Name        BIRTHDATE
---------------- ---------------- ---------
Paul             James            14-MAR-97
Brian            Anderson         06-MAR-48
Scott            James            01-MAR-33
Jason            Smith            12-DEC-99
Susan            Porter           14-NOV-67
Debbie           Saillez          09-SEP-55
Anthony          Rogers           07-DEC-41
Stephanie        Walters          01-JAN-45
Lynn             Westra           12-JUL-57
Jennifer         Poole            13-MAY-02
Ryan             Baily            25-DEC-77
```

```
Lewis          Crow              16-OCT-49
John           Cochran           03-MAR-48
Becky          Roach             08-SEP-75
John           Jackson           14-OCT-43
Paul           Kowalczyk         12-NOV-51
Linda          Davis             17-JUL-02
J.C.           Jones             17-JUL-02
Chasity        Wright            23-APR-73
Keith          Vanderchuck       08-AUG-68
Allen          Mcginnis          03-MAY-59
Joe            Sakic             16-SEP-76
```

22 rows selected.

Note: A combination of cases in the column aliases was used merely to illustrate the different options. Normally, the same format would be used for all column aliases on a SELECT statement.

Also note that the last alias is displayed in all uppercase even though it was entered in mixed case. This is intended to emphasize the requirement for double quotes around the alias whenever mixed case display is needed. Column aliases that are not enclosed in double quotes will be displayed in uppercase.

Common Error: Using single quotes instead of double quotes for a column alias.

| **Example 1.A.6** | Display all movie attributes with appropriate column headings. |

```
SQL: SELECT m_id "MOVIE ID", fee "RENTAL CHARGE", title, CATEGORY
     FROM movie;
```

Execution Results

```
MOVIE ID RENTAL CHARGE TITLE                  CATEGORY
---------- ------------- ---------------------- ----------
       204          1.99 City of Angels         Drama
       216          2.99 Ocean's Eleven         Action
       233          2.99 Gone in 60 Seconds     Action
       236           .99 Monsters, Inc.         Kids
       237           .99 E.T.                   Kids
       249          1.99 U-571                  Action
       254          2.99 Road to Perdition      Drama
       255          2.99 Amelie                 Foreign
       278          1.99 Monster's Ball         Drama
       287          2.99 A Knight's Tale
       289          1.99 The Royal Tenenbaums   Comedy
       304          2.99 Wild, Wild West        Comedy
       315          2.99 Himalaya               Foreign
       316           .99 Horse Whisperer        Drama
       320          1.99 A Beautiful Mind       Drama
       324          2.99 Field of Dreams        Family
       325          2.99 Beautiful Life         Foreign
       337          1.99 Grease
       349          1.99 Cast Away              Drama
       354          2.99 O Brother
       355          1.99 Spiderman              Kids
```

21 rows selected.

Part 2: Expressions in Calculated Columns

In addition to displaying existing columns, SELECT commands can also be used to display the results of expressions. These expressions may involve column names and/or literal values as operands for various operators. Column aliases may *not* be used as operands.

Numeric Expressions

Operators include + (addition), − (subtraction), * (multiplication), and / (division). As with most computer languages, multiplication and division are evaluated before addition and subtraction. Precedence can be overridden by using parentheses.

Example 1.A.7

For each doctor, display his or her name and annual income.

```
SQL: SELECT doc_name, salpermon * 12 + annual_bonus
     FROM doctor;
```

Execution Results

```
DOC_NAME   SALPERMON*12+ANNUAL_BONUS
---------  -------------------------
Harrison                      148500
Vester
Lewis                         122250
Cotner                        145500
Smith                          56850
James                         101900
James                         125300
Robertson                     134000
Thompson                       81200
Pronger
Borque                        204500
Stevenson

12 rows selected.
```

This example provides another opportunity to use column aliases, as they can be used to provide headings for calculated columns. A good habit to develop is to use a column alias for any column involving an expression or function.

Example 1.A.8

For each doctor, display his or her name and annual income.

```
SQL: SELECT doc_name,
            salpermon * 12 + annual_bonus "ANNUAL INCOME"
     FROM doctor;
```

Execution Results

```
DOC_NAME ANNUAL INCOME
-------- -------------
Harrison        148500
Vester
Lewis           122250
Cotner          145500
Smith            56850
James           101900
James           125300
```

```
Robertson          134000
Thompson            81200
Pronger
Borque             204500
Stevenson
```

```
12 rows selected.
```

Example 1.A.9

Display discounted movie rates ($0.50 off on Tuesdays).

```
SQL: SELECT title, fee-.5 "TUESDAY RATE"
     FROM movie;
```

Execution Results

```
TITLE                     TUESDAY RATE
-------------------- ------------
City of Angels                1.49
Ocean's Eleven                2.49
Gone in 60 Seconds            2.49
Monsters, Inc.                 .49
E.T.                           .49
U-571                         1.49
Road to Perdition             2.49
Amelie                        2.49
Monster's Ball                1.49
A Knight's Tale               2.49
The Royal Tenenbaums          1.49
Wild, Wild West               2.49
Himalaya                      2.49
Horse Whisperer                .49
A Beautiful Mind              1.49
Field of Dreams               2.49
Beautiful Life                2.49
Grease                        1.49
Cast Away                     1.49
O Brother                     2.49
Spiderman                     1.49
```

```
21 rows selected.
```

Example 1.A.10

Display movie rates for employees (either 20 percent or 25 percent off, depending on length of employment).

```
SQL: SELECT title, fee-fee * .20 "20% OFF", fee-fee * .25 "25% OFF"
     FROM movie;
```

Execution Results

```
TITLE                     20% OFF    25% OFF
---------------------- ------- ----------
City of Angels             1.592     1.4925
Ocean's Eleven             2.392     2.2425
Gone in 60 Seconds         2.392     2.2425
Monsters, Inc.              .792      .7425
E.T.                        .792      .7425
```

```
U-571                          1.592      1.4925
Road to Perdition              2.392      2.2425
Amelie                         2.392      2.2425
Monster's Ball                 1.592      1.4925
A Knight's Tale                2.392      2.2425
The Royal Tenenbaums           1.592      1.4925
Wild, Wild West                2.392      2.2425
Himalaya                       2.392      2.2425
Horse Whisperer                 .792       .7425
A Beautiful Mind               1.592      1.4925
Field of Dreams                2.392      2.2425
Beautiful Life                 2.392      2.2425
Grease                         1.592      1.4925
Cast Away                      1.592      1.4925
O Brother                      2.392      2.2425
Spiderman                      1.592      1.4925
```

```
21 rows selected.
```

Note: Functions used to format the display of numeric values will be presented in the next chapter. Until then, there is no facility for controlling the number of decimal positions in the display.

Character String Expressions

The concatenation operator (| |) is used to join two character strings. The character strings can come either from existing columns or from literal strings enclosed in single quotes. The concatenation operator works in a manner similar to the addition operator (+), and thus can be used to join several strings together by placing it between strings.

Example 1.A.11

6 + 4 + 5 gives a result of 15
'A' || 'B C' || ' D' gives a result of 'AB C D'

Example 1.A.12

Display each patient's name and street address in sentence form.

```
SQL: SELECT pt_fname || ' ' || pt_lname || ' was born on ' ||
        ptdob || '.' "PATIENT INFORMATION"
     FROM patient;
```

Execution Results

```
PATIENT INFORMATION
----------------------------------------
Paul James was born on 14-MAR-97.
Brian Anderson was born on 06-MAR-48.
Scott James was born on 01-MAR-33.
Jason Smith was born on 12-DEC-99.
Susan Porter was born on 14-NOV-67.
Debbie Saillez was born on 09-SEP-55.
Anthony Rogers was born on 07-DEC-41.
Stephanie Walters was born on 01-JAN-45.
Lynn Westra was born on 12-JUL-57.
Jennifer Poole was born on 13-MAY-02.
Ryan Baily was born on 25-DEC-77.
Lewis Crow was born on 16-OCT-49.
John Cochran was born on 03-MAR-48.
Becky Roach was born on 08-SEP-75.
```

```
John Jackson was born on 14-OCT-43.
Paul Kowalczyk was born on 12-NOV-51.
Linda Davis was born on 17-JUL-02.
J.C. Jones was born on 17-JUL-02.
Chasity Wright was born on 23-APR-73.
Keith Vanderchuck was born on 08-AUG-68.
Allen Mcginnis was born on 03-MAY-59.
Joe Sakic was born on 16-SEP-76.

22 rows selected.
```

Note: Again, a column alias is used to provide a heading for a column involving an expression.

Also note the single blank space enclosed within the single quotes. This is used to provide a blank space between the first name and the last name.

Common Errors:
1. Using || before the first item.
2. Using || after the last item.
3. Using double quotes instead of single quotes on character strings.
4. Using quotes around column names (just gives name instead of actual value).

Example 1.A.13

Display movie data in the following format (first row used as an example):
City of Angels is in the Drama category; fee is 1.99.

```
SQL: SELECT title || ' is in the ' || category ||
        ' category; fee is ' || fee || '.' "MOVIE INFORMATION"
    FROM movie;
```

Execution Results

```
MOVIE INFORMATION
------------------------------------------------------------
City of Angels is in the Drama category; fee is 1.99.
Ocean's Eleven is in the Action category; fee is 2.99.
Gone in 60 Seconds is in the Action category; fee is 2.99.
Monsters, Inc. is in the Kids category; fee is .99.
E.T. is in the Kids category; fee is .99.
U-571 is in the Action category; fee is 1.99.
Road to Perdition is in the Drama category; fee is 2.99.
Amelie is in the Foreign category; fee is 2.99.
Monster's Ball is in the Drama category; fee is 1.99.
A Knight's Tale is in the  category; fee is 2.99.
The Royal Tenenbaums is in the Comedy category; fee is 1.99.
Wild, Wild West is in the Comedy category; fee is 2.99.
Himalaya is in the Foreign category; fee is 2.99.
Horse Whisperer is in the Drama category; fee is .99.
A Beautiful Mind is in the Drama category; fee is 1.99.
Field of Dreams is in the Drama category; fee is 2.99.
Beautiful Life is in the Foreign category; fee is 2.99.
Grease is in the  category; fee is 1.99.
Cast Away is in the Drama category; fee is 1.99.
O Brother is in the  category; fee is 2.99.
Spiderman is in the Kids category; fee is 1.99.

21 rows selected.
```

Date Expressions

It is often necessary to use the built-in function SYSDATE to refer to the current date. This can be displayed by itself by using a dummy table named DUAL.

Example 1.A.14

Display the current date.

```
SQL: SELECT SYSDATE
     FROM DUAL;
```

Execution Results

```
SYSDATE
----------
01-JUL-03
```

Note: A system date of July 1, 2003, was used for the testing of all examples in this book.

One date can be subtracted from another date to determine the number of days between the two dates. Additionally, integers can be added or subtracted from dates, giving a new date.

Example 1.A.15

Determine the number of days that have elapsed since each patient's last visit.

```
SQL: SELECT pt_lname, pt_fname,
            sysdate - lastapptdate "DAYS SINCE LAST VISIT"
     FROM patient;
```

Execution Results

PT_LNAME	PT_FNAME	DAYS SINCE LAST VISIT
James	Paul	30
Anderson	Brian	30
James	Scott	11
Smith	Jason	47
Porter	Susan	122
Saillez	Debbie	30
Rogers	Anthony	181
Walters	Stephanie	201
Westra	Lynn	149
Poole	Jennifer	30
Baily	Ryan	25
Crow	Lewis	487
Cochran	John	546
Roach	Becky	546
Jackson	John	233
Kowalczyk	Paul	12
Davis	Linda	40
Jones	J.C.	40
Wright	Chasity	
Vanderchuck	Keith	16
Mcginnis	Allen	16
Sakic	Joe	16

```
22 rows selected.
```

Example 1.A.16

Display the number of days that each rental has been out and the number of days that each rental has left.

```
SQL: SELECT c_id "CUSTOMER", m_id "MOVIE",
            SYSDATE - date_out "DAYS OUT",
            due_date - SYSDATE "DAYS LEFT"
     FROM rental;
```

Execution Results

```
  CUSTOMER       MOVIE    DAYS OUT  DAYS LEFT
---------- ---------- ---------- ----------
       673         216 1.53362269 .466377315
       673         249 1.53362269 -.53362269
       388         320 .533622685 2.46637731
       400         354 2.53362269 -1.5336227
       579         354 .533622685 2.46637731
       673         304 2.53362269 -.53362269
       673         337 .533622685 2.46637731
       388         216 1.53362269 .466377315
       388         316 .533622685 2.46637731
       388         236 .533622685 2.46637731
       400         320 .533622685 2.46637731
       400         255 2.53362269 -.53362269
       701         216 1.53362269 .466377315
       701         278 2.53362269 -.53362269
       579         320 .533622685 1.46637731
```

```
15 rows selected.
```

Note: Functions used for rounding and truncating fractional values will be covered in the next chapter. Also note that without the use of such functions, the specific number of decimal positions displayed for the result of a calculation is implementation dependent.

Part 3: Special Cases

Null Values

If null (empty) values are included in an expression, the result will be null. This applies to all three types of values. For example, if a patient had not had a previous visit, then in the preceding example, SYSDATE − LASTAPPTDATe would yield a null result. Similarly, if a doctor didn't earn a bonus, then in example 1.5, SALPERMON * 12 + ANNUAL-BONUS would yield a null result. A look back at those examples will show that indeed there are null results due to null values in calculations.

Eventually, you will learn about a function that can be used to replace null values with a value of your choice, but at this point, just be aware that null values in expressions will give null results.

Duplicate Values

Duplicate rows can be eliminated from results by using DISTINCT before the column name.

Example 1.A.17

Display the IDs of all doctors assigned to patients.

```
SQL: SELECT doc_id
     FROM patient;
```

Execution Results

```
   DOC_ID
---------
      432
      235
```

```
                235
                509
                235
                235
                504
                504
                235
                389
                235
                235
                356
                235
                235
                558
                509
                509
                235
                504
                504
                504
22 rows selected.
```

Example 1.A.18	Eliminate display of duplicate values in the previous example by using DISTINCT.

```
SQL: SELECT DISTINCT doc_id
      FROM patient;
```

Execution Results

```
    DOC_ID
---------
       235
       356
       389
       432
       504
       509
       558

7 rows selected.
```

Example 1.A.19	Display the IDs of customers with current rentals.

```
SQL: SELECT c_id
      FROM rental;
```

Execution Results

```
      C_ID
----------
       673
       673
       388
       400
       579
       673
       673
```

```
        388
        388
        388
        400
        400
        701
        701
        579
```

```
15 rows selected.
```

Example 1.A.20

A better solution using DISTINCT:

```
SQL: SELECT DISTINCT c_id
       FROM rental;
```

Execution Results

```
      C_ID
----------
       388
       400
       579
       673
       701
```

Part 4: Ordering the Results

The ORDER BY clause is used to arrange the rows in the results of a query in a specific order. The actual order within the table does not change. The general syntax of the clause added after the FROM clause is as follows:

ORDER BY expression [DESC]

where the expression may consist of a column name, column alias, or calculated expression

and the default order is ascending (optionally include DESC for descending).

Reminder: The square brackets around the DESC keyword indicate that the contents are optional. The brackets are not actually typed as part of the syntax.

Example 1.A.21

Display all doctor's names and hire dates in chronological order with the person on staff the longest listed first.

```
SQL: SELECT doc_name, datehired
       FROM doctor
       ORDER BY datehired;
```

Execution Results

```
DOC_NAME   DATEHIRED
---------  ---------
Stevenson  30-JUN-79
Borque     30-JUN-89
Harrison   05-DEC-94
Robertson  02-MAR-95
James      02-MAY-95
Lewis      21-JAN-96
Thompson   18-MAR-97
```

```
Cotner      16-JUN-98
Smith       22-JUN-98
James       01-AUG-98
Pronger  .  18-DEC-99
Vester      09-JAN-00

12 rows selected.
```

Example 1.A.22

Modify the previous example to begin the list with the person on staff for the shortest time.

```
SQL: SELECT doc_name, datehired
     FROM doctor
     ORDER BY datehired DESC;
```

Execution Results

```
DOC_NAME   DATEHIRED
---------  ---------
Vester     09-JAN-00
Pronger    18-DEC-99
James      01-AUG-98
Smith      22-JUN-98
Cotner     16-JUN-98
Thompson   18-MAR-97
Lewis      21-JAN-96
James      02-MAY-95
Robertson  02-MAR-95
Harrison   05-DEC-94
Borque     30-JUN-89
Stevenson  30-JUN-79

12 rows selected.
```

Example 1.A.23

List all movies alphabetically.

```
SQL: SELECT *
     FROM movie
     ORDER BY title;
```

Execution Results

```
     M_ID        FEE  TITLE                 CATEGORY
----------  ---------- --------------------  ----------
       320       1.99  A Beautiful Mind      Drama
       287       2.99  A Knight's Tale
       255       2.99  Amelie                Foreign
       325       2.99  Beautiful Life        Foreign
       349       1.99  Cast Away             Drama
       204       1.99  City of Angels        Drama
       237        .99  E.T.                  Kids
       324       2.99  Field of Dreams       Family
       233       2.99  Gone in 60 Seconds    Action
       337       1.99  Grease
       315       2.99  Himalaya              Foreign
       316        .99  Horse Whisperer       Drama
       278       1.99  Monster's Ball        Drama
```

```
236        .99 Monsters, Inc.        Kids
354       2.99 O Brother
216       2.99 Ocean's Eleven        Action
254       2.99 Road to Perdition     Drama
355       1.99 Spiderman             Kids
289       1.99 The Royal Tenenbaums  Comedy
249       1.99 U-571                 Action
304       2.99 Wild, Wild West       Comedy
```

```
21 rows selected.
```

When calculated columns are involved, column aliases can be used on the ORDER BY clause. Be sure to exactly match the spelling on the SELECT clause and the spelling on the ORDER BY clause. If the column alias is enclosed in quotes on the SELECT clause, then it must also be enclosed in quotes on the ORDER BY clause.

Example 1.A.24

For each patient, display the patient ID and the number of days since their last appointment in order with the most recently seen patient listed first.

```
SQL: SELECT pt_id, SYSDATE - lastapptdate "DAYS SINCE APPT"
     FROM patient
     ORDER BY "DAYS SINCE APPT";
```

Execution Results

```
    PT_ID DAYS SINCE APPT
--------- ---------------
      313              11
      809              12
      696              16
      966              16
      669              16
      108              25
      168              30
      331              30
      103              30
      315              30
      307              40
      703              40
      816              47
      314             122
      267             149
      719             181
      264             201
      504             233
      943             487
      847             546
      163             546
      439
```

```
22 rows selected.
```

Note: Patient number 439 has a null value for LASTAPPTDATE. Therefore, the calculation involving LASTAPPTDATE yields a null result, as does any calculation involving a null value.

Common Errors: 1. Misspelling the alias; must be an exact match.
2. Not including the alias in quotes on the ORDER BY clause if it was included in quotes on the SELECT clause.
3. Not matching the case exactly (if enclosed in quotes).

Example 1.A.25

For each rental, display the number of days until due back from least to most.

```
SQL: SELECT m_id, due_date - SYSDATE "DAYS UNTIL DUE BACK"
     FROM rental
     ORDER BY "DAYS UNTIL DUE BACK";
```

Execution Results

M_ID	DAYS UNTIL DUE BACK
354	-1.5385995
249	-.53859954
304	-.53859954
255	-.53859954
278	-.53859954
216	.461400463
216	.461400463
216	.461400463
320	1.46140046
320	2.46140046
320	2.46140046
354	2.46140046
316	2.46140046
236	2.46140046
337	2.46140046

15 rows selected.

A multiple-level sort can be specified by listing more than one expression with commas for separators. The DESC specification may be included on each expression individually; it will not apply to the entire list of expressions.

Example 1.A.26

Display all patient data in alphabetic order. For patients with the same name, display the data in order of date of birth from youngest to oldest.

```
SQL: SELECT *
     FROM patient
     ORDER BY pt_lname, pt_fname, ptdob DESC;
```

Execution Results

PT_ID	PT_LNAME	PT_FNAME	PTDOB	DOC_ID	NEXTAPPTD	LASTAPPTD
331	Anderson	Brian	06-MAR-48	235	01-JUL-03	01-JUN-03
108	Baily	Ryan	25-DEC-77	235	06-JUN-05	06-JUN-03
847	Cochran	John	03-MAR-48	356	02-DEC-05	01-JAN-02
943	Crow	Lewis	16-OCT-49	235	01-JUL-05	01-MAR-02
703	Davis	Linda	17-JUL-02	509	21-JUL-03	22-MAY-03
504	Jackson	John	14-OCT-43	235	21-JUL-03	10-NOV-02
168	James	Paul	14-MAR-97	432	01-JUL-03	01-JUN-03
313	James	Scott	01-MAR-33	235	20-JUL-03	20-JUN-03

```
307 Jones          J.C.          17-JUL-02       509 21-JUL-03 22-MAY-03
809 Kowalczyk      Paul          12-NOV-51       558 29-JUL-03 19-JUN-03
966 Mcginnis       Allen         03-MAY-59       504           15-JUN-03
103 Poole          Jennifer      13-MAY-02       389 01-DEC-03 01-JUN-03
314 Porter         Susan         14-NOV-67       235 01-OCT-03 01-MAR-03
163 Roach          Becky         08-SEP-75       235 01-DEC-05 01-JAN-02
719 Rogers         Anthony       07-DEC-41       504 01-NOV-03 01-JAN-03
315 Saillez        Debbie        09-SEP-55       235 01-JUL-03 01-JUN-03
669 Sakic          Joe           16-SEP-76       504           15-JUN-03
816 Smith          Jason         12-DEC-99       509 15-NOV-03 15-MAY-03
696 Vanderchuck    Keith         08-AUG-68       504           15-JUN-03
264 Walters        Stephanie     01-JAN-45       504 12-DEC-03 12-DEC-02
267 Westra         Lynn          12-JUL-57       235 02-FEB-04 02-FEB-03
439 Wright         Chasity       23-APR-73       235
```

22 rows selected.

Example 1.A.27   Display all movie data in category order. Within a category, display titles in alphabetic order.

SQL: SELECT *
     FROM movie
     ORDER BY category, title;

Execution Results

```
      M_ID        FEE TITLE                   CATEGORY
---------- ---------- ---------------------- ----------
       233       2.99 Gone in 60 Seconds     Action
       216       2.99 Ocean's Eleven         Action
       249       1.99 U-571                  Action
       289       1.99 The Royal Tenenbaums   Comedy
       304       2.99 Wild, Wild West        Comedy
       320       1.99 A Beautiful Mind       Drama
       349       1.99 Cast Away              Drama
       204       1.99 City of Angels         Drama
       324       2.99 Field of Dreams        Family
       316        .99 Horse Whisperer        Drama
       278       1.99 Monster's Ball         Drama
       254       2.99 Road to Perdition      Drama
       255       2.99 Amelie                 Foreign
       325       2.99 Beautiful Life         Foreign
       315       2.99 Himalaya               Foreign
       237        .99 E.T.                   Kids
       236        .99 Monsters, Inc.         Kids
       355       1.99 Spiderman              Kids
       287       2.99 A Knight's Tale
       337       1.99 Grease
       354       2.99 O Brother
```

21 rows selected.

Section B: Row Selection with the WHERE Clause

All of the previous examples have displayed all or part of every row in the table; no rows have been eliminated. The WHERE clause can be added to the SELECT statement in order to restrict the results to rows that satisfy a specified condition.

Part 1: Comparisons

The general format for all comparisons is as follows:

> expression comparison-operator expression

> where an expression consists of a column name, literal value, or some combination involving operators (+, −, *, /, | |)

> and comparison-operators are >, <, =, >=, <=, and <> (not equal to)

The two expressions must be of the same type (numeric, character string, or date). Character string literals should be enclosed in single quotes. Whenever quotes are used within any SQL statements, the contents are case-sensitive. Date literals should be of the form 'DD-MON-YY', and numeric literals should consist of digits and optionally, a decimal and/or sign. Do not include commas or dollar signs in numeric literals.

Example 1.B.1

Display the names of doctors who charge at least $40 per appointment.

```
SQL: SELECT doc_name
     FROM doctor
     WHERE chgperappt >= 40;
```

Execution Results

```
DOC_NAME
---------
Harrison
Vester
Lewis
Cotner
James
James
Robertson
Thompson
Pronger
Borque

10 rows selected.
```

Common Error: Including a dollar sign or comma in the numeric literal.

Example 1.B.2

Display all data on movies with a fee of $1.99 or less.

```
SQL: SELECT *
     FROM movie
     WHERE fee <= 1.99;
```

Execution Results

M_ID	FEE	TITLE	CATEGORY
204	1.99	City of Angels	Drama
236	.99	Monsters, Inc.	Kids
237	.99	E.T.	Kids
249	1.99	U-571	Action
278	1.99	Monster's Ball	Drama
289	1.99	The Royal Tenenbaums	Comedy
316	.99	Horse Whisperer	Drama

```
320        1.99 A Beautiful Mind    Drama
337        1.99 Grease
349        1.99 Cast Away           Drama
355        1.99 Spiderman           Kids
```

```
11 rows selected.
```

Example 1.B.3

Display the names of patients whose next appointment is less than 60 days since their last appointment.

```
SQL: SELECT pt_lname, pt_fname
     FROM patient
     WHERE nextapptdate-lastapptdate < 60;
```

Execution Results

```
PT_LNAME          PT_FNAME
---------------   ---------------
James             Paul
Anderson          Brian
James             Scott
Saillez           Debbie
Kowalczyk         Paul
```

Example 1.B.4

Display movie IDs for yesterday's rentals.

```
SQL: SELECT *
     FROM rental
     WHERE date_out = SYSDATE - 1;
```

Execution Results

```
      C_ID       M_ID DATE_OUT  DUE_DATE
---------- ---------- --------- ---------
       673        216 30-JUN-03 02-JUL-03
       673        249 30-JUN-03 01-JUL-03
       388        216 30-JUN-03 02-JUL-03
       701        216 30-JUN-03 02-JUL-03
```

Note: A system date of 01-JUL-03 was used for all example testing.

Example 1.B.5

Display all data on patients whose last name is James.

```
SQL: SELECT *
     FROM patient
     WHERE pt_lname = 'James';
```

Execution Results

```
PT_ID PT_LNAME          PT_FNAME          PTDOB       DOC_ID NEXTAPPTD LASTAPPTD
--------- --------------- --------------- --------- --------- --------- ---------
  168 James             Paul              14-MAR-97     432 01-JUL-03 22-JUL-03
  313 James             Scott             01-MAR-33     235 20-JUL-03 10-JUL-03
```

Common Error: Not matching the case of literal string with the case used in the table.

Example 1.B.6

```
SQL: SELECT *
     FROM patient
     WHERE pt_lname = 'JAMES';
```

Execution Results

   no rows selected

Example 1.B.7

Customer 133 knows a late fee of 1 percent will be added to her balance tomorrow, and she wants to know the old and new balance amounts.

```
SQL: SELECT curr_bal "OLD BALANCE", curr_bal + curr_bal * .01
        "NEW BALANCE"
     FROM customer
     WHERE c_id = 133;
```

Execution Results

```
OLD BALANCE   NEW BALANCE
----------- -----------
      20.18       20.3818
```

Part 2: Special Operators

The BETWEEN Operator

There are several special operators that essentially serve as shortcuts for longer expressions. One of the most useful is the BETWEEN operator. It is used to determine whether or not a value lies within a specific range (including the end points).

Example 1.B.8

Display the IDs and balances of patients that owe at least $300 and no more than $500.

```
SQL: SELECT pt_id, balance
     FROM billing
     WHERE balance BETWEEN 300 AND 500;
```

Execution Results

```
    PT_ID   BALANCE
--------- ---------
      331       300
      809       450
      307       450
      439       500
```

Common Errors: 1. Including dollar signs and/or commas in the numeric literals.
   2. Including undesired end points (move end points in by one if necessary).

Example 1.B.9

Display title and fee for all movies costing more than $0.99, but under $2.99.

```
SQL: SELECT title, fee
     FROM movie
     WHERE fee BETWEEN 1.00 AND 2.98;
```

Execution Results

```
TITLE                     FEE
-------------------- ----------
City of Angels            1.99
U-571                     1.99
Monster's Ball            1.99
The Royal Tenenbaums      1.99
A Beautiful Mind          1.99
```

```
    Grease                      1.99
    Cast Away                   1.99
    Spiderman                   1.99

8 rows selected.
```

Example 1.B.10

Display all data on rentals due back today or tomorrow.

```
SQL: SELECT *
     FROM rental
     WHERE due_date BETWEEN SYSDATE AND SYSDATE + 1;
```

Execution Results

```
        C_ID       M_ID DATE_OUT  DUE_DATE
---------- ---------- --------- ---------
       673        216 30-JUN-03 02-JUL-03
       673        249 30-JUN-03 01-JUL-03
       673        304 29-JUN-03 01-JUL-03
       388        216 30-JUN-03 02-JUL-03
       400        255 29-JUN-03 01-JUL-03
       701        216 30-JUN-03 02-JUL-03
       701        278 29-JUN-03 01-JUL-03

7 rows selected.
```

Note: All date values actually include hours, minutes, and seconds as well, so an additional function is needed for most comparisons that involve SYSDATE. This is the TO_CHAR function, and it will be presented in the next chapter. For now, just be aware that the above results were achieved only by manipulating the system date and time.

The IN Operator

A second convenient special operator is IN. This is used to see if a value occurs in a set of possible values, and is a shortcut for separate, individual comparisons. The set of possible values are specified within parenthesis and separated by commas. As usual, character string values are enclosed in single quotes (column aliases are the only exception to this "when in doubt, use single quotes" rule so far).

Example 1.B.11

Display the names and areas of doctors specializing in pediatrics or family practice.

```
SQL: SELECT doc_name, area
     FROM doctor
     WHERE area IN ('Pediatrics', 'Family Practice');
```

Execution Results

```
DOC_NAME   AREA
--------- --------------------
Harrison   Pediatrics
Vester     Pediatrics
Lewis      Pediatrics
Smith      Family Practice
```

Common Errors: 1. Omitting the single quotes on character literals.

2. Using double quotes instead of single.

3. Not matching the case used in the database.

Example 1.B.12

Display the titles of movies in the foreign, comedy, and action categories.

```
SQL: SELECT title
     FROM movie
     WHERE category IN ('Foreign', 'Comedy', 'Action');
```

Execution Results

```
TITLE
--------------------
Ocean's Eleven
Gone in 60 Seconds
U-571
Amelie
The Royal Tenenbaums
Wild, Wild West
Himalaya
Beautiful Life

8 rows selected.
```

Example 1.B.13

Display all current rental data for movies 255, 354, and 315.

```
SQL: SELECT *
     FROM rental
     WHERE m_id IN (255, 354, 315);
```

Execution Results

```
     C_ID       M_ID DATE_OUT  DUE_DATE
---------- ---------- --------- ---------
       400        255 29-JUN-03 01-JUL-03
       400        354 29-JUN-03 30-JUN-03
       579        354 01-JUL-03 04-JUL-03
```

The IS NULL Operator

The third special operator is IS NULL. Any comparison to a null value that uses the standard comparison operators will not yield a match. Hence, if you need to check for null values, the IS NULL operator must be used.

Example 1.B.14

Display the IDs of doctors that do not receive annual bonuses.

```
SQL: SELECT doc_id
     FROM doctor
     WHERE annual_bonus IS NULL;
```

Execution Results

```
   DOC_ID
---------
      509
      239
      100
```

Common Error: Usage of = NULL rather than IS NULL.

Example 1.B.15

Display the IDs of customers with no balance due date.

```
SQL: SELECT c_id
     FROM customer
     WHERE duedate IS NULL;
```

Execution Results

```
     C_ID
----------
       388
       579
       239
```

The LIKE Operator

The LIKE operator is used in conjunction with wildcard characters to match character string patterns. The percent sign (%) is used to match zero or more characters, whereas the underscore (_) is used to match a single character. Wildcards cannot be used without the LIKE operator, and the LIKE operator should not be used without wildcards. If you need to match a specific character string (without wildcards), then just use one of the standard comparison operators.

Example 1.B.16

Display all billing data for patients living on N. Allen Street.

```
SQL: SELECT *
     FROM billing
     WHERE addr LIKE '%N. Allen%';
```

Execution Results

PT_ID	BALANCE	DUEDATE	PHONE	ADDR	CITY	ST	ZIP	PT_INS
504	0	01-JAN-03	549-6139	6657 N. Allen	Carbondale	IL	62901	QualityCare
307	450	31-AUG-03	457-6967	234 N. Allen	Carbondale	IL	62901	HealthCare

Common Errors: 1. Not matching case used in the database.
2. Using a wildcard without the LIKE operator.
3. Using the LIKE operator without a wildcard.

Example 1.B.17

Display the full name and phone number for customers whose phone number begins with 549-67.

```
SQL: SELECT lname || ',' || fname "FULL NAME", phone
     FROM customer
     WHERE phone LIKE '549-67__';
```

Execution Results

```
FULL NAME                PHONE
----------------------   --------
Woolard, Jessica         549-6730
Ackers, John             549-6711
```

Example 1.B.18

Display the ID, balance, and due date for customers with balances due in June.

```
SQL: SELECT c_id, curr_bal, duedate
     FROM customer
     WHERE duedate LIKE '%JUN%';
```

Execution Results

```
    C_ID   CURR_BAL DUEDATE
---------- ---------- ---------
       673       9.97 23-JUN-03
       767       14.9 30-JUN-03
       701         20 28-JUN-03
```

Part 3: Logical Operators

The three standard logical operators of AND, OR, and NOT are used to combine expressions. AND will return a value of true only if both expressions are true; OR will return a value of true if either or both of the expressions are true; and NOT will return the opposite value of the expression. Precedence is in the following order: NOT, AND, OR. You will occasionally need to use parenthesis to force evaluation of the OR before the AND.

Example 1.B.19

Display the IDs, balances, and due dates for patients that have balances owed past the due date.

```
SQL: SELECT pt_id, balance, duedate
     FROM billing
     WHERE balance > 0 AND duedate < SYSDATE;
```

Execution Results

```
    PT_ID   BALANCE DUEDATE
--------- ---------- ---------
      314       100 31-MAR-03
      264     35000 11-JAN-03
      847     98000 31-JAN-02
```

Example 1.B.20

Display all billing data on patients who either have balances of more than $90,000 or have insurance with SIH.

```
SQL: SELECT *
     FROM billing
     WHERE balance > 90000 OR pt_ins = 'SIH';
```

Execution Results

PT_ID	BALANCE	DUEDATE	PHONE	ADDR	CITY	ST	ZIP	PT_INS
168	15650	21-AUG-03	833-9569	128 W. Apple #4	Jonesboro	IL	62952	SIH
816	0	01-JAN-04	833-6654	8814 W. Apple	JONESBORO	IL	62952	SIH
847	98000	31-JAN-02	549-8854	6543 W. Parkview Ln.	Carbondale	IL	62901	BCBS
966	98700	15-JUL-03	833-5375	9009 Taylor Ave.	Anna	IL	62906	BCBS
669	128450	15-JUL-03	833-6654	353 Tin Bender Rd.	Jonesboro	IL	62952	BCBS

Note: No dollar sign or comma is included in the numeric literal 90000.

Example 1.B.21

Display the IDs and balances of customers who owe at least $10 and no more than $20.

```
SQL: SELECT c_id, curr_bal
     FROM customer
     WHERE curr_bal >= 10 AND curr_bal <= 20;
```

Execution Results

```
    C_ID   CURR_BAL
--------- ----------
      767       14.9
      701         20
```

Common Error: Omitting the second variable reference (for example, curr_bal $>=$ 10 AND $<=$ 20 will not work due to the missing variable).

Example 1.B.22

Display the opposite of the previous example by listing the IDs and balances of customers who do NOT owe between $10 and $20.

```
SQL: SELECT c_id, curr_bal
     FROM customer
     WHERE NOT (curr_bal >= 10 AND curr_bal <= 20);
```

Execution Results

```
    C_ID   CURR_BAL
--------- ----------
      402       4.99
      673       9.97
      799       1.99
      133      20.18
      400          5
```

Example 1.B.23

Display all data on movies either in the Action category with fees under $2.99 or in some other category with fees over $1.99.

```
SQL: SELECT *
     FROM movie
     WHERE category = 'Action' AND fee < 2.99
        OR category <> 'Action' AND fee > 1.99;
```

Execution Results

```
    M_ID        FEE  TITLE                 CATEGORY
--------- ---------- --------------------- ----------
      249       1.99 U-571                 Action
      254       2.99 Road to Perdition     Drama
      255       2.99 Amelie                Foreign
      304       2.99 Wild, Wild West       Comedy
      315       2.99 Himalaya              Foreign
      324       2.99 Field of Dreams       Family
      325       2.99 Beautiful Life        Foreign

7 rows selected.
```

Example 1.B.24

Display all data on patients except those with a last name of James, Jones, Wright, or Walters.

```
SQL: SELECT *
     FROM patient
     WHERE NOT pt_lname IN ('James', 'Jones', 'Wright', 'Walters');
```

Execution Results

PT_ID	PT_LNAME	PT_FNAME	PTDOB	DOC_ID	NEXTAPPTD	LASTAPPTD
331	Anderson	Brian	06-MAR-48	235	01-JUL-03	01-JUN-03
816	Smith	Jason	12-DEC-99	509	15-NOV-03	15-MAY-03
314	Porter	Susan	14-NOV-67	235	01-OCT-03	01-MAR-03
315	Saillez	Debbie	09-SEP-55	235	01-JUL-03	01-JUN-03
719	Rogers	Anthony	07-DEC-41	504	01-NOV-03	01-JAN-03
267	Westra	Lynn	12-JUL-57	235	02-FEB-04	02-FEB-03
103	Poole	Jennifer	13-MAY-02	389	01-DEC-03	01-JUN-03
108	Baily	Ryan	25-DEC-77	235	06-JUN-05	06-JUN-03
943	Crow	Lewis	16-OCT-49	235	01-JUL-05	01-MAR-02
847	Cochran	John	03-MAR-48	356	02-DEC-05	01-JAN-02
163	Roach	Becky	08-SEP-75	235	01-DEC-05	01-JAN-02
504	Jackson	John	14-OCT-43	235	21-JUL-03	10-NOV-02
809	Kowalczyk	Paul	12-NOV-51	558	29-JUL-03	19-JUN-03
703	Davis	Linda	17-JUL-02	509	21-JUL-03	22-MAY-03
696	Vanderchuck	Keith	08-AUG-68	504		15-JUN-03
966	Mcginnis	Allen	03-MAY-59	504		15-JUN-03
669	Sakic	Joe	16-SEP-76	504		15-JUN-03

17 rows selected.

The NOT operator can also be used in conjunction with the special operators as follows: NOT BETWEEN, NOT IN, IS NOT NULL, NOT LIKE. Hence, the previous example could have been written in a more readable format.

```
SQL: SELECT *
     FROM patient
     WHERE pt_lname NOT IN ('James', 'Jones', 'Wright', 'Walters');
```

Execution Results

PT_ID	PT_LNAME	PT_FNAME	PTDOB	DOC_ID	NEXTAPPTD	LASTAPPTD
331	Anderson	Brian	06-MAR-48	235	01-JUL-03	01-JUN-03
816	Smith	Jason	12-DEC-99	509	15-NOV-03	15-MAY-03
314	Porter	Susan	14-NOV-67	235	01-OCT-03	01-MAR-03
315	Saillez	Debbie	09-SEP-55	235	01-JUL-03	01-JUN-03
719	Rogers	Anthony	07-DEC-41	504	01-NOV-03	01-JAN-03
267	Westra	Lynn	12-JUL-57	235	02-FEB-04	02-FEB-03
103	Poole	Jennifer	13-MAY-02	389	01-DEC-03	01-JUN-03
108	Baily	Ryan	25-DEC-77	235	06-JUN-05	06-JUN-03
943	Crow	Lewis	16-OCT-49	235	01-JUL-05	01-MAR-02
847	Cochran	John	03-MAR-48	356	02-DEC-05	01-JAN-02
163	Roach	Becky	08-SEP-75	235	01-DEC-05	01-JAN-02
504	Jackson	John	14-OCT-43	235	21-JUL-03	10-NOV-02
809	Kowalczyk	Paul	12-NOV-51	558	29-JUL-03	19-JUN-03
703	Davis	Linda	17-JUL-02	509	21-JUL-03	22-MAY-03
696	Vanderchuck	Keith	08-AUG-68	504		15-JUN-03
966	Mcginnis	Allen	03-MAY-59	504		15-JUN-03
669	Sakic	Joe	16-SEP-76	504		15-JUN-03

17 rows selected.

Example 1.B.25   Display all data on movies other than those that cost between $1.99 and $2.99.

```
SQL: SELECT *
     FROM movie
     WHERE fee NOT BETWEEN 1.99 AND 2.99;
```

Execution Results

```
    M_ID          FEE TITLE                CATEGORY
---------- ---------- -------------------- ----------
       236        .99 Monsters, Inc.       Kids
       237        .99 E.T.                 Kids
       316        .99 Horse Whisperer      Drama
```

Part 4: Substitution Parameters

A substitution parameter is used to get a value from the user. Substitution parameters allow the user to enter a value before a query is executed, thus allowing the results to be customized at execution time. An additional SQL Plus command is used to provide the user with a prompt, and it is included at the beginning of the script file along with the SELECT command. Therefore, if you have not done so already, you will have to learn to create script files in order to be able to use these commands effectively. (See the Preface for a list of commonly used SQL Plus commands.)

General syntax of the ACCEPT command is as follows:

ACCEPT parameter-name PROMPT 'prompt string'

where the parameter-name should begin with a letter and contain nothing other than letters, digits, and underscores.

Once entered, the value is stored under the parameter name specified. To use the value within an SQL statement (such as SELECT), you must precede the parameter name with an ampersand (&). If the value entered is a character or date value, then both the ampersand and parameter name should be enclosed together in single quotes.

Example 1.B.26

Display all data on patients whose last name matches that entered by the user.

Script File Contents

```
ACCEPT last_name PROMPT 'Enter last name: '
SELECT *
FROM patient
WHERE pt_lname = '&last_name';
```

Execution Results

```
Enter last name: James
old   3:             WHERE pt_lname = '&last_name'
new   3:             WHERE pt_lname = 'James'

  PT_ID PT_LNAME  PT_FNAME  PTDOB       DOC_ID NEXTAPPTD LASTAPPTD
------- --------- --------- --------- -------- --------- ---------
    168 James     Paul      14-MAR-97      432 01-JUL-03 01-JUN-03
    313 James     Scott     01-MAR-33      235 20-JUL-03 20-JUN-03
```

Note: Each substitution parameter produces three extra lines of output before the results are displayed. Line 1 displays the prompt and echoes the value entered by the user. Line 2 shows the "old" part of the statement before the substitution is made, and line 3 shows the "new" part of the statement after the substitution is made. A means of turning the old/new line display off will be presented in Chapter 4.

Common Errors: 1. Enclosing the prompt in double quotes instead of single.
2. Within the SQL statement, not enclosing the & parameter name in single quotes (required for character and date values).

Example 1.B.27

Display all data on the movie whose title is entered by the user.

Script File Contents

```
ACCEPT movie_title PROMPT 'Enter title of movie: '
SELECT *
FROM movie
WHERE title = '&movie_title';
```

Execution Results

```
Enter title of movie: A Beautiful Mind
old   3:                WHERE title = '&movie_title'
new   3:                WHERE title = 'A Beautiful Mind'

      M_ID         FEE TITLE                 CATEGORY
---------- ----------- -------------------- ----------
       320        1.99 A Beautiful Mind      Drama
```

You should be aware that the case of the value typed must match the case of the values in the table exactly, or else no rows will satisfy the condition on the WHERE clause. In the next chapter, you will learn to use a function to get around this potential problem.

It is sometimes more convenient to use numeric columns for retrievals to avoid this situation, as illustrated by the next example. Quotes are not used around the substitution parameter reference for numeric values.

Example 1.B.28

Display all data on the movie whose ID is entered by the user.

Script File Contents

```
ACCEPT movie_id PROMPT 'Enter the ID of movie: '
SELECT *
FROM movie
WHERE m_id = &movie_id;
```

Execution Results

```
Enter the ID of movie:  354
old   3:                WHERE m_id = &movie_id
new   3:                WHERE m_id = 354

      M_ID         FEE TITLE                 CATEGORY
---------- ----------- -------------------- ----------
       354        2.99 O Brother
```

It is often desirable to use a single quote within the prompt string (as in patient's last name). When this is needed, you must place two single quotes together in order to have one single quote displayed in the output. Additionally, notice that spaces are also included at the end of the string (before the closing quote) to provide space between the prompt and the value entered during execution.

Example 1.B.29

Display all data on patients whose full name matches that entered by the user.

Script File Contents

```
ACCEPT last_name PROMPT 'What is the patient"s last name? '
ACCEPT first_name PROMPT 'And the patient"s first name? '
SELECT *
FROM patient
WHERE pt_lname = '&last_name'
      AND pt_fname = '&first_name';
```

Execution Results

```
What is the patient's last name? Saillez
And the patient's first name? Debbie
old   3:                    WHERE pt_lname = '&last_name'
new   3:                    WHERE pt_lname = 'Saillez'
old   4:                        AND pt_fname = '&first_name'
new   4:                        AND pt_fname = 'Debbie'


    PT_ID PT_LNAME         PT_FNAME          PTDOB        DOC_ID NEXTAPPTD LASTAPPTD
--------- ---------------- ---------------- --------- --------- --------- ---------
      315 Saillez          Debbie            09-SEP-55       235 01-JUL-03 01-JUN-03
```

Note: The prompt on both of the ACCEPT commands contains two single quotes (even though it looks like one double quote).

Some people find it more understandable to make the names of the substitution parameters exactly match the names of the columns, as illustrated in the next example.

Example 1.B.30

Display all data on the patient whose ID is entered by the user.

Script File Contents

```
ACCEPT pt_id PROMPT 'Enter patient"s ID: '
SELECT *
FROM patient
WHERE pt_id = &pt_id;
```

Execution Results

```
Enter patient's ID: 267
old   3:                    WHERE pt_id = &pt_id
new   3:                    WHERE pt_id = 267


    PT_ID PT_LNAME         PT_FNAME          PTDOB        DOC_ID NEXTAPPTD LASTAPPTD
--------- ---------------- ---------------- --------- --------- --------- ---------
      267 Westra           Lynn              12-JUL-57       235 02-FEB-04 02-FEB-03
```

Note: All ACCEPT examples thus far have focused on receiving numeric or character values from the user. Dates can also be handled with substitution parameters. However, an additional function is needed for dates entered by the user, and it will be covered in the next chapter.

A script file may require more than one substitution parameter, as illustrated by the following example.

Example 1.B.31

Display all data on movies whose category is the same as the one entered by the user, and also, whose fee is in the range whose end points are entered by the user.

Script File Contents

```
ACCEPT category PROMPT 'Enter movie category: '
ACCEPT low_fee PROMPT 'Enter low end of movie fee range: '
ACCEPT high_fee PROMPT 'Enter high end of movie fee range: '
SELECT *
FROM movie
WHERE category = '&category' AND
      fee BETWEEN &low_fee AND &high_fee;
```

Execution Results

```
Enter movie category: Action
Enter low end of movie fee range: .99
Enter high end of movie fee range: 1.99
old    3:                  WHERE category = '&category' AND
new    3:                  WHERE category = 'Action' AND
old    4:                       fee BETWEEN &low_fee AND
                                   &high_fee
new    4:                       fee BETWEEN .99 AND 1.99

      M_ID       FEE TITLE                    CATEGORY
---------- ---------- -------------------- ----------
       249      1.99 U-571                  Action
```

Chapter Summary

The SELECT statement is used to query a database. It can be used to display all columns or just specific columns, either from the table contents or calculated using expressions. Column aliases can be used to display improved column headings. Results can be sorted by including the ORDER BY clause. Specific rows can be selected by using the WHERE clause with a variety of operators. Substitution parameters can be used to allow the user to enter specifications to be included on the query.

Exercises

Section A: Fundamentals

1. Display movie titles and fees.
2. Display current rental data. Use appropriate column headings for all solutions.
3. All movie prices are going up. Display each movie ID, the current fee, fee including a 5 percent increase, and fee including a 10 percent increase.
4. Show current rental data in a sentence form of your choice.
5. For each patient, show his or her name and the number of days until his or her next visit.
6. Display the number of weeks and number of months until each patient's next visit.
7. Display the IDs of movies currently rented.
8. List customer data by current balance (highest to lowest).
9. List customer data by current balance (lowest to highest).
10. List customer data in alphabetic order.
11. List current rentals by customer, and for a specific customer, in chronological order of due date.
12. Display names and annual salaries of all doctors by increasing annual salaries.

Section B: Row Selection with the WHERE Clause

1. Display all data on movies due to be returned today.

2. Display all data on movies to be returned tomorrow. Arrange the results by customer ID, and for multiple rentals per customer, arrange in order by movie ID.

3. List the full name and balance for customers whose last name is Akers.

4. Doctors may receive a 10 percent increase in the annual bonus. Display the name, current bonus, and projected bonus for all doctors who earn no more than $10,000 per month. Be sure to use a column alias for the calculated column.

5. Display the full names of customers owing more than $10 and less than $20. List the results in alphabetic order.

6. Show the IDs of movies rented yesterday and today.

7. List the full names and phone numbers of all Akers and Ackers.

8. Show the name and due date of customers with balances due within the next five days (including today).

9. Display the names and current balances for customers whose phone number is either 549-1234 or 549-1235.

10. Display all data on movies in the unknown category.

11. Show the IDs and full names of patients whose last name ends with "an."

12. A customer remembers only a part of his or her phone number, and doesn't know the third and sixth digits. The first two are "54," digits four and five are "84," and the last digit is "0." Display the names and phone numbers of customers whose phone number matches that pattern.

13. Display all data on customers with balances of more than $50 due within the next week.

14. Show the names of doctors who are in either pediatrics or rehab, and also charge more than $50 per appointment.

15. Display the opposite of the previous problem: the names of all doctors *other than* those who are in either pediatrics or rehab charging more than $50 per appointment.

16. Display the names and phone numbers of customers with phone prefixes other than 453 and 529.

17. List all data on the current rentals for the customer whose ID is entered by the user.

18. Display the current balance of the customer whose full name is entered by the user.

19. Show all data on doctors whose area of specialization is the same as one of two areas entered by the user.

20. Modify the previous problem to restrict the results further to those doctors that earn a monthly salary over the cutoff entered by the user.

21. Display all current rental data in order of the column name entered by the user.

Chapter 2

Functions Applied to Single Values

There is a wide variety of functions that can be used on single values within a row. Some of them are used to convert values from one type to another, while others modify a value and give a result of the same type as the original value. All of these functions are used to provide more powerful querying abilities. When used in a SELECT statement, these functions do not change the table contents, but rather, they are used to change the results that are displayed or used in comparisons.

Eleven of the most commonly used functions are presented in this chapter and more than 70 built-in functions are available. The general syntax for all of these functions is function name followed by arguments enclosed within parentheses and separated by commas, as in ROUND (rate, 2).

Section A: Input and Output of the Same Type

Part 1: Character-to-Character Functions

Three character-to-character functions accept a character string as input and return a character string as the result. All three are for case specification: UPPER returns the string in all uppercase letters; LOWER returns the string in all lowercase letters; and INITCAP returns the string with the first letter of each word capitalized and the rest of the string in lowercase. When used on the SELECT clause, these functions are a form of calculated column, and as such, column aliases should be used.

Example 2.A.1

To illustrate the differences in these three functions, display the street address for patient number 816 in the three formats.

```
SQL: SELECT UPPER(addr) "UPPERCASE", LOWER(addr) "LOWERCASE",
            INITCAP(addr) "INITIAL CAP FORM"
     FROM billing
     WHERE pt_id = 816;
```

Execution Results

```
UPPERCASE           LOWERCASE           INITIAL CAP FORM
------------------  ------------------  ------------------
8814 W. APPLE       8814 w. apple       8814 W. Apple
```

Note: Double quotes are required only on the last column alias because it contains a space. The other column aliases are enclosed in quotes solely for the purpose of improving readability.

Example 2.A.2

Show all data on the patient whose full name is entered by the user (in any case).

Script File Contents

```
ACCEPT last_name PROMPT 'Enter patient"s last name: '
ACCEPT first_name PROMPT 'Enter patient"s first name: '
SELECT *
FROM patient
WHERE pt_lname = INITCAP ('&last_name')
     AND pt_fname = INITCAP ('&first_name');
```

Execution Results

```
Enter patient's last name: westra
Enter patient's first name: LYNN
old   3:              WHERE pt_lname = INITCAP ('&last_name')
new   3:              WHERE pt_lname = INITCAP ('westra')
old   4:                    AND pt_fname = INITCAP ('&first_name')
new   4:                    AND pt_fname = INITCAP ('LYNN')
```

PT_ID	PT_LNAME	PT_FNAME	PTDOB	DOC_ID	NEXTAPPTD	LASTAPPTD
267	Westra	Lynn	12-JUL-57	235	02-FEB-04	02-FEB-03

Note: INITCAP was used on the substitution parameter because the names in the table are stored in initcap form. If the names are stored in all uppercase letters in the table, then UPPER should be used. If the names are in a combination of forms or in unknown forms, then the function (any of the three) should be applied both to the column and to the substitution parameter.

Also note that even though what appears to be a double quote is used in the PROMPT string, this is actually a pair of single quotes. Two single quotes are used to display one single quote within a prompt.

Example 2.A.3

Display complete addresses for patients living in the city specified by the user. Allow for the possibility that some rows may have the city in initcap form (such as Makanda), whereas others may have the city in all caps (such as MAKANDA).

Script File Contents

```
ACCEPT city PROMPT 'Please enter desired city: '
SELECT pt_id, addr, city, st, zip
FROM billing
WHERE UPPER (city) = UPPER ('&city');
```

Execution Results

```
Please enter desired city:   jonesboro
old   3: WHERE UPPER (city) = UPPER ('&city')
new   3: WHERE UPPER (city) = UPPER ('jonesboro')
```

PT_ID	ADDR	CITY	ST	ZIP
168	128 W. Apple #4	Jonesboro	IL	62952
816	8814 W. Apple	JONESBORO	IL	62952

```
108 334 Pansie Hill Rd.   JONESBORO   IL      62952
315 404 Williford Rd.     JONESBORO   IL      62952
669 353 Tin Bender Rd.    Jonesboro   IL      62952
```

Note: These results would have been exactly the same if either LOWER or INITCAP had been used on both sides of the equal sign.

Example 2.A.4

Display customer names in all caps using this format:

```
Customer Names
-------------------------------------
FIRST: XXXXXXXXXXXX   LAST: XXXXXXXXXXXXX
FIRST: XXXXXXXXXXXX   LAST: XXXXXXXXXXXXX

SQL: SELECT 'FIRST: ' ||UPPER(fname) || ' LAST: ' || UPPER(lname)
          "Customer Names"
     FROM customer;
```

Execution Results

```
Customer Names
-------------------------------
FIRST:   JESSICA LAST: WOOLARD
FIRST:   ELLEN LAST: ST. JAMES
FIRST:   JANET LAST: AKERS
FIRST:   BLAINE LAST: POSTON
FIRST:   JOHN LAST: ACKERS
FIRST:   CHERI LAST: RALSTON
FIRST:   LEITA LAST: AKERS
FIRST:   GREG LAST: MACKE
FIRST:   LORETTA LAST: SALYERS
FIRST:   TISHA LAST: WILLIAMS

10 rows selected.
```

Part 2: Number-to-Number Functions

The two functions available that accept a number as input and return a number as the result are ROUND and TRUNC. The general syntax is as follows:

ROUND (numeric expression [, position])

where numeric expression may be a numeric column or a calculated value and position is an integer as follows:

If position is positive, it indicates the decimal place to which to round.

If position is zero, the value will be rounded to an integer.

If position is negative, it indicates the position to which to round to the left of the decimal.

If position is not specified, a default value of zero is used.

Reminder: [ ] indicates optional contents, and the brackets are not actually typed as part of the syntax.

Example 2.A.5

ROUND (138.547, 2) gives a result of 138.55
ROUND (138.547, 1) gives a result of 138.5
ROUND (138.547, 0) gives a result of 139
ROUND (138.547, −1) gives a result of 140
ROUND (138.547, −2) gives a result of 100

Note: These could each be tested by selecting the expression from DUAL in a manner similar to SYSDATE, as in SELECT ROUND(138.547,2) FROM DUAL;

Example 2.A.6

Ten percent raises are being considered for doctors of neurology. For each of them, show the current monthly salary, raise amount, and new salary, each rounded to whole dollars.

```
SQL: SELECT doc_id, salpermon,
        ROUND(salpermon * .10, 0) "RAISE AMOUNT",
        ROUND(salpermon + salpermon * .10, 0) "NEW SALARY"
        FROM doctor
        where area = 'Neurology';
```

Execution Results

DOC_ID	SALPERMON	RAISE AMOUNT	NEW SALARY
504	11500	1150	12650
356	7950	795	8745
289	16500	1650	18150

TRUNC works in a manner similar to ROUND, except the value is truncated at the specified position rather than rounded.

Example 2.A.7

For doctor number 235's patients, display the number of full weeks since each patient's last visit.

```
SQL: SELECT pt_id, TRUNC ((SYSDATE -lastapptdate) / 7)
        "NUMBER OF WEEKS"
    FROM patient
    WHERE doc_id = 235;
```

Execution Results

PT_ID	NUMBER OF WEEKS
331	4
313	1
314	17
315	4
267	21
108	3
943	69
163	78
504	33
439	

10 rows selected.

Note: If parenthesis had *not* been used around the expression SYSDATE−LASTAPPTDATE, then an attempt would have been made to divide LASTAPPTDATE by 7, and then subtract that result from SYSDATE.

Part 3: Date-to-Date Functions

The ADD_MONTHS Function

The ADD_MONTHS function can be used to add a specific number of months to a date, with the result being a date value. The number of months can be a literal value or a calculated value. General syntax is ADD_MONTHS (date value, number of months).

Example 2.A.8

Keith Vanderchuck called the clinic and wants to know when he's due for his annual physical. He hasn't been to the clinic since his last physical.

```
SQL: SELECT ADD_MONTHS (lastapptdate, 12) " PHYS. DUE"
     FROM patient
     WHERE pt_lname = 'Vanderchuck'
         AND pt_fname = 'Keith';
```

Execution Results

```
PHYS. DUE
---------
15-JUN-04
```

Note: The default displayed column size for dates is nine characters, so even if a longer, less abbreviated column alias had been used, it would have been truncated to the first nine characters. This will be modified in Chapter 4 using the COLUMN command.

Example 2.A.9

Physicians begin receiving annual bonuses after they have been employed at the clinic for five years. For each physician who does not yet receive an annual bonus (other than the Director), display his or her name and the date on which he or she will be eligible to receive a bonus.

```
SQL: SELECT doc_name,
            ADD_MONTHS (datehired, 5 * 12) ELIGIBLE
     FROM doctor
     WHERE annual_bonus IS NULL
     AND area <> 'Director';
```

Execution Results

```
DOC_NAME  ELIGIBLE
--------- ---------
Vester    09-JAN-05
Pronger   18-DEC-04
```

The NEXT_DAY Function

The NEXT_DAY function returns the date that is the next occurrence of the day specified following the given date. The general syntax is NEXT_DAY (date value, day of week), where day of week is enclosed in single quotes.

Example 2.A.10

When bills aren't paid on time, reminders are sent out on the first Friday following the due date. For patients with balances due that were not paid on time, print the patient ID and date on which reminders should be sent.

```
SQL: SELECT pt_id, NEXT_DAY (duedate,'FRIDAY') REMIND
     FROM billing
     WHERE balance > 0 AND duedate < SYSDATE;
```

Execution Results

```
    PT_ID REMIND
---------- ---------
      314 04-APR-03
      264 17-JAN-03
      847 01-FEB-02
```

Common Errors: 1. Using double quotes instead of single quotes around the day name.

2. Missing quotes around the day name.

Example 2.A.11

When movies aren't returned, notices are mailed on the first Monday following the due date. For current rentals that were due to be returned within the past seven days, display the customer ID and due date.

```
SQL: SELECT c_id, NEXT_DAY (duedate,'MONDAY') "SEND NOTE"
     FROM customer
     WHERE duedate BETWEEN SYSDATE-6 AND SYSDATE;
```

Execution Results

```
      C_ID SEND NOTE
---------- ---------
       799 07-JUL-03
       767 07-JUL-03
       701 30-JUN-03
```

Example 2.A.12

A modification to the previous example: allow the user to enter the day of the week, (for example, Monday) and the number of days to be used (for example, 7).

Script File Contents

```
ACCEPT day PROMPT 'Please enter day of week on which notices will be sent: '
ACCEPT num_days PROMPT 'Please enter number of days in range: '
SELECT c_id, NEXT_DAY (duedate,'&day') "SEND NOTE"
FROM customer
WHERE duedate BETWEEN
    SYSDATE - &num_days + 1 AND SYSDATE;
```

Execution Results

```
Please enter day of week on which notices will be sent:    MONDAY
Please enter number of days in range: 7
old   1:        SELECT c_id, NEXT_DAY (duedate,'&day') "SEND NOTE"
new   1:        SELECT c_id, NEXT_DAY (duedate,'MONDAY') "SEND NOTE"
old   4:            SYSDATE - &num_days + 1   AND    SYSDATE
new   4:            SYSDATE - 7 + 1   AND    SYSDATE

      C_ID SEND NOTE
---------- ---------
       799 07-JUL-03
       767 07-JUL-03
       701 30-JUN-03
```

The MONTHS_BETWEEN Function

The MONTHS_BETWEEN function doesn't return a date value as the two previous functions do, but rather, it returns an integer representing the number of months between two date values. It performs the calculation by taking the first date and subtracting the second date to get the number of days between the two dates, dividing by approximately 30 to get the number of months, and then truncating the result to get a whole number of months. In actuality, the calculation is much more accurate than this description in that the exact number of days per month is accounted for, and leap years are also taken into consideration.

Example 2.A.13

For all patients except patients of doctor number 235, display their ID, date of birth, age in months, and age in whole years in order from oldest to youngest.

```
SQL: SELECT pt_id, ptdob,
            MONTHS_BETWEEN (SYSDATE, ptdob) "AGE IN MONTHS",
            TRUNC(MONTHS_BETWEEN(SYSDATE, ptdob) / 12) "AGE IN YEARS"
     FROM patient
     WHERE doc_id <> 235
     ORDER BY "AGE IN MONTHS" DESC;
```

Execution Results

PT_ID	PTDOB	AGE IN MONTHS	AGE IN YEARS
719	07-DEC-41	738.806452	61
264	01-JAN-45	702	58
847	03-MAR-48	663.935484	55
809	12-NOV-51	619.645161	51
966	03-MAY-59	529.935484	44
696	08-AUG-68	418.774194	34
669	16-SEP-76	321.516129	26
168	14-MAR-97	75.5806452	6
816	12-DEC-99	42.6451613	3
103	13-MAY-02	13.6129032	1
703	17-JUL-02	11.483871	0
307	17-JUL-02	11.483871	0

12 rows selected.

Note: This is the first example of using functions within functions, which are called *nested functions*. When functions are nested, evaluation begins with the innermost function and then works outward. There may be several levels of nesting.

Example 2.A.14

For each of doctor number 509's patients, list the patient ID, last appointment date, and number of months since his or her last appointment, rounded to one decimal place.

```
SQL: SELECT pt_id, lastapptdate,
            ROUND(MONTHS_BETWEEN (SYSDATE, lastapptdate) ,1)
     "MONTHS SINCE LAST APPT"
     FROM patient
     WHERE doc_id = 509;
```

Execution Results

PT_ID	LASTAPPTD	MONTHS SINCE LAST APPT
816	15-MAY-03	1.5
703	22-MAY-03	1.3
307	22-MAY-03	1.3

Common Errors:
1. With MONTHS_ BETWEEN, putting the earlier date first rather than second.
2. With nested functions, assuming that evaluation proceeds from left to right rather than from innermost to outermost.

Section B: Input and Output of Different Types

Part 1: Number-to-Character Conversion

The TO_CHAR function is used to convert numeric values to character values. This is especially useful for formatting numeric values, such as adding a dollar sign or a comma for thousands.

General Syntax

```
TO_CHAR (numeric expression, format model)
```

where the format model is a character string enclosed in single quotes containing one or more of the following format elements:

9   Uses one per digit position
0   Forces display of leading or trailing zeros when used in place of a leading or trailing 9
$ Displays dollar sign
.   Displays decimal
,   Displays comma
fm Suppresses spaces in the results (acts as a toggle switch)

Example 2.B.1

For each patient who owes a payment on his or her account, display his or her ID and balance due, appropriately formatted.

```
SQL: SELECT pt_id, TO_CHAR (balance, '$999,999') " AMT. DUE"
     FROM billing
     WHERE balance > 0;
```

Execution Results

```
    PT_ID   AMT. DUE
--------- ---------
      168    $15,650
      331       $300
      314       $100
      264    $35,000
      103     $4,500
      847    $98,000
      809       $450
      703       $225
      696    $79,850
      966    $98,700
      307       $450
      439       $500
      315     $5,000
      669   $128,450

14 rows selected.
```

Example 2.B.2

For each movie in the action or foreign category, show the title and the fee (appropriately formatted).

```
SQL: SELECT title, TO_CHAR (fee, '$9.99') " FEE "
     FROM movie
     WHERE category IN ('Action','Foreign');
```

Execution Results

```
TITLE                      FEE
------------------------   ------
Ocean's Eleven             $2.99
Gone in 60 Seconds         $2.99
U-571                      $1.99
Amelie                     $2.99
Himalaya                   $2.99
Beautiful Life             $2.99

6 rows selected.
```

Example 2.B.3

For each doctor in pediatrics, display his or her name and annual income (appropriately formatted).

```
SQL: SELECT doc_name,
            TO_CHAR (salpermon * 12 + annual_bonus,
            '$999,999.99') "TOTAL INCOME "
       FROM doctor
       WHERE area = 'Pediatrics';
```

Execution Results

```
DOC_NAME   TOTAL INCOME
---------  ------------
Harrison   $148,500.00
Vester
Lewis      $122,250.00
```

Note: Dr. Vester's total income is empty because a null value (his annual bonus) was used on the calculation on the SELECT. The NVL function can be used to solve this problem, and it will be presented in the last part of this section.

Common Errors: 1. Using double quotes instead of single quotes on the format model.
2. Missing quotes around the format model.

Part 2: Date-to-Character Conversion

In addition to converting numeric values to character values, the TO_CHAR function is also used to convert date values to character values. This is especially useful when there is a need to display date values in a format other than the default display format of DD-MON-YY. It is also required when a date value is compared to a string value (such as the value of a substitution parameter), and this situation occurs frequently for tables that involve dates. Therefore, you will probably refer back to this section of the book with some regularity.

Internally, dates are stored in a full format including the year (four digits), day of the year, hours, minutes, and seconds. From these values, month, day, and day of the week can also be determined. Any of these values can be displayed by using the TO_CHAR function.

The general syntax is the same as for numeric conversion: TO_CHAR (date expression, format model). However, different format elements are used for dates, with some of the more commonly used elements listed here.

DD	Day of the month
DAY	Name of the day of the week
DY	Three-letter abbreviation of the name of the day of the week

MM	Two-digit month of the year
MONTH	Name of the month
MON	Three-letter abbreviation of the name of the month
RR (or YY)	Last two digits of year
RRRR (YYYY)	Four-digit year
/ - , : .	Punctuation as needed
"…"	Included the character string specified

Note: If the format model is omitted, then the default of 'DD-MON-YY' will be used.

Also note an important situation related to the Y2K issue. Now that the current date is in the first half of a new century the majority of the dates that appear in the database will most likely be either in the first half of this century or in the last half of the previous century. Therefore, the RR (or RRRR) format model should generally be used instead of YY (or YYYY), as it is specifically intended for this situation.

This has the additional effect of rendering the default date format ineffective for use in comparisons, as the default format uses YY instead of RR. Its usage in comparisons will often lead to erroneous results, and the source of the error in this case can be quite difficult to find. Hence, a much better solution is to *always specify a format model,* and *always use RR (or RRRR) for years.*

Example 2.B.4

Display the current date in sentence format.

```
SQL: SELECT TO_CHAR (SYSDATE,'"Today is" Day, Month DD, RRRR')
          "Current Date"
     FROM DUAL;
```

Execution Results

```
Current Date
------------------------------------
Today is Tuesday  , July      01, 2003
```

As you can see, default sizes for day and month are nine characters. To suppress the extra spaces, include fm at the beginning of the format model.

```
SQL: SELECT TO_CHAR (SYSDATE,' fm "Today is" Day, Month DD, RRRR')
          "Current Date"
     FROM DUAL;
```

Execution Results

```
Current Date
 ------------------------------------
 Today is Tuesday, July 1, 2003
```

Also notice the capitalization in the results. The characters in double quotes will appear exactly in the case entered. However, the format elements work differently. If the first letter of the day (or month) should be capitalized, then capitalize only the first letter of the corresponding format element. Alternatively, if the entire day (or month) should be capitalized, then capitalize the entire corresponding format element.

```
SQL: SELECT TO_CHAR (SYSDATE,'fm "TODAY IS" DAY, MONTH DD, RRRR')
          "Current Date"
     FROM DUAL;
```

Execution Results

```
Current Date
----------------------------------------
TODAY IS TUESDAY, JULY 1, 2003
```

Character strings can be included at any position in the format model. Note that this is the second occurrence of double quotes in SQL statements (the first being column aliases). At all other times, single quotes are used, so when in doubt, use single quotes.

All three versions of this particular example could have been written using concatenation rather than including the character string within the format model. However, the resulting code is often more difficult to debug. Therefore, literals within format models should be used instead of concatenation whenever possible.

Common Errors: 1. Using double quotes around the format model.

2. Using single quotes around the character literal(s).

Format Element Suffixes

To control numeric display, suffixes can be added to some of the format elements. The case is still determined by the format element (not the suffix). Options include two suffixes plus a suffix consisting of a combination of the two.

TH	Ordinal number (1st, 2nd, 3rd, 4th, etc.)
SP	Spelled-out number (one, two, etc.)
SPTH	Spelled-out ordinal number (first, second, etc.)

Example 2.B.5

For the patients of doctor 235, display ID and next appointment date in this sample format: Monday, the twenty-first (21st) of May

```
SQL: SELECT pt_id, TO_CHAR (nextapptdate,
          'fm Day, "the" Ddspth (ddth) "of" Month ')
       "Next Appointment Date"
    FROM patient
    WHERE doc_id = 235;
```

Execution Results

```
    PT_ID Next Appointment Date
--------- ---------------------------------------------
      331 Tuesday, the First (1st) of July
      313 Sunday, the Twentieth (20th) of July
      314 Wednesday, the First (1st) of October
      315 Tuesday, the First (1st) of July
      267 Monday, the Second (2nd) of February
      108 Monday, the Sixth (6th) of June
      943 Friday, the First (1st) of July
      163 Thursday, the First (1st) of December
      504 Monday, the Twenty-first (21st) of July
      439

10 rows selected.
```

Example 2.B.6

For the customer whose phone number is entered by the user, display the customer ID, balance, and due date for balance (month and day).

Script File Contents

```
ACCEPT phone   PROMPT 'Enter customer"s phone number: '
SELECT c_id, TO_CHAR(duedate, 'fmMonth DD') "DUE DATE"
FROM customer
WHERE phone = '&phone';
```

Execution Results

```
Enter customer's phone number:  549-8440
old    3:                  WHERE phone = '&phone'
new    3:                  WHERE phone = '549-8440'


     C_ID DUE DATE
---------- ------------
      400 July 6
```

Example 2.B.7

For the customer whose ID is entered by the user, show billing data in this format: Balance of $XXX.XX is due on Month DD, YYYY

Script File Contents

```
ACCEPT cust_id PROMPT 'Enter customer"s identification number: '
SELECT TO_CHAR (curr_bal,' "Balance of" $999.00')
     || TO_CHAR (duedate,'  "due on " Month DD, RRRR')
     "Billing Report"
FROM customer
WHERE c_id = &cust_id;
```

Execution Results

```
Enter customer's identification number: 767
old    3:                  WHERE c_id = &cust_id
new    3:                  WHERE c_id = 767


Billing Report
-----------------------
Balance of $14.90 due on June  30, 2003
```

Note: Date-to-character and character-to-date conversions will be used quite frequently, so you should familiarize yourself with the formatting elements that are available. Again, be aware that the value stored for each date is not at all the same as the default date display format; other formats can be easily extracted from the stored date values.

Part 3: Character-to-Date Conversions

Date-to-character conversion is accomplished with the TO_CHAR function, and character-to-date conversion uses the TO_DATE function. Format models and syntax are identical between the two functions. You can determine which one to use by focusing on the output of the function. If the output will be a character value, then use TO_CHAR. If the output will be a date value, then use TO_DATE.

Character-to-date conversion is needed for various purposes and is often used when the user enters a date value. Date values must be entered in character form and then converted to date format for any needed comparisons. General syntax is TO_DATE (character string expression, format model), and the format models are the same as those used for conversion from date to character using the TO_CHAR function. Another similarity is the required usage of the RR format model elements for years rather than YY, as the current date is near the beginning of a century.

Be sure to let the user know what format should be used; otherwise, the attempted character-to-date conversion may not work.

Example 2.B.8

Display the names of all patients who have appointments on the date entered by the user.

Script File Contents

```
ACCEPT target_date PROMPT 'Enter date in MM/DD/YY format: '
SELECT pt_lname, pt_fname
FROM patient
WHERE nextapptdate = TO_DATE('&target_date', 'MM/DD/RR');
```

Execution Results

```
Enter date in MM/DD/YY format:  07/21/03
old   3:   WHERE nextapptdate = TO_DATE('&target_date', 'MM/DD/RR')
new   3:   WHERE nextapptdate = TO_DATE('07/21/03', 'MM/DD/RR')


PT_LNAME          PT_FNAME
--------------    --------------
Jackson           John
Davis             Linda
Jones             J.C.
```

Converting the appointment date to a character string rather than converting the input character string to a date value could have yielded the same results.

Script File Contents

```
ACCEPT target_date PROMPT 'Enter date in MM/DD/YY format:'
SELECT pt_lname, pt_fname
FROM patient
WHERE TO_CHAR(nextapptdate, 'MM/DD/RR')= '&target_date';
```

Execution Results

```
Enter date in MM/DD/YY format: 07/21/03
old   3:   WHERE TO_CHAR(nextapptdate, 'MM/DD/RR')= '&target_date'
new   3:   WHERE TO_CHAR(nextapptdate, 'MM/DD/RR')= '07/21/03'


PT_LNAME          PT_FNAME
------------      --------------
Jackson           John
Davis             Linda
Jones             J.C.
```

Notice that in both cases the substitution parameter is included in single quotes, because it is a character string. Also notice that YY is used in the prompt to the user even though RR is used in the function, because most users will be more familiar with the meaning of the characters YY than with RR.

Example 2.B.9

Show all data on current rentals that were checked out within two days either before or after the date entered by the user. Any date format may be used, as long as the format specified by the user matches the format coded on the TO_DATE function.

Script File Contents

```
ACCEPT target_date  PROMPT 'Enter target date (MM/DD/YY): '
SELECT *
FROM rental
```

```
WHERE date_out
    BETWEEN TO_DATE('&target_date', 'MM/DD/RR') - 2
    AND TO_DATE('&target_date', 'MM/DD/RR') + 2;
```

Execution Results

```
Enter target date (MM/DD/YY):  06/28/03
old    4:         BETWEEN TO_DATE('&target_date', 'MM/DD/RR') - 2
new    4:         BETWEEN TO_DATE('06/28/03', 'MM/DD/RR') - 2
old    5:             AND TO_DATE('&target_date', 'MM/DD/RR') + 2
new    5:             AND TO_DATE('06/28/03', 'MM/DD/RR') + 2


        C_ID      M_ID DATE_OUT  DUE_DATE
---------- ---------- --------- ---------
 .      673       216 30-JUN-03 02-JUL-03
        673       249 30-JUN-03 01-JUL-03
        400       354 29-JUN-03 30-JUN-03
        673       304 29-JUN-03 01-JUL-03
        388       216 30-JUN-03 02-JUL-03
        400       255 29-JUN-03 01-JUL-03
        701       216 30-JUN-03 02-JUL-03
        701       278 29-JUN-03 01-JUL-03

8 rows selected.
```

Part 4: Null-to-Value Conversions

The NVL function is used to replace a null value with a specific value. This can be used in expressions or for displaying output. General syntax is NVL (first expression, second expression). If the first expression is null, the function returns the second expression. Otherwise, the function returns the first expression. In other words, if the column in a particular row contains a value, then that value is used. However, if there is nothing there (i.e., a null value), then the value listed in the function call is used. If a character string is specified, it should be enclosed in single quotes.

Both expressions must be of the same type. If it is necessary to display a character value for a null date or numeric value, then TO_CHAR must first be applied to the date or numeric value before the application of NVL. Hence, TO_CHAR would be nested inside NVL.

Example 2.B.10

For each doctor in pediatrics, display doctor ID and annual bonus. If no bonus is received, display a zero.

```
SQL: SELECT doc_id, NVL(annual_bonus,0) "ANNUAL BONUS"
    FROM doctor
    WHERE area = 'Pediatrics';
```

Execution Results

```
    DOC_ID ANNUAL BONUS
---------- ------------
       432         4500
       509            0
       389         2250
```

Example 2.B.11

Same as example 2.B.10, except if no bonus is received, display the word NONE.

```
SQL: SELECT doc_id, NVL (TO_CHAR (annual_bonus , '999999'),
               ' NONE') BONUS
        FROM doctor
        WHERE area = 'Pediatrics';
```

Execution Results

```
     DOC_ID BONUS
---------- -------
        432    4500
        509    NONE
        389    2250
```

Example 2.B.12

For all patients except those that see doctor number 235, display their full names and next appointment dates. If none is scheduled, display "None scheduled".

```
SQL: SELECT pt_fname ||''|| pt_lname "PATIENT NAME",
         NVL(TO_CHAR(nextapptdate, 'Mon. DD, RRRR'),
           'None Scheduled') "NEXT APPT DATE"
        FROM patient
        WHERE doc_id <> 235;
```

Execution Results

```
PATIENT NAME                      NEXT APPT DATE
-------------------------------- ---------------
Paul James                        Jul. 01, 2003
Jason Smith                       Nov. 15, 2003
Anthony Rogers                    Nov. 01, 2003
Stephanie Walters                 Dec. 12, 2003
Jennifer Poole                    Dec. 01, 2003
John Cochran                      Dec. 02, 2005
Paul Kowalczyk                    Jul. 29, 2003
Linda Davis                       Jul. 21, 2003
J.C. Jones                        Jul. 21, 2003
Keith Vanderchuck                 None Scheduled
Allen Mcginnis                    None Scheduled
Joe Sakic                         None Scheduled

12 rows selected.
```

Note: TO_CHAR must be nested inside NVL in order to convert the date to character string so that it matches the type of the replacement value.

Example 2.B.13

List data on all movies costing less than the amount entered by the user. For empty categories, display "UNKNOWN".

Script File Contents

```
ACCEPT cutoff  PROMPT 'Enter amount of fee cutoff: '
SELECT m_id, TO_CHAR(fee, '$9.99') "FEE", title,
     NVL(category, 'UNKNOWN') "CATEGORY"
FROM movie
WHERE fee < &cutoff;
```

Execution Results

```
Enter amount of fee cutoff: 2.00
old   4:               WHERE fee < &cutoff
new   4:               WHERE fee < 2.00
```

```
     M_ID FEE    TITLE                 CATEGORY
---------- ------ -------------------- ----------
      204  $1.99 City of Angels        Drama
      236   $.99 Monsters, Inc.        Kids
      237   $.99 E.T.                  Kids
      249  $1.99 U-571                 Action
      278  $1.99 Monster's Ball        Drama
      289  $1.99 The Royal Tenenbaums  Comedy
      316   $.99 Horse Whisperer       Drama
      320  $1.99 A Beautiful Mind      Drama
      337  $1.99 Grease                UNKNOWN
      349  $1.99 Cast Away             Drama
      355  $1.99 Spiderman             Kids
```

11 rows selected.

Example 2.B.14

Display each doctor's annual income. If no annual bonus is earned, use zero in its place. Appropriately format the income amount.

```
SQL: SELECT doc_name,
            TO_CHAR(salpermon * 12 + NVL (annual_bonus, 0),
       '$999,999,999')   " INCOME"
     FROM DOCTOR;
```

Execution Results

```
DOC_NAME          INCOME
--------- -------------
Harrison        $148,500
Vester           $97,200
Lewis           $122,250
Cotner          $145,500
Smith            $56,850
James           $101,900
James           $125,300
Robertson       $134,900
Thompson         $81,200
Pronger          $42,000
Borque          $204,500
Stevenson       $282,000
```

12 rows selected.

Example 2.B.15

Put it all together. Show the patient ID, date of birth, and last appointment date for patients born in the month entered by the user. List the results in chronological order of date of birth. For empty last appointment date values, show "New Patient".

Script File Contents

```
ACCEPT target_month PROMPT 'Enter 2-digit target birth month (01 -12): '
SELECT pt_id, TO_CHAR(ptdob, 'fmMonth DD, RRRR') "BIRTH DATE",
     NVL(TO_CHAR(nextapptdate, 'fmMonth DD, RRRR'), 'New Patient')
     "NEXT APPT DATE"
FROM patient
WHERE TO_CHAR(ptdob, 'mm') = '&target_month'
ORDER BY ptdob;
```

Execution Results

```
Enter 2-digit target birth month (01 -12): 05
old   4:        WHERE TO_CHAR(ptdob, 'mm') = '&target_month'
new   4:        WHERE TO_CHAR(ptdob, 'mm') = '05'

    PT_ID BIRTH DATE          NEXT APPT DATE
---------- ------------------  -------------------
      966 May 3, 1959         New Patient
      103 May 13, 2002        December 1, 2003
```

Chapter Summary

Functions can be used to manipulate individual values from tables. Case changes can be made for character values, numeric values can be rounded or truncated, and dates can be adjusted. Character, numeric, and date values can be formatted using format models. Functions can be nested inside other functions, and evaluation begins with the innermost function and works its way outward. The following list summarizes the functions used in this chapter:

Character-to-character functions

UPPER (string expression)

LOWER (string expression)

INITCAP (string expression)

Number-to-number functions

ROUND (numeric expression [, position])

TRUNC (numeric expression [, position])

Date-to-date functions

ADD_MONTHS (date value, number of months)

NEXT_DAY (date value, day of week)

Other date function

MONTHS_BETWEEN (later-date, earlier-date)

Number-to-character function

TO_CHAR (numeric expression, format model)

Date-to-character function

TO_CHAR (date expression, format model)

Character-to-date function

TO_DATE (string expression, format model)

Null-to-value function

NVL (first expression, second expression)

Exercises

Section A: INPUT and OUTPUT of the Same Type

1. Display all data on the movie whose title is entered by the user (in any letter case).

2. Modify the previous problem to allow for the possibility that some titles in the database may be in all caps, while others are in initial cap form.

3. Show doctor data in this format: "XXXX's area is XXXX." Be sure to include an appropriate column alias.

4. The fee for all movies in the "Foreign" category is being increased by 15 percent. Display the movie title and both old and new fees, each rounded to the nearest cent and appropriately formatted.

5. At the beginning of each month, a 2 percent fee is added to each past due customer balance. For all customers with balances due during the past month, show customer ID, the balance, and the increased balance. Monetary amounts should be appropriately formatted.

6. Appointment reminders are mailed each Thursday for the following week. For each patient with a next appointment scheduled, display the patient ID, the patient's next appointment date, and the reminder date.

7. For each patient whose last appointment was over a year ago, display the name and date of last appointment. Order the list chronologically.

Section B: INPUT and OUTPUT of Different Types

1. Give an alphabetic display of each doctor's name, monthly salary, and annual bonus (appropriately formatted).

2. Allow the user to enter an area of specialization and a raise percent (as a whole number). Then for each doctor in that area, display the doctor ID, current monthly salary, raise amount, and new monthly salary. Round the raise and the new salary to the nearest dollar.

3. Display the customer IDs and due dates in this form: Day of week, the XXst.

4. For the customers whose last name is entered by the user, display customer ID and due date including the month and day of month in one column, and the day of week in another column (with separate column headings).

5. For each doctor hired in the year entered by the user, display each of the following fully spelled-out values in four separate columns: Day of week hired, month hired, day of month hired, and year hired. Include doctor name, and show the results in chronological order.

6. Show the ID and phone number of the customer whose full name is entered by the user in the format first name, space, last name. For unknown phone numbers, display the word "Unlisted".

7. Modify the previous problem to include balances and due dates. For empty balances, display a zero. For empty due dates, display the phrase "Nothing due".

8. Display the ID, due date, and balance for customers who do not have balances more than seven days past due. For null balances, display $.00, and appropriately format nonnull balances. Display due dates in the format of this sample: Apr. 4, 2003. For null due dates, display *** none ***.

3

Advanced SELECT Statements

Now that the basics of the SELECT command, ORDER BY clause, WHERE clause, and single-value functions have been presented, it's time to examine some of the more complex features of the SELECT command. These include joining tables, performing summary functions, grouping rows, and specifying subqueries.

Section A: Joins

One of the best features of relational database management systems is the ability to join related tables. This is usually accomplished through the use of foreign keys. As you should remember from your previous study of database design, a relationship between two tables is implemented by adding a "relationship link" called a foreign key to one of the tables (usually the table on the "many" side of a one-to-many relationship). This foreign key is a column that contains values that match primary key values in the related table.

For example, the DOC_ID column in the PATIENT table represents a relationship between that table and the DOCTOR table. Values in the PATIENT table's DOC_ID column should match values found in the DOCTOR table's DOC_ID column, or be empty (if no doctor is yet assigned to that patient). This shared attribute is called a foreign key in the PATIENT table.

Equijoins (or Equality Joins)

In order to join tables in SQL by using the foreign key, an equijoin is used. This type of join is based on equal values in related tables. The first step is to list the tables involved on the FROM clause. Second, include a condition matching the foreign key and the related primary key on the WHERE clause. Without such a condition, the results just would be a Cartesian product, and would be of no value. The Cartesian product of the two tables consists of every possible combination of one row from the first table and one row from the second table. Hence, the number of rows initially resulting from a join is equal to the number of rows in the first table multiplied by the number of rows from the second table.

For example, if the first table contains 200 rows and the second table contains 500 rows, then the resulting Cartesian product will contain 100,000 rows. Out of this set, the only rows that are of any value are those where there is some relationship between the row from the first table and the joined row from the second table. In the example, that would be a maximum of either 200 or 500 rows, depending on which table contains the relationship link. All other row combinations are of no use, and should be discarded.

General Syntax for Joining Two Tables (Equijoin)

```
SELECT column-list
FROM table1, table2
WHERE table1.primary key column = table2.foreign key column;
```

Since the name of the primary key column in the first table is usually the same as the name of the foreign key column in the second table, the column names must be qualified by preceding each one with the appropriate table name and a period. This also applies to any other columns whose names may be the same in both tables.

Example 3.A.1

For each patient, display his or her name and the name of his or her doctor.

```
SQL: SELECT pt_lname, pt_fname, doc_name
     FROM doctor, patient
     WHERE doctor.doc_id = patient.doc_id;
```

Execution Results

PT_LNAME	PT_FNAME	DOC_NAME
James	Paul	Harrison
Anderson	Brian	Smith
James	Scott	Smith
Smith	Jason	Vester
Porter	Susan	Smith
Saillez	Debbie	Smith
Rogers	Anthony	Cotner
Walters	Stephanie	Cotner
Westra	Lynn	Smith
Poole	Jennifer	Lewis
Baily	Ryan	Smith
Crow	Lewis	Smith
Cochran	John	James
Roach	Becky	Smith
Jackson	John	Smith
Kowalczyk	Paul	James
Davis	Linda	Vester
Jones	J.C.	Vester
Wright	Chasity	Smith
Vanderchuck	Keith	Cotner
Mcginnis	Allen	Cotner
Sakic	Joe	Cotner

```
22 rows selected.
```

Common Error: Missing the WHERE clause matching the foreign key of one table with the primary key of the other. Such a join results in an unusual, unusable, large number of rows. In this example, if the WHERE clause had been incorrectly omitted, the resulting 264 rows (12 times 22) would clearly not make sense, as there are only 22 patients—not 264. This is a very common error, so if the number of rows in the results displayed is extremely large for the table sizes being used, then the WHERE clause has probably been mistakenly omitted.

Example 3.A.2

For illustration purposes only, repeat example 3.A.1 without the WHERE clause.

```
SQL: SELECT pt_lname, pt_fname, doc_name
     FROM doctor, patient;
```

Execution Results

PT_LNAME	PT_FNAME	DOC_NAME
James	Paul	Harrison
James	Paul	Vester
James	Paul	Lewis
James	Paul	Cotner
James	Paul	Smith
James	Paul	James
James	Paul	James
James	Paul	Robertson
James	Paul	Thompson
James	Paul	Pronger
James	Paul	Borque
James	Paul	Stevenson
Anderson	Brian	Harrison
Anderson	Brian	Vester
Anderson	Brian	Lewis
Anderson	Brian	Cotner
Anderson	Brian	Smith

(and so on...)

264 rows selected.

Note: A quick look at the table contents in Appendix B verifies that these results are inaccurate, as only 22 patients exist in the PATIENT table—not 264 patients. Without the WHERE clause to link the foreign key and the related primary key, the results are useless.

Table aliases are often used with joins to provide shorter table names for qualifiers. This becomes even more useful when more than two tables are joined. When table aliases are used, they are specified on the FROM clause following each table name. The first letter of the table name is commonly used for the alias.

Example 3.A.3

For each pediatrics patient, display his or her ID and his or her doctor's ID and name.

```
SQL: SELECT pt_id, p.doc_id, doc_name
     FROM patient p, doctor d
     WHERE p.doc_id = d.doc_id
     AND area = 'Pediatrics';
```

Execution Results

PT_ID	DOC_ID	DOC_NAME
168	432	Harrison
816	509	Vester
103	389	Lewis
703	509	Vester
307	509	Vester

Note: On the SELECT clause, either one of the table aliases can be used to qualify the DOC_ID column. Also, the comparison on the WHERE clause can be listed in any order (such as primary key = foreign key, or foreign key = primary key), as illustrated in the previous example.

Example 3.A.4

For each current rental by the customer whose phone number is entered by the user, display the customer name, movie ID, and due date.

Script File Contents

```
ACCEPT target_phone PROMPT 'Enter phone number: '
SELECT lname || ',' || fname "CUSTOMER NAME", m_id, duedate
FROM customer c, rental r
WHERE c.c_id = r.c_id
    AND phone = '&target_phone';
```

Execution Results

```
Enter phone number:      549-8440
old   4:                        AND phone = '&target_phone'
new   4:                        AND phone = '549-8440'


CUSTOMER NAME                      M_ID DUEDATE
---------------------- ---------- ---------
Salyers, Loretta                   354 06-JUL-03
Salyers, Loretta                   320 06-JUL-03
Salyers, Loretta                   255 06-JUL-03
```

Example 3.A.5

Modify the previous example to include customer ID instead of name.

Script File Contents

```
ACCEPT target_phone PROMPT 'Enter phone number: '
SELECT r.c_id cust_id, m_id, due_date
FROM rental r, customer c
WHERE r.c_id = c.c_id
    AND phone = '&target_phone';
```

Execution Results

```
Enter phone number:  549-8440
old   4:                        AND phone = '&target_phone'
new   4:                        AND phone = '549-8440'


   CUST_ID      M_ID DUEDATE
---------- ---------- ---------
       400        255 06-JUL-03
       400        320 06-JUL-03
       400        354 06-JUL-03
```

Note: Table qualifier is needed on the C_ID reference on the SELECT clause because more than one of the tables listed on the FROM clause contains a column by that name. Omission of the table qualifier would result in an "ambiguous reference" error message.

Also note that the join is still needed even though the displayed columns (listed on the SELECT clause) can be retrieved from just one table. The restricting column on the second part of the WHERE clause comes from the second table, thus requiring its inclusion.

Self-Joins

A table may be involved in a unary or a recursive relationship, where one row in the table is related to another row in the same table. This is often the case when a supervisory relationship exists, such as manager, supervisor, director, department chair, and so forth. In this situation, the table is joined with itself by using a different table alias for each of the two copies. It may help to try to visualize one copy as being employee (or subordinate) data, and the other copy as being manager (or supervisor) data.

Example 3.A.6

For each doctor, display the name and the name of the doctor's supervisor in alphabetic order of supervisor's name. Include column aliases for clarity.

```
SQL: SELECT d.doc_name "DOCTOR", s.doc_name "SUPERVISOR"
     FROM doctor d, doctor s
     WHERE d.supervisor_id = s.doc_id
     ORDER BY "SUPERVISOR";
```

Execution Results

```
DOCTOR      SUPERVISOR
---------   ----------
Cotner      Borque
James       Borque
Vester      Harrison
Lewis       Harrison
James       Robertson
Harrison    Stevenson
Borque      Stevenson
Robertson   Stevenson
Thompson    Stevenson
Smith       Stevenson
Pronger     Thompson

11 rows selected.
```

Note: The columns joined on the WHERE clause are crucial. In this example, the desired joined rows are those where the doctor's supervisor's ID matches the supervisor's doctor ID.

Common Error: Matching an incorrect column on the WHERE clause, as illustrated by the following modification to the previous example:

```
SQL: SELECT d.doc_name "DOCTOR", s.doc_name "SUPERVISOR"
     FROM doctor d, doctor s
     WHERE d.doc_id = s.supervisor_id
     ORDER BY "SUPERVISOR";
```

Execution Results

```
DOCTOR      SUPERVISOR
---------   ---------
Stevenson   Borque
Borque      Cotner
Stevenson   Harrison
Borque      James
Robertson   James
Harrison    Lewis
Thompson    Pronger
Stevenson   Robertson
Stevenson   Smith
Stevenson   Thompson
Harrison    Vester

11 rows selected.
```

A quick look at the tables should verify that Borque is not Stevenson's supervisor, but rather, Stevenson is Borque's supervisor. This WHERE clause is clearly incorrect, though the error is commonly made.

Example 3.A.7

Put it together. For each doctor in one of the two areas entered by the user, show the doctor's name and annual salary (including bonus), and his or her supervisor's name and annual salary.

Script File Contents

```
ACCEPT target_area1 PROMPT 'Enter first area of specialization: '
ACCEPT target_area2 PROMPT 'Enter second area of specialization: '
SELECT d.doc_name "DOC. NAME",
       TO_CHAR(d.salpermon * 12 + NVL(d.annual_bonus,0), '$999,999')
       " DOC. SAL", s.doc_name "SUP. NAME",
       TO_CHAR(s.salpermon * 12 + NVL(s.annual_bonus,0), '$999,999')
       " SUP. SAL"
FROM doctor d, doctor s
WHERE d.supervisor_id = s.doc_id
      AND d.area IN ('&target_area1', '&target_area2');
```

Execution Results

```
Enter first area of specialization: Pediatrics
Enter second area of specialization: Orthopedics
old   6:    AND d.area  IN ('&target_area1', '&target_area2')
new   6:    AND d.area  IN ('Pediatrics', 'Orthopedics')

DOC. NAME  DOC. SAL SUP. NAME  SUP. SAL
---------  -------- ---------  ---------
Harrison   $148,500 Stevenson  $282,000
Vester      $97,200 Harrison   $148,500
Lewis      $122,250 Harrison   $148,500
James      $125,300 Robertson  $134,900
Robertson  $134,900 Stevenson  $282,000
```

Nonequality Joins

There may be occasions on which two tables need to be joined on the basis of something other than matching key values. In those instances, a nonequality join is used. As with the equijoin, both tables are listed on the FROM clause and a WHERE clause is included. However, the WHERE clause contains a condition based on comparison to a range of values from the other table rather than a condition based on an exact match. Though such situations are rare and are not included in the tables used in this book, you should be aware that not all joins are based on equality conditions.

Joining More Than Two Tables

The techniques used to join two tables can be extended to join more than two tables. List all tables on the FROM clause (include a table alias for each), and then match the primary keys and foreign keys on the WHERE clause. If three tables are being joined, then two matches are combined with the AND operator. If four tables are being joined, then three matches are combined with two uses of the AND operator, and so on.

Example 3.A.8

For patients whose last name matches the name entered by the user, display their first name, phone number, and doctor's name.

Script File Contents

```
ACCEPT target_name PROMPT 'Enter patient"s last name: '
SELECT pt_fname, phone, doc_name
FROM patient p, doctor d, billing b
```

```
WHERE p.doc_id = d.doc_id
    AND b.pt_id = p.pt_id
    AND UPPER(pt_lname) = UPPER('&target_name');
```

Execution Results

```
Enter patient's last name: Davis
old   5:                AND UPPER(pt_lname) = UPPER('&target_name')
new   5:                AND UPPER(pt_lname) = UPPER('Davis')


PT_FNAME           PHONE     DOC_NAME
---------------    --------  ---------
Linda              529-8332  Vester
```

Example 3.A.9

For each patient, display his or her name, the amount each doctor charges per appointment, and the amount each doctor's supervisor charges per appointment. Display the data from highest charge to lowest.

```
SQL: SELECT pt_fname || '' || pt_lname "PATIENT",
         d.chgperappt "DOCTOR'S CHARGE",
         s.chgperappt "SUPERVISOR'S CHARGE"
     FROM patient p, doctor d, doctor s
     WHERE p.doc_id = d.doc_id
         AND d.supervisor_id = s.doc_id
     ORDER BY d.chgperappt DESC, s.chgperappt DESC;
```

Execution Results

PATIENT	DOCTOR'S CHARGE	SUPERVISOR'S CHARGE
Anthony Rogers	85	95
Stephanie Walters	85	95
Keith Vanderchuck	85	95
Allen Mcginnis	85	95
Joe Sakic	85	95
Paul Kowalczyk	85	90
John Cochran	80	95
Paul James	75	
Jason Smith	40	75
Jennifer Poole	40	75
Linda Davis	40	75
J.C. Jones	40	75
Brian Anderson	25	
Becky Roach	25	
Chasity Wright	25	
John Jackson	25	
Lewis Crow	25	
Ryan Baily	25	
Lynn Westra	25	
Debbie Saillez	25	
Susan Porter	25	
Scott James	25	

```
22 rows selected.
```

Example 3.A.10

For the patient whose full name is entered by the user, display the patient's balance, doctor's name, area, and the doctor's supervisor's name.

Script File Contents

```
ACCEPT lname PROMPT 'Enter patient"s last name: '
ACCEPT fname PROMPT 'Enter first name: '

SELECT TO_CHAR(balance, '$999,999') "BALANCE", d.doc_name, d.area,
      s.doc_name
FROM patient p, doctor d, billing b, doctor s
WHERE p.doc_id = d.doc_id
     AND b.pt_id = p.pt_id
     AND d.supervisor_id = s.doc_id
     AND UPPER(pt_lname) = UPPER('&lname')
          AND UPPER(pt_fname) = UPPER('&fname');
```

Execution Results

```
Enter patient's last name: Walters
Enter first name:  Stephanie
old    7:         AND UPPER(pt_lname) = UPPER('&lname')
new    7:         AND UPPER(pt_lname) = UPPER('Walters')
old    8:             AND UPPER(pt_fname) = UPPER('&fname')
new    8:             AND UPPER(pt_fname) = UPPER('Stephanie')


BALANCE    DOC_NAME   AREA                 DOC_NAME
---------  ---------  -------------------- ---------
  $35,000 Cotner     Neurology            Borque
```

Section B: Summary Functions and Row Grouping

Part 1: Summary Functions

Several functions are used to calculate and return summary information. They are COUNT, SUM, AVG, MAX, and MIN. In each case, the function name is followed by a parameter enclosed in parenthesis.

The Count Function

COUNT returns the number of rows selected in a query, and the general syntax is COUNT (*), COUNT (column-name), or COUNT ([DISTINCT] column-name). Use the DISTINCT keyword when duplicates are to be eliminated from the results displayed.

Example 3.B.1

Display the number of patients who have balances past due.

```
SQL: SELECT COUNT (*) "NUMBER OF PAST DUE BALANCES"
     FROM billing
     WHERE duedate < SYSDATE;
```

Execution Results

```
NUMBER OF PAST DUE BALANCES
---------------------------
                          4
```

Example 3.B.2

Display the number of doctors that currently have patients.

```
SQL: SELECT COUNT (doc_id) "DOCTORS WITH PATIENTS"
     FROM patient;
```

Execution Results

```
DOCTORS WITH PATIENTS
---------------------
                   22
```

Note: These results are clearly inaccurate because there are only 12 doctors in the database. In this example, each occurrence of a doctor ID is counted, rather than each occurrence of a *different* doctor ID. Therefore, the DISTINCT keyword needs to be included in order to give accurate results.

```
SQL: SELECT COUNT (DISTINCT doc_id) "DOCTORS WITH PATIENTS"
     FROM patient;
```

Execution Results

```
DOCTORS WITH PATIENTS
---------------------
                   7
```

Example 3.B.3

Display the number of customers that currently have movies rented.

```
SQL: SELECT COUNT (DISTINCT c_id) "CUSTOMERS WITH RENTALS"
     FROM rental;
```

Execution Results

```
CUSTOMERS WITH RENTALS
----------------------
                    10
```

The Sum Function

SUM is used to calculate a total. The parameter can be either a column or an expression.

Example 3.B.4

Display the total amount past due for all patients.

```
SQL: SELECT SUM (balance) "TOTAL PAST DUE"
     FROM billing
     WHERE duedate < SYSDATE;
```

Execution Results

```
TOTAL PAST DUE
--------------
        133000
```

Note: Formatting can (and often should) be applied to the results of the summary functions.

```
SQL: SELECT TO_CHAR(SUM (balance), '$9,999,999,999')
          "TOTAL PAST DUE"
     FROM billing
     WHERE duedate < SYSDATE;
```

Execution Results

```
TOTAL PAST DUE
--------------
      $133,000
```

Example 3.B.5

Show the total annual bonus earned by doctors hired in the year entered by the user.

Script File Contents

```
ACCEPT target_year PROMPT 'Enter a 4-digit year: '
SELECT TO_CHAR(SUM (annual_bonus), '$999,999') " TOTAL"
FROM doctor
WHERE TO_CHAR(datehired, 'RRRR') = '&target_year';
```

Execution Results

```
Enter a 4-digit year: 1998
old   3:        WHERE TO_CHAR(datehired, 'RRRR') = '&target_year'
new   3:        WHERE TO_CHAR(datehired, 'RRRR') = '1998'

     TOTAL
   ---------
   $16,250
```

Note: Spaces were included within the quotes at the beginning of the column alias to align the heading with the value. A better method of achieving this result is the COLUMN command, which will be presented in the next chapter.

Common Error: Assuming evaluation of nested functions proceeds from left to right. Evaluation is always from the innermost nested function to the outermost.

Example 3.B.6

Display the total that will be charged for appointments today.

```
SQL: SELECT TO_CHAR(SUM (chgperappt), '$9,999,999,999')
          "TODAY'S CHARGES"
     FROM patient p, doctor d
     WHERE p.doc_id = d.doc_id
        AND nextapptdate = SYSDATE;
```

Execution Results

```
TODAY'S CHARGES
---------------
          $125
```

Note: Even though the total charges for one day will most likely never approach $9,999,999,999 (as specified in the format model of the TO_CHAR function), adding extra positions to the format model is one of the simplest ways to increase the displayed column size. If the extra positions had not been included, the column heading would have been truncated. This illustrates the availability of an additional method for controlling column heading display (see note on previous example). Alternatively, the COLUMN command could be used to increase the column display size (covered in Chapter 4).

Example 3.B.7

Display the total annual salary (including bonuses) earned by all doctors.

```
SQL: SELECT TO_CHAR(SUM (salpermon * 12 + NVL (annual_bonus, 0)),
          '$9,999,999,999') " TOTAL EARNED"
     FROM doctor;
```

Execution Results

```
   TOTAL EARNED
   -------------
    $1,542,100
```

Note: NVL was needed in the previous example because calculations that use null values will return null results. Hence, a new doctor earning a monthly salary but not yet earning a bonus would have added *nothing* to the total (not even the monthly salary) if the NVL function had not been used.

The AVG Function

AVG is used to calculate and determine an average by summing the values and dividing by the number of values. Null values will not be included in the number of values used for the division unless the NVL function is used.

Example 3.B.8

Display the average annual bonus earned by doctors that receive a bonus.

```
SQL: SELECT TO_CHAR(AVG (annual_bonus), '$999,999,999')
        "AVERAGE BONUS"
    FROM doctor
    WHERE annual_bonus IS NOT NULL;
```

Execution Results

```
AVERAGE BONUS
-------------
     $5,478
```

Note: The WHERE clause is included here only for clarification. As illustrated by the following modification, the results would have been exactly the same without it, because nulls are not included by the AVG function.

```
SQL: SELECT TO_CHAR(AVG (annual_bonus), '$999,999,999')
        "AVERAGE BONUS"
    FROM doctor;
```

Execution Results

```
AVERAGE BONUS
-------------
     $5,478
```

Also notice that this value differs significantly from the results in the next example, which uses the NVL function. Of course, the difference is not found in the sum of the bonuses, but rather, in the number of values used for the division.

Example 3.B.9

Display the average annual bonus earned by all doctors.

```
SQL: SELECT TO_CHAR(AVG (NVL (annual_bonus, 0)), '$999,999,999')
        "AVERAGE BONUS"
    FROM doctor;
```

Execution Results

```
AVERAGE BONUS
-------------
     $4,108
```

Example 3.B.10

Display the average fee charged for movies rented today.

```
SQL: SELECT AVG (fee) "AVG. FOR TODAY'S RENTALS"
    FROM rental r, movie m
    WHERE r.m_id = m.m_id
        AND date_out = SYSDATE;
```

Execution Results

```
AVG. FOR TODAY'S RENTALS
------------------------
              1.84714286
```

Example 3.B.11

Modify the previous example to include formatting and rounding to two decimal places.

```
SQL: SELECT TO_CHAR (ROUND (AVG (fee), 2), '$9.99') "AVG"
     FROM rental r, movie m
     WHERE r.m_id = m.m_id
        AND date_out = SYSDATE;
```

Execution Results

```
AVG.
------
 $1.85
```

The MAX and MIN Functions

The MAX function is used to determine the highest value, and the MIN function is used to determine the lowest value. They can be used on numeric, character string, and date values.

Example 3.B.12

Display the lowest and highest charge per appointment.

```
SQL: SELECT MIN (chgperappt) "LOWEST CHARGE",
         MAX (chgperappt) "HIGHEST CHARGE"
     FROM doctor;
```

Execution Results

```
LOWEST CHARGE HIGHEST CHARGE
------------- --------------
           25             95
```

Note: The charges are not formatted because using a format model of '$99' would truncate the column headings to three characters (to be corrected in Chapter 4). Again, if formatting is needed, then extra nines could be used in the format model to avoid truncation.

Example 3.B.13

List the highest, lowest, and average fee for all movies in the category entered by the user (formatted appropriately).

Script File Contents

```
ACCEPT category PROMPT 'Enter the desired category: '
SELECT TO_CHAR(MAX(fee), '$99.99') MAX,
     TO_CHAR(MIN(fee), '$99.99') MIN,
     TO_CHAR(AVG(fee), '$99.99') AVG
FROM movie
WHERE UPPER(category) = UPPER('&category');
```

Execution Results

```
Enter the desired category: Drama
old   5:        WHERE UPPER(category) = UPPER('&category')
new   5:        WHERE UPPER(category) = UPPER('Drama')

MAX     MIN     AVG
------- ------- -------
  $2.99   $.99   $1.99
```

Part 2: Grouping Rows

Rows can be rearranged temporarily and arranged in groups of like values for the purpose of applying the summary functions to the groups. Grouping in no way changes the order of the rows in the tables, but rather, a temporary reordering is used only for the purpose of the individual query evaluation.

The GROUP BY clause is used to specify the column to use for the grouping. General syntax is GROUP BY expression where the expression usually consists of a column name.

Example 3.B.14

Display the number of patients currently assigned to each doctor.

```
SQL: SELECT doc_id, COUNT (*) "NUMBER OF PATIENTS"
    FROM patient
    GROUP BY doc_id;
```

Execution Results

```
    DOC_ID NUMBER OF PATIENTS
--------- ------------------
       235                10
       356                 1
       389                 1
       432                 1
       504                 5
       509                 3
       558                 1
```

7 rows selected.

Example 3.B.15

Display the number of movies currently rented by each customer.

```
SQL: SELECT c_id, COUNT (*) "NUMBER OF MOVIES"
    FROM rental
    GROUP BY c_id;
```

Execution Results

```
C_ID NUMBER OF MOVIES
---------- ----------------
       388                4
       400                3
       579                2
       673                4
       701                2
```

Example 3.B.16

For each area of specialization, display the average monthly salary.

```
SQL: SELECT area, TO_CHAR(AVG (salpermon),'$9,999,999')
        "AVG. SALARY"
    FROM doctor
    GROUP BY area;
```

Execution Results

```
AREA                 AVG. SALARY
-------------------- -----------
Director                 $23,500
Family Practice           $4,550
Neurology                $11,983
```

```
Orthopedics                        $10,150
Pediatrics                         $10,033
Rehab                               $5,000
```

```
6 rows selected.
```

There may be times when it is necessary to specify groups within groups. In this case, two or more columns may be specified on the GROUP BY clause.

Example 3.B.17

For each area of specialization, display the number of patients from each town represented.

```
SQL: SELECT area, INITCAP(city) "CITY",
            COUNT (*) "NUMBER OF PATIENTS"
     FROM patient p, doctor d, billing b
     WHERE p.doc_id = d.doc_id
     AND p.pt_id = b.pt_id
     GROUP BY area, INITCAP(city);
```

Execution Results

```
AREA                     CITY          NUMBER OF PATIENTS
--------------------     -----------   ------------------
Family Practice          Anna                           3
Family Practice          Carbondale                     3
Family Practice          Cobden                         1
Family Practice          Herrin                         1
Family Practice          Jonesboro                      2
Neurology                Anna                           1
Neurology                Carbondale                     3
Neurology                Herrin                         1
Neurology                Jonesboro                      1
Orthopedics              Murphysboro                    1
Pediatrics               Anna                           1
Pediatrics               Carbondale                     2
Pediatrics               Jonesboro                      2
```

```
13 rows selected.
```

Note: INITCAP was used on the SELECT clause so that cities would be displayed in a consistent format. INITCAP was used on the GROUP BY clause so that cases such as JONESBORO and Jonesboro would be included within the same group. This example also serves to illustrate that calculations and/or formatting functions may be included on the GROUP BY clause.

Also note that all three tables are needed, because the patient table provides the only link to the billing table's city column (through the P_ID column) and also to the doctor table's area column (through the DOC_ID column).

Example 3.B.18

For each category, display the number of different titles available at each fee. Use "Unknown" for empty categories.

```
SQL: SELECT NVL(category, 'Unknown') "CATEGORY", fee,
            COUNT(*) "NUMBER OF TITLES"
     FROM movie
     GROUP BY category, fee;
```

Execution Results

```
CATEGORY          FEE NUMBER OF TITLES
----------  ----------  ----------------
Unknown         1.99                   1
Unknown         2.99                   2
Kids             .99                   2
Kids            1.99                   1
Drama            .99                   1
Drama           1.99                   4
Drama           2.99                   2
Action          1.99                   1
Action          2.99                   2
Comedy          1.99                   1
Comedy          2.99                   1
Family          2.99                   1
Foreign         2.99                   3
```

13 rows selected.

The HAVING Clause

The HAVING clause can be added after the GROUP BY clause to specify the inclusion only of groups that meet a certain condition. The HAVING clause applies to groups in the same manner that the WHERE clause applies to rows. The general syntax is HAVING condition, where the condition is a logical expression of the same format as that used on the WHERE clause. Additionally, the summary functions presented earlier in this section may also be used on the HAVING clause.

Example 3.B.19

For all areas with at least two doctors, display the average charge per appointment, rounded to the nearest dollar and appropriately formatted.

```
SQL: SELECT area, TO_CHAR(ROUND(AVG (chgperappt)), '$99,999')
            "AVG. CHG"
     FROM doctor
     GROUP BY area
     HAVING COUNT (doc_id) >= 2;
```

Execution Results

```
AREA                AVG. CHG
-------------------- --------
Neurology                $87
Orthopedics              $88
Pediatrics               $52
Rehab                    $53
```

Example 3.B.20

For all areas with three or more different fees available, display the average fee per category, rounded to the nearest cent.

```
SQL: SELECT category,
            TO_CHAR(ROUND(AVG (fee) ,2), '$999.99') "AVG. FEE"
     FROM movie
     GROUP BY category, fee
     HAVING COUNT (m_id) >= 3;
```

Execution Results

```
CATEGORY    AVG. FEE
----------  --------
Drama         $1.99
Foreign       $2.99
```

Any combination of the clauses presented thus far may be included in one SELECT statement. The order of *specification* is as follows:

1. SELECT
2. FROM
3. WHERE
4. GROUP BY
5. HAVING
6. ORDER BY

The order of *evaluation* is as follows:

1. The tables listed on the FROM clause are copied to temporary storage.
2. The rows that do not satisfy the condition listed on the WHERE clause are eliminated.
3. The rows are rearranged and grouped by like values as specified on the GROUP BY clause.
4. The groups that do not satisfy the condition listed on the HAVING clause are eliminated.
5. Group functions are applied as specified on the SELECT clause.
6. Results are displayed in the order specified on the ORDER BY clause.

Example 3.B.21

For all doctors except numbers 432 and 509, display the average balance owed by their patients in ascending order. Ignore groups with a total of less than $100 owed.

```
SQL: SELECT doc_id, TO_CHAR(AVG (balance), '$99,999,999')
            "AVERAGE OWED"
        FROM billing b, patient p
        WHERE b.pt_id = p.pt_id
            AND doc_id NOT IN (432, 509)
        GROUP BY doc_id
        HAVING SUM (balance) >= 100
        ORDER BY AVG (balance);
```

Execution Results

```
DOC_ID AVERAGE OWED
--------- ------------
    235        $240
    558        $450
    389      $4,500
    504     $68,400
    356     $98,000
```

Example 3.B.22

For each customer except the Woolards and Mackes, display the total owed for each day of current rentals. Exclude daily rentals consisting of more than four movies. Order the results by customer, and for each customer, place the list in chronological order.

```
SQL: SELECT c.c_id, due_date, TO_CHAR(SUM (fee), '$99.99') "TOTAL"
     FROM movie m, rental r, customer c
     WHERE m.m_id = r.m_id
         AND c.c_id = r.c_id
         AND lname NOT IN ('Woolard', 'Macke')
     GROUP BY c.c_id, due_date
     HAVING COUNT (m.m_id) <= 4
     ORDER BY c.c_id, due_date;
```

Execution Results

```
    C_ID DUE_DATE  TOTAL
---------- --------- -------
     400 30-JUN-03  $2.99
     400 01-JUL-03  $2.99
     400 04-JUL-03  $1.99
     579 03-JUL-03  $1.99
     579 04-JUL-03  $2.99
     673 01-JUL-03  $4.98
     673 02-JUL-03  $2.99
     673 04-JUL-03  $1.99
     701 01-JUL-03  $1.99
     701 02-JUL-03  $2.99

10 rows selected.
```

Section C: Single-Column Subqueries

Subqueries can be used to determine results that cannot be found in one step, but rather, require two or more steps. As with the queries covered thus far, subqueries can return a single value, several columns of values, and/or several rows. Each subquery is enclosed in parentheses, and the innermost query is evaluated before the outermost query.

Part 1: Single-Column, Single-Row Results

A subquery is used to determine a value (or values) before the rest of the query is completed. For example, in order to display the names of doctors that earn more than the average, a subquery would have to be used to first determine the average salary. Then the rest of the query (also known as the outer query) can be executed.

The key to understanding subqueries lies in deciding which piece of information needs to be determined first. It may help to try to figure out how you would determine the answer by hand while looking at a portion of the table contents. Be aware of what you looked up first and how you used that on your second pass through the table. Then write a query for only the item that you looked up first (this will eventually become the subquery), and get it to run correctly. Don't bother with formatting the output or using column aliases because they'll just be buried in the subquery eventually and not displayed. Finally, add the outer query, thus changing your original query into a subquery.

Always take the time to execute the subquery by itself first before adding the outer query, even if you think you can do it all in one pass. This helps focus your attention on the subquery results, thereby enabling verification that exactly one value is indeed returned by the subquery, also assisting in using the correct type of value on the comparison. The overall time required to execute queries with subqueries will be shortened if you can develop the important habit of executing the subquery by itself first.

As far as syntax is concerned, a subquery that returns one value (single column, single row) may be used as part of the condition on the WHERE clause. It must be contained within parentheses, but other than that, the syntax is exactly the same as that used in the queries thus far.

Example 3.C.1

Display the names of doctors in Dr. Harrison's area. (*Hint:* The piece of information that needs to be determined first is Dr. Harrison's area.)

```
SQL: SELECT doc_name
     FROM doctor
     WHERE area =
         (SELECT area
          FROM doctor
          WHERE doc_name = 'Harrison');
```

Execution Results

```
DOC_NAME
---------
Harrison
Vester
Lewis
```

Note: The same effect can be achieved by using a join of the table used on the outer query and the table used on the inner subquery. In this case, the two tables are the same, so a self-join is used as follows:

```
SQL: SELECT cowork.doc_name
     FROM doctor harr, doctor cowork
     WHERE harr.area = cowork.area
         AND harr.doc_name = 'Harrison';
```

Execution Results

```
DOC_NAME
---------
Harrison
Vester
Lewis
```

However, consider which version might be more efficient. In the first version, the subquery makes one pass through the DOCTOR table, finds the correct row, and then chooses the value for AREA from that row. Then the outer query makes one pass through the DOCTOR table, and chooses the rows with areas that match the area from the subquery. Finally, the doctor names from those chosen rows are displayed.

Conversely, the second version forms a join by taking every possible combination of one row from the HARR version, and one row from the COWORK version, for a total of 144 rows. Then the rows with matching areas and a doctor's name of Harrison are chosen. Finally, the doctor names from those chosen rows are displayed.

Overall, the production of the potentially large number of rows involved with the join is much less efficient than a quick subquery. This example involved only 144 rows, but more realistically, the tables involved may have hundreds or thousands of rows, and the resulting join could be a very slow process. Therefore, when you have the option, use a subquery instead of a join.

Example 3.C.2

For each copy of *Ocean's Eleven* currently rented, display the due date and the customer ID.

```
SQL: SELECT due_date, c_id
     FROM rental
     WHERE m_id =
        (SELECT m_id
         FROM movie
         WHERE title = 'Ocean"s Eleven');
```

Execution Results

```
DUE_DATE          C_ID
---------      ----------
02-JUL-03            673
02-JUL-03            388
02-JUL-03            701
```

Example 3.C.3

Display the names and salaries of doctors who earn more than the average salary.

```
SQL: SELECT doc_name, TO_CHAR(salpermon, '$999,999') "SALARY"
     FROM doctor
     WHERE salpermon >
        (SELECT AVG (salpermon) FROM doctor);
```

Execution Results

```
DOC_NAME   SALARY
---------  ---------
Harrison   $12,000
Cotner     $11,500
Robertson  $10,500
Borque     $16,500
Stevenson  $23,500
```

Note: How can we tell whether or not these results are correct? It would help to know what the average salary per month is, so the subquery should have first been executed by itself. This provides further justification for executing the subquery before adding the outer query. And FYI, the average salary per month is approximately $10,367, so the above results are indeed correct.

Example 3.C.4

Display the name of the customer with the highest current balance.

```
SQL: SELECT fname || '' || lname "CUST. W/HIGHEST BAL."
     FROM customer
     WHERE curr_bal =
        (SELECT MAX (curr_bal) FROM customer);
```

Execution Results

```
CUST. W/HIGHEST BAL.
--------------------
Leita Akers
```

Part 2: Single-Column, Multiple-Row Results

The need may arise for several values to be returned by a subquery, such as checking to see if a value occurs in a list returned by a subquery, or checking to see if a value is greater than (or less than) the values in a list. These situations call for a subquery that returns the value for only one column, but for several rows, resulting in a list of several values rather than just one. In this case, simple comparison operators are inappropriate, so other operators must be used.

The IN Operator

This operator is used to determine whether or not a value appears in a set of values, as it does when used without subqueries. When a subquery is used, however, the set of values is determined by the subquery rather than by listing literal values within parentheses.

Example 3.C.5

Display the names of doctors who are also supervisors.

```
SQL: SELECT doc_name
     FROM doctor
     WHERE doc_id IN
         (SELECT DISTINCT supervisor_id
         FROM doctor);
```

Execution Results

```
DOC_NAME
---------
Stevenson
Borque
Harrison
Robertson
Thompson
```

Note: As is sometimes the case, this could have been handled with a join instead of a subquery as follows:

```
SQL: SELECT DISTINCT s.doc_name
     FROM doctor d, doctor s
     WHERE d.supervisor_id = s.doc_id;
```

Execution Results

```
DOC_NAME
---------
Borque
Harrison
Robertson
Stevenson
Thompson
```

However, as mentioned previously, joining tables requires more resources (in time and memory) than subqueries do, so again, when given a choice, use a subquery instead of a join.

Example 3.C.6

Display the names of patients insured by HealthCare. Use a subquery instead of a join.

```
SQL: SELECT pt_fname || ' ' || pt_lname "NAME"
     FROM patient
     WHERE pt_id IN
                 (SELECT pt_id
                 FROM billing
                 WHERE pt_ins = 'HealthCare');
```

Execution Results

```
NAME
---------------------
Jennifer Poole
Ryan Baily
```

```
Becky Roach
J.C. Jones
Debbie Saillez
Linda Davis
Anthony Rogers

7 rows selected.
```

Example 3.C.7

Display the names of movies due back today that were rented during the past week. Use a subquery instead of a join.

```
SQL: SELECT title
     FROM movie
     WHERE m_id IN
          (SELECT DISTINCT m_id
          FROM rental
          WHERE due_date = SYSDATE
               AND date_out BETWEEN SYSDATE-6 AND SYSDATE);
```

Execution Results

```
TITLE
----------
U-571
Amelie
Monster's Ball
Wild, Wild, West
```

Note: The DISTINCT operator was used on the subquery, because there is no need to keep duplicate values in this case.

The ALL Operator

This operator can be used in conjunction with any of the basic comparison operators (<, =, <=, etc.) to determine how a value compares to all of the values in the list. For example, > ALL means more than the maximum, <> ALL is the same as NOT IN, and < ALL means less than the minimum.

Example 3.C.8

Display the names and monthly salaries of doctors who earn more than all of the doctors in pediatrics.

```
SQL: SELECT doc_name, TO_CHAR(salpermon, '$999,999') SALARY
     FROM doctor
     WHERE salpermon > ALL
          (SELECT salpermon
          FROM doctor
          WHERE area = 'Pediatrics');
```

Execution Results

```
DOC_NAME   SALARY
---------  ---------
Borque       $16,500
Stevenson    $23,500
```

Note: The ALL operator could have been replaced with the usage of MAX on the subquery as follows:

```
SQL: SELECT doc_name, TO_CHAR(salpermon, '$999,999') SALARY
     FROM doctor
     WHERE salpermon >
          (SELECT MAX(salpermon)
           FROM doctor
           WHERE area = 'Pediatrics');
```

Execution Results

```
DOC_NAME   SALARY
---------  ---------
Borque        $16,500
Stevenson     $23,500
```

Example 3.C.9

Same as previous solution (using ALL). But for this example assume that we don't know the doctor's area of specialty, but rather, only that it is Dr. Vester's area.

```
SQL: SELECT doc_name, TO_CHAR(salpermon, '$999,999') "SALARY"
     FROM doctor
     WHERE salpermon > ALL
          (SELECT salpermon
           FROM doctor
           WHERE area =
                (SELECT area
                 FROM doctor
                 WHERE doc_name = 'Vester'));
```

Execution Results

```
DOC_NAME   SALARY
---------  ---------
Borque        $16,500
Stevenson     $23,500
```

Note: This example illustrates that subqueries may be contained within subqueries. Again, the innermost query (the one in parentheses) is evaluated first, working outward to the outermost query. Therefore, Dr. Vester's area is selected, then the salaries in that area are selected, and then the comparison is made on the WHERE clause of the outermost query.

Example 3.C.10

Display the titles and categories of movies that cost less than all of the foreign movies.

```
SQL: SELECT title, category
     FROM movie
     WHERE fee < ALL
          (SELECT fee
           FROM movie
           WHERE category = 'Foreign');
```

Execution Results

```
TITLE                   CATEGORY
--------------------    ----------
City of Angels          Drama
Monsters, Inc.          Kids
E.T.                    Kids
```

```
U-571                    Action
Monster's Ball           Drama
The Royal Tenenbaums     Comedy
Horse Whisperer          Drama
A Beautiful Mind         Drama
Grease
Cast Away                Drama
Spiderman                Kids
```

```
11 rows selected.
```

The ANY Operator

As with the ALL operator, the ANY operator is used in conjunction with the basic comparison operators to determine how a value compares to any of the values in the list. For example, > ANY means more than the minimum, = ANY is the same as IN, and < ANY means less than the maximum.

Example 3.C.11

Display the names and charges per appointment for doctors that charge more per appointment than any one of the doctors in neurology.

```
SQL: SELECT doc_name, chgperappt
     FROM doctor
     WHERE chgperappt > ANY
         (SELECT chgperappt
          FROM doctor
          WHERE area = 'Neurology');
```

Execution Results

```
DOC_NAME   CHGPERAPPT
---------  ----------
Cotner            85
James             85
Robertson         90
Borque            95
```

Note: The ANY operator could have been replaced with the usage of MIN on the subquery as follows:

```
SQL: SELECT doc_name, chgperappt
     FROM doctor
     WHERE chgperappt >
         (SELECT MIN(chgperappt)
          FROM doctor
          WHERE area = 'Neurology');
```

Execution Results

```
DOC_NAME   CHGPERAPPT
---------  ----------
Cotner            85
James             85
Robertson         90
Borque            95
```

Example 3.C.12

Show the titles of movies that cost less than any one of the action flicks (though perhaps not costing less than all of the action flicks).

```
SQL: SELECT title
     FROM movie
     WHERE fee < ANY
         (SELECT fee
          FROM movie
          WHERE category = 'Action');
```

Execution Results

```
TITLE
--------------------
City of Angels
Monsters, Inc.
E.T.
U-571
Monster's Ball
The Royal Tenenbaums
Horse Whisperer
A Beautiful Mind
Grease
Cast Away
Spiderman

11 rows selected.
```

Example 3.C.13

Display the IDs, salaries, and year hired for doctors that earn more than any one of the doctors hired during the year entered by the user. Order the results by year hired. Exclude doctors hired during the target year.

Script File Contents

```
ACCEPT target_year PROMPT 'Enter a 4-digit year: '
SELECT doc_id, TO_CHAR(salpermon, '$999,999') "SALARY",
    TO_CHAR(datehired, 'RRRR') "YEAR"
FROM doctor
WHERE salpermon > ANY
      (SELECT salpermon
       FROM doctor
       WHERE TO_CHAR(datehired, 'RRRR') = '&target_year')
AND TO_CHAR(datehired, 'RRRR') <> '&target_year'
ORDER BY "YEAR";
```

Execution Results

```
Enter a 4-digit year: 1996
old   7:       WHERE TO_CHAR(datehired, 'RRRR') = '&target_year')
new   7:       WHERE TO_CHAR(datehired, 'RRRR') = '1996')
old   8:       AND TO_CHAR(datehired, 'RRRR') <> '&target_year'
new   8:       AND TO_CHAR(datehired, 'RRRR') <> '1996'

   DOC_ID SALARY      YEAR
--------- --------- ----
      100 $23,500 1979
      289 $16,500 1989
      432 $12,000 1994
      876 $10,500 1995
      504 $11,500 1998
```

Note: The two conditions on the WHERE clause of the outer query could have been performed in the opposite order (comparison on year first and then the condition involving the subquery). The results would have been the same.

Section D: Advanced Subqueries

Part 1: Multiple Column Results

A **pairwise** multiple-column subquery is used to match values in two columns rather than one. As with the single-column subqueries, results may contain one row or multiple rows. In either case, the pair of columns is enclosed in parenthesis on the WHERE clause followed by the IN operator.

Example 3.D.1

Display the names of doctors that have the same area and charge per appointment as Dr. Lewis does.

```
SQL: SELECT doc_name
     FROM doctor
     WHERE doc_name <> 'Lewis'
     AND (area, chgperappt) IN
          (SELECT area, chgperappt
           FROM doctor
           WHERE doc_name = 'Lewis');
```

Execution Results

```
DOC_NAME
----------
Vester
```

Example 3.D.2

Display the IDs of customers who have rented at least one of the same movies as Jessica Woolard, and also have it due back on the same date.

```
SQL: SELECT c_id
     FROM rental
     WHERE (m_id,due_date) IN
         (SELECT m_id, due_date
          FROM rental
          WHERE c_id =
              (SELECT c_id
               FROM customer
               WHERE lname = 'Woolard' AND fname = 'Jessica'));
```

Execution Results

```
      C_ID
----------
       673
       388
       701
       388
       388
       388
       400
```

7 rows selected.

Example 3.D.3

Display the names, hire dates, and areas of doctors who were hired the same year as Dr. Cotner and also work in his area.

```
SQL: SELECT doc_name, datehired, area
     FROM doctor
     WHERE (TO_CHAR (datehired,'RRRR'), AREA) IN
         (SELECT TO_CHAR (datehired, 'RRRR'), area
         FROM doctor
         WHERE doc_name = 'Cotner')
     AND doc_name <> 'Cotner';
```

Execution Results

```
DOC_NAME   DATEHIRED AREA
---------  --------- --------------------
James      01-AUG-98 Neurology
```

Example 3.D.4

Show the IDs of the patients who live in the same town as patient number 168.

```
SQL: SELECT pt_id
     FROM billing
     WHERE (city, st) IN
                 (SELECT city, st
                 FROM billing
                 WHERE pt_id = 168)
         AND pt_id <> 168;
```

Execution Results

```
    PT_ID
----------
      669
```

Note: Due to the mixture of cases used in the database, not all of the city names met the condition in this example. A better solution would include one of the case-related functions, as follows:

```
SQL: SELECT pt_id
     FROM billing
     WHERE (UPPER(city), st) IN
                 (SELECT UPPER(city), st
                 FROM billing
                 WHERE pt_id = 168)
         AND pt_id <> 168;
```

Execution Results

```
    PT_ID
----------
      816
      108
      315
      669
```

This example also illustrates the ability to use functions on the condition that references a subquery. As long as the types match (characters compared to characters, numbers compared to numbers, and dates compared to dates), any of the functions covered thus far may be included on conditions involving subqueries.

Example 3.D.5

Modify the previous example to allow the user to enter the name of the patient rather than the specific patient number (168).

Script File Contents

```
ACCEPT last PROMPT 'Enter patient"s last name: '
ACCEPT first PROMPT 'Enter patient"s first name: '
SELECT pt_id
FROM billing
WHERE (UPPER(city), st) IN
    (SELECT UPPER(city), st
    FROM billing
    WHERE pt_id =
        (SELECT pt_id
        FROM patient
        WHERE pt_lname = '&last' AND pt_fname = '&first'))
AND pt_id <>
    (SELECT pt_id
    FROM patient
    WHERE pt_lname = '&last' AND pt_fname = '&first');
```

Execution Results

```
Enter patient's last name: James
Enter patient's first name: Paul
old    9:        WHERE pt_lname = '&last' AND pt_fname = '&first'))
new    9:        WHERE pt_lname = 'James' AND pt_fname = 'Paul'))
old   13:        WHERE pt_lname = '&last' AND pt_fname = '&first')
new   13:        WHERE pt_lname = 'James' AND pt_fname = 'Paul')

     PT_ID
----------
       108
       816
       669
       315
```

Nonpairwise subqueries can be used when two or more values need to be matched, but they don't necessarily come from the same row. This case is just an extension of single-column subqueries, and as such, is unrelated to pairwise queries.

Example 3.D.6

Susan Porter has canceled her next appointment. In order to try to fill her spot, display the names and next appointment dates of patients who have appointments with her doctor on a later date.

```
SQL: SELECT pt_lname, pt_fname, nextapptdate
    FROM patient
    WHERE doc_id =
        (SELECT doc_id
        FROM patient
        WHERE pt_lname = 'Porter'
        AND pt_fname = 'Susan')
    AND nextapptdate >
        (SELECT nextapptdate
        FROM patient
        WHERE pt_lname = 'Porter'
        AND pt_fname = 'Susan');
```

Execution Results

```
PT_LNAME          PT_FNAME           NEXTAPPTD
---------------   ---------------    ---------
Westra            Lynn               02-FEB-02
Baily             Ryan               06-JUN-05
Crow              Lewis              01-JUL-05
Roach             Becky              01-DEC-05
```

Note: Since the appointment date selected was later than (not equal to) Susan Porter's appointment date, there was no need to include a condition to eliminate her data from the outer query (as was necessary in the previous example).

Also note that upon initial examination of the solution, it appears that a pairwise query could have been used. However, because the comparison operators are different (equal to for DOC_ID and greater than for NEXTAPPTDATE), only the nonpairwise format will work.

Example 3.D.7

Show all data on rentals due back today of either action movies or movies that cost less than the cheapest foreign movies.

```sql
SQL: SELECT *
     FROM rental
     WHERE (m_id IN
         (SELECT m_id
          FROM movie
          WHERE category = 'Action')
     OR m_id IN
         (SELECT m_id
          FROM movie
          WHERE fee <
              (SELECT MIN(fee)
               FROM movie
               WHERE category = 'Foreign')))
     AND due_date = SYSDATE;
```

Execution Results

```
    C_ID       M_ID DATE_OUT   DUE_DATE
---------- ---------- --------- ---------
    673        249 30-JUN-03 01-JUL-03
    701        278 29-JUN-03 01-JUL-03
```

Note: The extra parentheses are required around the two conditions used with the OR operator in order to force the evaluation of the OR before the AND.

Example 3.D.8

Display the names, salaries, charges per appointment and bonuses of doctors who either earn more per month than the doctors in pediatrics, charge more per appointment than at least one of the doctors in orthopedics, or receive a larger annual bonus than Dr. Vester. Exclude pediatricians, orthopedists, and Dr. Vester from the results.

```sql
SQL: SELECT doc_name, TO_CHAR(salpermon, '$999,999') "SALARY",
            chgperappt, TO_CHAR(annual_bonus, '$999,999') "BONUS"
     FROM doctor
     WHERE (salpermon > ALL
                (SELECT salpermon
                 FROM doctor
                 WHERE area = 'Pediatrics')
```

```
     OR chgperappt > ANY
             (SELECT chgperappt
             FROM doctor
             WHERE area = 'Orthopedics')
     OR annual_bonus >
             (SELECT NVL (annual_bonus, 0)
             FROM doctor
             WHERE doc_name = 'Vester'))
     AND area NOT IN ('Pediatrics', 'Orthopedics')
     AND doc_name <> 'Vester';
```

Execution Results

```
DOC_NAME   SALARY     CHGPERAPPT BONUS
---------  ---------  ---------- ---------
Cotner     $11,500            85  $7,500
Smith       $4,550            25  $2,250
James       $7,950            80  $6,500
Thompson    $6,500            65  $3,200
Borque     $16,500            95  $6,500
Stevenson  $23,500

6 rows selected.
```

Note: The ALL operator could have been replaced with MAX on the subquery, whereas the ANY operator could have been replaced with MIN on the subquery. NVL was used on the subquery on the chance that Dr. Vester does not yet earn a bonus. Parenthesis were used around the first three conditions on the WHERE clause in order to force their evaluation to occur before the AND operators. The charges per appointment are not formatted, because using a format model of '$99' would truncate the column headings to three characters (to be corrected in Chapter 4).

Part 2: Subquery on the FROM Clause

When the GROUP BY clause is used on a standard query, there is no means for displaying information from individual rows; only the summary information is available. However, a subquery on the FROM clause can be used in this case. It allows summary results to be joined and displayed for individual rows. The subquery should be enclosed in parenthesis with a "table" alias specified outside of the parenthesis.

Example 3.D.9

For each movie, show the title, category, and number of movies in that category. Display the titles in alphabetic order.

```
SQL: SELECT title, m.category,
          s.num_in_cat "NUMBER OF MOVIES IN CATEGORY"
     FROM movie m, (SELECT category, COUNT(*) num_in_cat
                    FROM movie
                    GROUP BY category) s
     WHERE m.category = s.category
     ORDER BY title;
```

Execution Results

```
TITLE                CATEGORY   NUMBER OF MOVIES IN CATEGORY
-------------------- ---------- ----------------------------
A Beautiful Mind     Drama                                 6
Amelie               Foreign                               3
Beautiful Life       Foreign                               3
```

Cast Away	Drama	6
City of Angels	Drama	6
E.T.	Kids	3
Field of Dreams	Family	1
Gone in 60 Seconds	Action	3
Himalaya	Foreign	3
Horse Whisperer	Drama	6
Monster's Ball	Drama	6
Monsters, Inc.	Kids	3
Ocean's Eleven	Action	3
Road to Perdition	Drama	6
Spiderman	Kids	3
The Royal Tenenbaums	Comedy	2
U-571	Action	3
Wild, Wild West	Comedy	2

18 rows selected.

Example 3.D.10

Modify the previous example to include the movies with no category (requiring several usages of NVL).

```
SQL: SELECT title, NVL(m.category, 'NONE') category,
            s.num_in_cat "NUMBER OF MOVIES IN CATEGORY"
       FROM movie m, (SELECT NVL(category, 'NONE') category,
                             COUNT(*) num_in_cat
                        FROM movie
                        GROUP BY NVL(category, 'NONE')) s
      WHERE NVL(m.category, 'NONE') = s.category
      ORDER BY title;
```

Execution Results

TITLE	CATEGORY	NUMBER OF MOVIES IN CATEGORY
A Beautiful Mind	Drama	6
A Knight's Tale	NONE	3
Amelie	Foreign	3
Beautiful Life	Foreign	3
Cast Away	Drama	6
City of Angels	Drama	6
E.T.	Kids	3
Field of Dreams	Family	6
Gone in 60 Seconds	Action	3
Grease	NONE	3
Himalaya	Foreign	3
Horse Whisperer	Drama	6
Monster's Ball	Drama	6
Monsters, Inc.	Kids	3
O Brother	NONE	3
Ocean's Eleven	Action	3
Road to Perdition	Drama	6
Spiderman	Kids	3
The Royal Tenenbaums	Comedy	2
U-571	Action	3
Wild, Wild West	Comedy	2

21 rows selected.

Example 3.D.11

For each patient with an appointment this month, list his or her name, doctor's ID number, and number of patients that each doctor currently sees.

```
SQL: SELECT pt_lname, pt_fname, d.doc_id, d.num_patients
       FROM patient p, (SELECT doc_id, COUNT(*) num_patients
                          FROM patient
                          GROUP BY doc_id) d
      WHERE p.doc_id = d.doc_id
        AND TO_CHAR(nextapptdate, 'MMRRRR') LIKE
             TO_CHAR(SYSDATE, 'MMRRRR');
```

Execution Results

PT_LNAME	PT_FNAME	DOC_ID	NUM_PATIENTS
Anderson	Brian	235	10
James	Scott	235	10
Saillez	Debbie	235	10
Jackson	John	235	10
James	Paul	432	1
Davis	Linda	509	3
Jones	J.C.	509	3
Kowalczyk	Paul	558	1

```
8 rows selected.
```

Example 3.D.12

Modify the previous example to include the doctor's name instead of ID number.

```
SQL: SELECT pt_lname, pt_fname, n.doc_name, d.num_patients
       FROM patient p,
            (SELECT doc_id, COUNT(*) "NUM_PATIENTS"
             FROM patient
             GROUP BY doc_id) d,
            (SELECT doc_id, doc_name
             FROM doctor) n
      WHERE p.doc_id = d.doc_id
        AND d.doc_id = n.doc_id
        AND TO_CHAR(nextapptdate, 'MMRRRR') LIKE
             TO_CHAR(SYSDATE, 'MMRRRR');
```

Execution Results

PT_LNAME	PT_FNAME	DOC_NAME	NUM_PATIENTS
Anderson	Brian	Smith	10
James	Scott	Smith	10
Saillez	Debbie	Smith	10
Jackson	John	Smith	10
James	Paul	Harrison	1
Davis	Linda	Vester	3
Jones	J.C.	Vester	3
Kowalczyk	Paul	James	1

```
8 rows selected.
```

Example 3.D.13

For each doctor, display his or her name, area, salary, and the highest and lowest salaries in his or her area. Exclude the director. Order the list alphabetically by doctor's name.

```
SQL: SELECT doc_name, d.area, TO_CHAR(salpermon, '$999,999') "SALARY",
        TO_CHAR(high, '$999,999') "HIGHEST",
            TO_CHAR(low, '$999,999') "LOWEST"
     FROM doctor d,  (SELECT area, MAX (salpermon) high,
                             MIN (salpermon) low
                      FROM doctor
                      WHERE area <> 'Director'
                      GROUP BY area) S
     WHERE d.area = s.area
     ORDER BY doc_name;
```

Execution Results

DOC_NAME	AREA	SALARY	HIGHEST	LOWEST
Borque	Neurology	$16,500	$16,500	$7,950
Cotner	Neurology	$11,500	$16,500	$7,950
Harrison	Pediatrics	$12,000	$12,000	$8,100
James	Neurology	$7,950	$16,500	$7,950
James	Orthopedics	$9,800	$10,500	$9,800
Lewis	Pediatrics	$10,000	$12,000	$8,100
Pronger	Rehab	$3,500	$6,500	$3,500
Robertson	Orthopedics	$10,500	$10,500	$9,800
Smith	Family Practice	$4,550	$4,550	$4,550
Thompson	Rehab	$6,500	$6,500	$3,500
Vester	Pediatrics	$8,100	$12,000	$8,100

```
11 rows selected.
```

Chapter Summary

Two or more tables can be joined by listing the table names on the FROM clause and matching the primary and foreign keys on the WHERE clause. Table aliases provide a shorter means of qualifying column names when joins are involved.

Summary functions can be used on all rows of a table or on groups of rows as specified on a GROUP BY clause. Groups can be restricted with a HAVING clause in a manner similar to row restriction with a WHERE clause.

Subqueries can be used to determine results requiring more than one step. It is usually helpful to try to isolate the piece (or pieces) of information that must be determined first when writing the subquery. Single-column, single-row subqueries return a single value, while multiple-column and/or multiple-row subqueries may return many values. In all cases, the subquery should be executed by itself first before adding the outer query. A subquery may also be specified on the FROM clause to allow summary information to be displayed along with individual rows.

There will often be two seemingly equivalent ways of writing a query: one that uses a join and one that uses a subquery. Joins are less efficient, thus using more processing and memory resources, so subqueries should be used instead of joins whenever possible.

Exercises

Section A: Joins

1. For each movie rented in the category entered by the user, display the title and due date.
2. Modify the previous problem to include the name of the customer renting each movie.
3. For each rented movie due back on the month and day entered by the user, list the title, fee (appropriately formatted), and due date (month, day, and day of week).

4. For patients with appointments within the next month, list full name (in one column), phone number, and date of next appointment (format of your choice).

5. For patients with balances within the range entered by the user, list full name and balance (appropriately formatted).

6. For all doctors hired in the year entered by the user, display their ID and hire date, and their supervisor's ID and hire date.

7. For each movie rented in the category entered by the user, display the movie title, due date, and customer name. Show the listing in reverse chronological order, and for a particular day, list the movie titles in alphabetic order.

8. For the patient whose phone number is entered by the user, list the insurance type and doctor's area.

9. For each doctor working for the supervisor whose name is entered by the user, display doctor ID, and patient names arranged in descending order of doctor ID. Also, for a particular doctor, list patient names in alphabetic order.

10. Modify the previous problem to include patient phone number.

Section B: Summary Functions and Grouping Rows

1. Display the total number of movies rented.

2. Display the number of different movies rented.

3. Show the total fees charged for movies rented today.

4. Show the total owed by all customers in the household whose phone number is entered by the user. List it in this form: The household at XXX-XXXX owes $XXX.XX.

5. Display the average balance for customers whose last name is entered by the user.

6. Modify the previous problem to exclude customers who have an empty balance.

7. List the highest, lowest, and average balance for patients with balances more than 10 days past due (formatted appropriately).

8. Modify the previous problem to allow the user to enter the number of days (i.e., 10).

9. For each movie currently rented, display the number of copies rented.

10. For all patients, show the total of the balances due on each date, ordered chronologically, and appropriately formatted.

11. Display counts based on groups of the column whose name is specified by the user. Also allow the user to specify the table name.

12. For each customer with one or more current rentals, display the number of movies due each day (out of those days when movies are due).

13. For each fee, show the number of different movies in each category.

14. Modify the previous example to order the results from highest fee to lowest, and within a particular fee, by decreasing counts.

15. For each supervisor of only one or two doctors, list the total bonus earned by doctors under their supervision.

16. For each area with at least $20,000 allocated for salaries each month, show the average annual bonus earned. Include doctors who don't earn bonuses in the determination of the average. Show the results in reverse alpha order of area.

Section C: Single Column Subqueries

1. Display the titles of movies in the same category as U-571.

2. Modify the previous problem to allow the user to enter the movie title (i.e., U-571).

3. List the names of patients who see the same doctor as the patient whose name is entered by the user.

4. Display the titles of action movies that cost less than the average for action movies.

5. For the customer whose ID number is entered by the user, display the IDs of movies checked out on the same day that the customer rented *Monsters, Inc.*

6. Modify the previous problem to allow the user to enter the movie title (i.e., *Monsters, Inc.*).

7. Display the names of patients who live in Carbondale (use a subquery instead of a join).

8. Allow the user to enter a column name and a target value to be used on a condition (as in, column name equal target value). Display the names of patients who live in the same city as any one of the patients satisfying the condition.

9. List the names of doctors who charge more per appointment than all of the doctors in pediatrics.

10. Show the names and hire dates of doctors who were hired after all of the doctors in orthopedics.

11. Display the IDs of any customers who currently have more movies rented than any of the Postons.

12. A customer said he wanted to rent the same movie his neighbor, Janet Akers, rented last week. Display all data on the movies rented by the customer whose name is entered by the user.

Section D: Advanced Subqueries

1. There has been a problem with one of the patient insurance providers for patients in a certain town. List the names of patients with the same insurance provider as Anthony Rogers who also live in the same town that he does.

2. Scott James needs an earlier appointment; show the names of patients who are scheduled to see his doctor earlier than his next scheduled appointment.

3. Show the names of patients who owe more than Jason Smith, excluding those who have the same phone number that he does.

4. For each customer, list name, balance, and number of movies currently rented.

5. For each movie, list title, number of copies currently rented, and total fee charged for those rentals.

Chapter

Report Formatting

All queries thus far have displayed results in a rather primitive report format. This chapter covers some of the SQL* Plus commands that can be used to produce nicely formatted reports. SQL* Plus commands are not SQL statements, and as such, do not require semicolons. The ACCEPT command is an example of an SQL* Plus command. These SQL* Plus commands are not stored in the buffer, and therefore cannot be saved to a file with the SAVE command. Hence, you should create a new script file by using the EDIT command every time your solution includes SQL* Plus commands. Hopefully, you will have already developed this habit when creating solutions involving the ACCEPT command, but if not, now is the time to do so.

The first section of this chapter focuses on the system variables that can be manipulated to improve the format of reports, while the second section focuses on specific formatting commands.

Section A: Setting System Variables

There are more than 50 system variables that can be set to adjust the environment settings. They can be modified by using the SQL* Plus SET command. For report formatting, these SET commands should be included in the script file that generates the report. Including the commands within the script file also allows you to reset the variable after report generation, and this is a good programming practice to follow.

The general syntax for the set command is SET system-variable value. The most commonly used report-formatting system variables are presented in this section.

VERIFY

This system variable is used to verify the results of a substitution that was made involving a substitution parameter. By default, the setting is ON, which indicates that the portion of the SQL statement involving the substitution parameter will be displayed both before the substitution is made (labeled OLD) and after the substitution is made (labeled NEW). This is mainly useful for debugging purposes when the value entered causes an error. Once the script file runs correctly, the VERIFY variable can be set OFF.

In general, setting VERIFY OFF can be used to clean up the screen output when substitution parameters are used.

Example 4.A.1	Display the next appointment date of the patient whose ID is entered by the user.

Script File Contents

```
ACCEPT id PROMPT 'Enter patient ID: '
SELECT nextapptdate
FROM patient
WHERE pt_id = &id;
```

Execution Results

```
Enter patient ID: 264
old   3:                  WHERE pt_id = &id
new   3:                  WHERE pt_id = 264


NEXTAPPTD
---------
12-DEC-03
```

Example 4.A.2

Follow the directions for example 4.A.1, except eliminate verification of the substitution.

Script File Contents

```
SET VERIFY OFF
ACCEPT id PROMPT 'Enter patient ID: '
SELECT nextapptdate
FROM patient
WHERE pt_id = &id;
SET VERIFY ON
```

Execution Results

```
Enter patient ID: 264


NEXTAPPTD
---------
12-DEC-03
```

Note: It is a good programming practice to reset system variables at the end of the script file.

Example 4.A.3

Display the current balance of the customer whose name is entered by the user.

Script File Contents

```
SET VERIFY OFF
ACCEPT lname PROMPT 'Enter customer"s last name: '
ACCEPT fname PROMPT 'Enter first name: '
SELECT TO_CHAR(curr_bal,'$999.99') "BALANCE"
FROM customer
WHERE UPPER(lname) = UPPER('&lname')
    AND UPPER(fname) = UPPER('&fname');
SET VERIFY ON
```

Execution Results

```
Enter customer's last name: Akers
Enter first name: Janet


BALANCE
--------
   $9.97
```

FEEDBACK

This system variable controls the display of the number of rows returned by a query, as shown by the last line of many of the examples. If the number of rows returned is greater than or equal to the current setting of the FEEDBACK variable, then this count will be displayed at the end of the query. The default value is system dependent, but is frequently set to 6. If you prefer to see this count regardless of the number of rows returned, then set this variable to 1. If you instead prefer to eliminate this extraneous line from a report, then set this variable to OFF. When FEEDBACK is on, it also verifies the completion of a COMMIT statement. More information on the COMMIT statement is contained in the next chapter.

Example 4.A.4

Display all information on patients with appointments this month. Eliminate the line of feedback at the end of this report.

Script File Contents

```
SET FEEDBACK OFF
SELECT *
FROM patient
WHERE TO_CHAR(nextapptdate, 'Month') =
     TO_CHAR( SYSDATE, 'Month');
SET FEEDBACK ON
```

Execution Results

```
  PT_ID PT_LNAME          PT_FNAME         PTDOB         DOC_ID NEXTAPPTD LASTAPPTD
------- ----------------  ---------------- --------- --------- --------- ---------
    168 James             Paul             14-MAR-97       432 01-JUL-03 01-JUN-03
    331 Anderson          Brian            06-MAR-48       235 01-JUL-03 01-JUN-03
    313 James             Scott            01-MAR-33       235 20-JUL-03 20-JUN-03
    315 Saillez           Debbie           09-SEP-55       235 01-JUL-03 01-JUN-03
    943 Crow              Lewis            16-OCT-49       235 01-JUL-05 01-MAR-02
    504 Jackson           John             14-OCT-43       235 21-JUL-03 10-NOV-02
    809 Kowalczyk         Paul             12-NOV-51       558 29-JUL-03 19-JUN-03
    703 Davis             Linda            17-JUL-02       509 21-JUL-03 22-MAY-03
    307 Jones             J.C.             17-JUL-02       509 21-JUL-03 22-MAY-03
```

Example 4.A.5

Display all data on rentals due back on the date entered by the user. Prevent the display of substitution parameter replacements. Eliminate the line of feedback at the end of this report.

Script File Contents

```
SET FEEDBACK OFF
SET VERIFY OFF
ACCEPT target_date PROMPT 'Please enter due date in form MM/DD/YY: '
SELECT *
FROM rental
WHERE due_date =
     TO_DATE('&target_date', 'MM/DD/RR');
SET FEEDBACK ON
SET VERIFY ON
```

Execution Results

```
Please enter due date in form MM/DD/YY:  07/04/03

      C_ID       M_ID DATE_OUT  DUE_DATE
---------- ---------- --------- ---------
       388        320 01-JUL-03 04-JUL-03
       579        354 01-JUL-03 04-JUL-03
```

```
       673          337 01-JUL-03 04-JUL-03
       388          316 01-JUL-03 04-JUL-03
       388          236 01-JUL-03 04-JUL-03
       400          320 01-JUL-03 04-JUL-03
```

PAGESIZE

This determines the number of lines that will be displayed on each "page," though this term has little meaning in a spool file. Essentially, it controls the frequency with which headings will be displayed and page numbers will increase. The default size is implementation dependent, but is usually 14 lines. This can be set to any nonnegative integer. Setting PAGESIZE to zero will cause the suppression of all headings and other formatting specifications. The purpose of this system variable will become more apparent when other formatting commands are covered in the next section.

Example 4.A.6

For illustration purposes only, use a page size of 5 to display the names of pediatricians.

Script File Contents

```
SET PAGESIZE 5
SELECT doc_name
FROM doctor
WHERE area = 'Pediatrics';
SET PAGESIZE 14
```

Execution Results

```
DOC_NAME
---------
Harrison
Vester


DOC_NAME
---------
Lewis


3 rows selected.
```

Note: The page size includes one line for the column heading, one line for the line of dashes beneath the column heading, and one blank line at the end of each page. Thus, a page size of 5 displays two rows per page, while a page size of 14, for example, displays 11 rows per page.

Example 4.A.7

For illustration purposes only, display all customer IDs and phone numbers using a page size that gives four customers per page.

Script File Contents

```
SET PAGESIZE 7
SELECT c_id, phone
FROM customer;
SET PAGESIZE 14
```

Execution Results

```
      C_ID PHONE
---------- --------
       388 549-6730
       402 529-8420
```

```
        673 549-8400
        579 549-1234


      C_ID PHONE
---------- --------
        799 549-6711
        767 453-8228
        133 453-2271
        239 549-1235


      C_ID PHONE
---------- --------
        400 549-8440
        701 549-8840


10 rows selected.
```

Example 4.A.8

Modify example 4.A.7 to allow the user to enter the last name of the customer(s) to be displayed. Prevent the display of substitution parameter replacements.

Script File Contents

```
SET PAGESIZE 7
SET VERIFY OFF
ACCEPT last PROMPT 'Enter customer last name: '
SELECT c_id, phone
FROM customer
WHERE UPPER(lname) = UPPER('&last');
SET VERIFY ON
SET PAGESIZE 14
```

Execution Results

```
Enter customer last name: Poston


      C_ID PHONE
---------- --------
        579 549-1234


1 row selected.
```

LINESIZE

This variable determines the number of characters that will be displayed on each line before text is wrapped around to the next line. It also controls the position of centered titles specified with the TTITLE command (covered in the next section). The default line size is implementation dependent, but is usually 80 characters. This is another case where the purpose of this system variable will become more apparent when other related formatting commands are covered in the next section.

Example 4.A.9

For illustration purposes only, use a line size of 40 to display all data on patient number 108.

Script File Contents

```
SET LINESIZE 40
SELECT *
FROM patient
WHERE pt_id = 108;
SET LINESIZE 80
```

Execution Results

```
     PT_ID PT_LNAME
--------- ---------------
PT_FNAME        PTDOB       DOC_ID
--------------- --------- ---------
NEXTAPPTD LASTAPPTD
--------- ---------
      108 Baily
Ryan            25-DEC-77       235
06-JUN-05 06-JUN-03
```

Note: Output that wraps around should serve as a reminder to either increase the page size or decrease the displayed column size, as the results above are certainly difficult to interpret.

Example 4.A.10

Display all data on movies in the category entered by the user. Prevent the display of substitution parameter replacements. Eliminate the line of feedback at the end of this report, show 20 movies per page, and use a line size of 60.

Script File Contents

```
SET LINESIZE 60
SET VERIFY OFF
SET FEEDBACK OFF
SET PAGESIZE 23

ACCEPT category PROMPT 'Enter desired movie category: '
SELECT *
FROM movie
WHERE category = '&category';

SET LINESIZE 80
SET VERIFY ON
SET FEEDBACK ON
SET PAGESIZE 14
```

Execution Results

```
Enter desired movie category: Comedy

      M_ID        FEE TITLE                CATEGORY
---------- ---------- -------------------- ----------
       289       1.99 The Royal Tenenbaums Comedy
       304       2.99 Wild, Wild West      Comedy
```

NUMWIDTH

This system variable controls the number of columns displayed for each numeric value. The default size is implementation dependent, but is frequently set at 10 columns. When numeric values are always smaller than 10 positions, setting this variable to a lower value will allow for compressed output with more information displayed in less space, thus decreasing the possibility of wraparound.

Example 4.A.11

For illustration purposes only, display doctor IDs and salaries for pediatric doctors using the default number width of 10, and then display it again using a width of 5.

Script File Contents

```
SELECT doc_id, salpermon
FROM doctor
WHERE area = 'Pediatrics';
SET NUMWIDTH 5
SELECT doc_id, salpermon
FROM doctor
WHERE area = 'Pediatrics';
SET NUMWIDTH 10
```

Execution Results

```
    DOC_ID   SALPERMON
---------- ----------
       432      12002
       509       8100
       389      10000


DOC_ID SALPERMON
------ ---------
   432     12002
   509      8100
   389     10000
```

Note: Displayed column size for numeric values is also affected by the size of the column name or column alias. Hence, the results from the second SELECT in the previous example used a column size of 9 for SALPERMON (there are nine characters in the column alias), even though NUMWIDTH was set to 5. However, the size of the column name does not affect the display of date values.

Example 4.A.12

Display all data for Dr. Cotner's patients. Compress the numeric value display as much as possible.

Script File Contents

```
SET NUMWIDTH 3
SELECT pt_id "PT.", pt_lname "LNAME", pt_fname "FNAME",
     ptdob "DOB", doc_id "DOC", nextapptdate "NEXTAPPT",
     lastapptdate "LASTAPPT"
FROM patient
WHERE doc_id =
     (SELECT doc_id
      FROM doctor
      WHERE doc_name = 'Cotner');
SET NUMWIDTH 10
```

Execution Results

```
PT. LNAME           FNAME            DOB       DOC NEXTAPPT  LASTAPPT
--- --------------- ---------------- --------- --- --------- ---------
719 Rogers          Anthony          01-JAN-42 504 01-NOV-03 01-JAN-03
264 Walters         Stephanie        26-JAN-45 504 12-DEC-03 12-DEC-02
696 Vanderchuck     Keith            08-AUG-68 504           15-JUN-03
966 Mcginnis        Allen            03-MAY-59 504           15-JUN-03
669 Sakic           Joe              16-SEP-76 504           15-JUN-03

5 rows selected.
```

Note: In addition to the lower setting for NUMWIDTH, shorter column aliases were used for the numeric values to avoid having the larger heading length override the new NUMWIDTH setting.

PAUSE

Query results often involve more than a screenful of rows. By setting this system variable ON, display will pause after each page (depending on the PAGESIZE), thus allowing the user to control the scrolling by pressing the ENTER key. The default setting is OFF. A third possible setting is to specify a character string (enclosed in single quotes) to be shown to the user as a prompt when display is paused. The default setting is no text.

Example 4.A.13

For illustration purposes only, set the page size to 6 and the pause variable to ON. Then display the names of doctor number 504's patients.

Script File Contents

```
SET PAGESIZE 6
SET PAUSE ON
SET PAUSE '*** Press ENTER to continue: ***'
SELECT pt_lname, pt_fname
FROM patient
WHERE doc_id = 504;
SET PAGESIZE 14
SET PAUSE OFF
```

Execution Results

```
*** Press ENTER to continue: ***


PT_LNAME        PT_FNAME
--------------- ---------------
Rogers          Anthony
Walters         Stephanie
Vanderchuck     Keith
*** Press ENTER to continue: ***


PT_LNAME        PT_FNAME
--------------- ---------------
Mcginnis        Allen
Sakic           Joe
```

Example 4.A.14

Show all movie data, 10 rows per page, pausing after each page.

Script File Contents

```
SET PAGESIZE 13
SET PAUSE ON
SET PAUSE '-------------- ENTER to continue ---------------'
SELECT *
FROM movie;
SET PAGESIZE 14
SET PAUSE OFF
```

Execution Results

```
------------------ ENTER to continue ----------------

      M_ID        FEE TITLE                CATEGORY
---------- ---------- -------------------- ----------
       204       1.99 City of Angels       Drama
       216       2.99 Ocean's Eleven       Action
       233       2.99 Gone in 60 Seconds   Action
       236        .99 Monsters, Inc.       Kids
       237        .99 E.T.                 Kids
       249       1.99 U-571                Action
       254       2.99 Road to Perdition    Drama
       255       2.99 Amelie               Foreign
       278       1.99 Monster's Ball       Drama
       287       2.99 A Knight's Tale
------------------ ENTER to continue ----------------

      M_ID        FEE TITLE                CATEGORY
---------- ---------- -------------------- ----------
       289       1.99 The Royal Tenenbaums Comedy
       304       2.99 Wild, Wild West      Comedy
       315       2.99 Himalaya             Foreign
       316        .99 Horse Whisperer      Drama
       320       1.99 A Beautiful Mind     Drama
       324       2.99 Field of Dreams      Family
       325       2.99 Beautiful Life       Foreign
       337       1.99 Grease
       349       1.99 Cast Away            Drama
       354       2.99 O Brother
------------------ ENTER to continue ----------------

      M_ID        FEE TITLE                CATEGORY
---------- ---------- -------------------- ----------
       355       1.99 Spiderman            Kids

21 rows selected.
```

SHOW

This is a command rather than a system variable. It is used to show the current setting of any system variable. General syntax is SHOW system-variable-name.

Example 4.A.15

Display the current PAUSE and PAGESIZE settings.

At the prompt, type the following:

```
SHOW PAUSE
SHOW PAGESIZE
```

Execution Results

```
SQL> SHOW PAUSE
PAUSE is OFF
SQL> SHOW PAGESIZE
pagesize 14
```

Section B: Format Commands

This next set of SQL* Plus commands are used to improve the report format of query results. As with the SET command, you should develop the habit of clearing formatting at the end of report generation. Only the most common options on each command will be presented, but there are many more options available.

TTITLE

This command is used to specify a top title (as opposed to BTITLE for bottom title) for a report. General syntax is TTITLE 'character string'. This will usually display at least two lines of top title, though this is installation dependent. The first line will consist of the current date at the left and the current page number at the right. The second line will consist of the text specified in the character string. If this text is to be spread over two or more lines, then the vertical bar can be used to indicate a linefeed.

The title text will be centered, and the alignment of all lines of the title will be determined by the current PAGESIZE. Hence, the page size will usually be set anytime the TTITLE command is used. At the end of the report, the title should be turned off with the command TTITLE OFF.

Example 4.B.1

Display doctor names, salaries, and hire dates using the title "Physician Report."

Script File Contents

```
SET FEEDBACK OFF
SET PAGESIZE 25
SET LINESIZE 30
TTITLE 'Physician Report'

SELECT doc_name, salpermon, datehired
FROM doctor
ORDER BY doc_name;

SET FEEDBACK ON
SET PAGESIZE 14
SET LINESIZE 80
TTITLE OFF
```

Execution Results

```
Tue Jul 01              page    1
        Physician Report

DOC_NAME   SALPERMON DATEHIRED
---------- ---------- ---------
Borque         16500 30-JUN-89
Cotner         11500 16-JUN-98
Harrison       12002 05-DEC-94
James           7950 01-AUG-98
James           9800 02-MAY-95
Lewis          10000 21-JAN-96
Pronger         3500 18-DEC-99
Robertson      10500 02-MAR-95
Smith           4550 22-JUN-98
```

```
Stevenson        23500 30-JUN-79
Thompson          6500 18-MAR-97
Vester            8100 09-JAN-02
```

Note: The linesize can be determined by eyeballing the results and either increasing or decreasing the linesize as needed. Alternatively, the sum of the column sizes can be calculated. Then add one for each space of column separator, as in 9 (DOC_NAME is Varchar2(9)) + 10 (default numwidth display for SALPERMON is 10) + 9 (default date display size is 9) + 2 (for 2 column separators) = 30.

Another available feature is useful for customized reporting. The user may specify all or part of the title when the script file is executed by using a substitution parameter within the character string.

Example 4.B.2

Display the names, salaries, and hire dates of doctors who work in the area specified by the user.

Script File Contents

```
ACCEPT area PROMPT 'Which area should be displayed? '
SET VERIFY OFF
SET FEEDBACK OFF
SET PAGESIZE 25
SET LINESIZE 30
TTITLE ' |Physicians in the Area of |&AREA '

SELECT doc_name, salpermon, datehired
from doctor
WHERE area = '&area'
ORDER BY doc_name;

SET VERIFY ON
SET FEEDBACK ON
SET PAGESIZE 14
SET LINESIZE 80
TTITLE OFF
```

Execution Results

```
Which area should be displayed? Pediatrics

Tue Jul 01                  page     1

   Physicians in the Area of
           Pediatrics


DOC_NAME    SALPERMON DATEHIRED
--------- ---------- ---------
Harrison        12002 05-DEC-94
Lewis           10000 21-JAN-96
Vester           8100 09-JAN-02
```

Note: The vertical bar (|) is used as the linefeed character within the TTITLE character string.

Example 4.B.3

Produce a nicely formatted report of movie titles and categories.

Script File Contents

```
SET FEEDBACK OFF
SET PAGESIZE 30
SET LINESIZE 31
TTITLE '||Current Movie | Information'

SELECT title, category
FROM movie;

SET FEEDBACK ON
SET PAGESIZE 14
SET LINESIZE 80
TTITLE OFF
```

Execution Results

```
Tue Jul 01             page    1


        Current Movie
          Information


TITLE                CATEGORY
-------------------- ----------
City of Angels       Drama
Ocean's Eleven       Action
Gone in 60 Seconds   Action
Monsters, Inc.       Kids
E.T.                 Kids
U-571                Action
Road to Perdition    Drama
Amelie               Foreign
Monster's Ball       Drama
A Knight's Tale
The Royal Tenenbaums Comedy
Wild, Wild West      Comedy
Himalaya             Foreign
Horse Whisperer      Drama
A Beautiful Mind     Drama
Field of Dreams      Family
Beautiful Life       Foreign
Grease
Cast Away            Drama
O Brother
Spiderman            Kids
```

COLUMN

This command is used to define formatting for an individual column. The column name used on this command must exactly match the column name used on the SELECT command. If a column alias is used on the SELECT command, then the alias may be used on the COLUMN command (including double quotes, if present). One frequently needed specification that may *not* be used is table qualifiers, so if a qualified column is being selected, use a column alias so that it can be used on the COLUMN command.

The three commonly used options available on the COLUMN command are HEAD-ING, FORMAT, and JUSTIFY. Any or all of the options may be included and listed in any order. General syntax is as follows:

COLUMN column-name HEADING 'character string' FORMAT format JUSTIFY position where the character string may be split over more than one line by including a vertical bar and the format is one of two forms:

1. The letter *A* followed by a number *n* indicating an alphanumeric column displayed in n columns.
2. A numeric format consisting of a 9 for each digit position, and optionally, a period, comma, and/or dollar sign.

and the heading justification position is *L* for left, *R* for right, and *C* for centered.

For date columns, formatting must be performed by using TO_CHAR on the SELECT statement, as there is no facility for formatting date values on the COLUMN command.

At the end of the report, all column formatting can be cleared by using the CLEAR COLUMNS command.

Example 4.B.4

Display a nicely formatted report of patient names, balances due, and due dates for all patients with appointments today (*Note:* script file continues on the next page).

Script File Contents

```
SET FEEDBACK OFF
SET LINESIZE 49
TTITLE 'Daily Patient Report'
COLUMN last HEADING 'Last|Name' FORMAT A15
COLUMN first HEADING 'First|Name' FORMAT A10
COLUMN balance HEADING 'Balance Due' FORMAT $999,999.99
COLUMN due HEADING 'Due Date'

SELECT pt_lname last, pt_fname first, balance,
    TO_CHAR(duedate, 'MM/DD/RR') due
FROM patient p, billing b
WHERE p.pt_id = b.pt_id
    AND nextapptdate = SYSDATE;

SET FEEDBACK ON
SET LINESIZE 80
TTITLE OFF
CLEAR COLUMNS
```

Execution Results

```
Tue Jul 01                                     page    1
                   Daily Patient Report


Last                 First
Name                 Name         Balance Due Due Date
--------------- ---------- ------------ --------
James                Paul         $15,650.00 08/21/03
Anderson             Brian           $300.00 09/09/03
Saillez              Debbie        $5,000.00 09/14/03
```

Note: For each column, be aware of the difference between the column name in the table, the column alias on the SELECT statement, the column name on the COLUMN command,

and the column heading on the COLUMN command. *The column alias on the SELECT statement must exactly match the column name on the COLUMN command;* the others do not make a difference.

BREAK

This command is used in conjunction with the ORDER BY clause of the SELECT statement. When rows are arranged in groups, the BREAK command can be used to specify formatting to be performed when the group value changes. This is also called control-break reporting. If there is more than one level specified on the BREAK command, then duplicate values will be eliminated from the display of the outer levels. General syntax is as follows:

> BREAK ON column [SKIP n]
>> where column is the column name or alias (see details under COLUMN command)
>> and n is the number of lines to skip when the column value changes (SKIP clause is optional)
>> and the ON and SKIP specifications can be repeated for additional columns.

Breaks can be cleared at the end of the report with the CLEAR BREAKS command.

Example 4.B.5	Display doctor IDs, patient names, and next appointment dates. Arrange the list in order of doctor ID, and for each doctor, in chronological order of next appointment date.

Script File Contents

```
SET FEEDBACK OFF
SET LINESIZE 65
SET PAGESIZE 40
TTITLE 'Doctor Appointment Report'
BREAK ON doc_id SKIP 2 ON APPT
COLUMN doc_id HEADING 'Doctor ID'
COLUMN pt_lname HEADING 'Last Name'
COLUMN pt_fname HEADING 'First Name'
COLUMN appt HEADING 'Date of Appointment(s)' FORMAT A22

SELECT doc_id,TO_CHAR(nextapptdate,'Month DD, RRRR') appt,
       pt_lname, pt_fname
FROM patient
WHERE nextapptdate IS NOT NULL
ORDER BY doc_id, nextapptdate;

SET FEEDBACK ON
SET LINESIZE 80
SET PAGESIZE 14
TTITLE OFF
CLEAR BREAKS
CLEAR COLUMNS
```

Execution Results

```
Tue Jul 01                                              page    1
                    Doctor Appointment Report

Doctor ID Date of Appointment(s) Last Name       First Name
---------- ---------------------- --------------- ---------------
      235 July       01, 2003     Anderson        Brian
                                  Saillez         Debbie
```

```
                 July        20, 2003      James        Scott
                 July        21, 2003      Jackson      John
                 October     01, 2003      Porter       Susan
                 February    02, 2004      Westra       Lynn
                 June        06, 2005      Baily        Ryan
                 July        01, 2005      Crow         Lewis
                 December    01, 2005      Roach        Becky

          356    December    02, 2005      Cochran      John

          389    December    01, 2003      Poole        Jennifer

          432    July        01, 2003      James        Paul

          504    November    01, 2003      Rogers       Anthony
                 December    12, 2003      Walters      Stephanie

          509    July        21, 2003      Davis        Linda
                 Jones                     J..C.
                 November    15, 2003      Smith        Jason

          558    July        29, 2003      Kowalczyk    Paul
```

Note: Each doctor ID and next appointment date for that doctor is displayed only once due to the BREAK command.

Common Errors: Using BREAK ON without ORDER BY, or using ORDER BY without BREAK ON. These two must be used together rather than separately in report formatting situations.

Example 4.B.6

Display movie categories, titles, and number of whole days until due back for all current rentals. Arrange the list in alphabetic order of category, and for each specific category, in alphabetic order of titles. Within a specific title, order the results by decreasing number of days until due back. Include "None" for unknown categories. *Note:* The small page size was chosen to illustrate the repetition of headings at the top of each new page.

Script File Contents

```
SET FEEDBACK OFF
SET LINESIZE 53
SET PAGESIZE 20
TTITLE 'Summary Report | of Current Rentals'
BREAK ON CATEGORY SKIP 2 ON TITLE SKIP 1

SELECT NVL(CATEGORY,'None') CATEGORY, TITLE, C_ID,
      ROUND(DUE_DATE - SYSDATE) "DAYS LEFT"
FROM MOVIE M, RENTAL R
WHERE M.M_ID = R.M_ID
ORDER BY CATEGORY, TITLE, DUE_DATE - SYSDATE DESC;

SET FEEDBACK ON
SET LINESIZE 80
SET PAGESIZE 14
TTITLE OFF
CLEAR BREAKS
CLEAR COLUMNS
```

Execution Results

```
Tue Jul 01                                        page     1
                        Summary Report
                       of Current Rentals

CATEGORY    TITLE                    C_ID  DAYS LEFT
----------  --------------------  ----------  ----------
Action      Ocean's Eleven           673          1
                                     388          1
                                     701          1

            U-571                    673          0


Comedy      Wild, Wild West          673          0


Drama       A Beautiful Mind         388          3

Tue Jul 01                                        page     2
                        Summary Report
                       of Current Rentals

CATEGORY    TITLE                    C_ID  DAYS LEFT
----------  --------------------  ----------  ----------
Drama       A Beautiful Mind         400          3
                                     579          2

            Horse Whisperer          388          3

            Monster's Ball           701          0


Foreign     Amelie                   400          0


Tue Jul 01                                        page     3
                        Summary Report
                       of Current Rentals

CATEGORY    TITLE                    C_ID  DAYS LEFT
----------  --------------------  ----------  ----------
Kids        Monsters, Inc.           388          3

None        Grease                   673          3

            O Brother                579          3
                                     400         -1
```

Chapter Summary

A variety of SQL*Plus commands can be used to improve the appearance of query results. TTITLE is used to specify top title lines, COLUMN is used to specify column headings, format, and/or justification, BREAK is used for control-break reporting, and CLEAR is used to clear settings. Additionally, the SET command is used to set new values for system variables such as VERIFY, FEEDBACK, PAGESIZE, LINESIZE, NUMWIDTH, and PAUSE. The SHOW command can be used to display current system variable settings.

Exercises

Section A: Setting System Variables

1. Display the names of customers who owe more than the amount entered by the user. Prevent the display of substitution parameter replacements.

2. Modify the previous problem to allow the user to enter the entire condition to be used on the WHERE clause.

3. Show a listing of all movies other than those in the category entered by the user. Prevent the display of substitution parameter replacements. Eliminate the line of feedback at the end of this report.

4. List the title and due date of all current rentals, six per page.

5. Display the names and current balances of customers whose balance is within the range entered by the user. Prevent the display of substitution parameter replacements. Eliminate the line of feedback at the end of this report, and show 10 customers per page.

6. Display all data on customer 673 using 30 characters per line. Then gradually increase the line size until exactly the required number of characters is specified to avoid wraparound.

7. Modify the previous problem to allow the user to enter the customer number (i.e., 673). Prevent the display of substitution parameter replacements.

8. Show a listing of all patients born earlier than the year entered by the user. Prevent the display of substitution parameter replacements. Eliminate the line of feedback at the end of this report, show 20 patients per page, and use a line size of 84.

9. Show a listing of doctor IDs, monthly salaries, charges per appointment, and supervisor IDs for all doctors earning a monthly salary in the range entered by the user. Format monetary values appropriately. Prevent the display of substitution parameter replacements. Eliminate the line of feedback at the end of this report, show six doctors per page (pausing after each page), compress numeric values as much as possible, and use the smallest line size needed to avoid wraparound.

10. Display the current numeric display width, line size, and page size.

Section B: Format Commands

1. Produce a nicely formatted report of customer names and balances for those customers whose name matches the last name entered by the user. Prevent the display of substitution parameter replacements. Include all of the appropriate system variable settings and an overall report heading.

2. Produce a nicely formatted report of patient full names and addresses for those that have insurance provided by one of the two insurers entered by the user. Prevent the display of substitution parameter replacements. Include all of the appropriate system variable settings and an overall report heading.

3. Produce a nicely formatted report of all current rental data, sorted by customer, and within a particular customer's data, sorted in chronological order by due date. Use a format of your choice (other than the default) for the date values. Include all of the appropriate system variable settings and an overall report heading.

4. Modify the previous problem so that it includes detailed column headings for the output. Justify each of the column headings in the same manner that the column values are justified.

5. Produce a nicely formatted report of customer IDs, names, and balances for those customers whose balance is due within the range of dates entered by the user. Include all of the appropriate system variable settings, an overall report heading, and column headings.

6. Produce a nicely formatted report of doctor areas, names, year hired (not date hired), and IDs in alphabetic order of area, and within a particular area, within chronological order of year hired. Include all of the appropriate system variable settings, an overall report heading, and column headings. Eliminate the display of duplicate area names and hire dates.

7. Produce a nicely formatted report of patient names, addresses, and insurance provider in alphabetic order of city, and within a particular city, within alphabetic order of insurance provider. Do not include patients that live in the city specified by the user. Prevent the display of substitution parameter replacements. Include all of the appropriate system variable settings, an overall report heading, and column headings. Eliminate the display of duplicate city listings and last names. Leave three blank lines between different cities, and one blank line between different last names. Show 10 patients per page, and pause before displaying each page.

Chapter 5

Making Changes
to Table Contents

All of the previous chapters have focused on only one of the four DML (Data Manipulation Language) statements available in SQL. In addition to SELECT, the other DML statements are INSERT, DELETE, and UPDATE. These three statements are used to make changes to table contents. Additionally, three TCO (Transaction Control Operations) statements are used to support these changes, and they are ROLLBACK, COMMIT, and SAVEPOINT. This chapter covers the fundamentals of using these six statements.

As you practice writing SQL by solving the exercises at the end of the chapter, you may need to use the TCO commands to either save or undo the modified table contents. Hence, those commands are presented first, and they are followed by the commands that actually perform the modifications.

So that the printouts of the table contents shown in Appendix B can be used consistently throughout this book, none of the changes made to the tables in this chapter are saved with the COMMIT statement. Instead, they are each rolled back.

Section A: Transaction Control Operations

Transaction Control Operations (TCO) statements control whether or not changes to the tables are made permanent. General syntax and execution effects are as follows:

General Syntax:

```
COMMIT;
```

This statement permanently saves all changes performed by INSERT, UPDATE, and DELETE statements since the last COMMIT (or since the beginning of the current session if no COMMIT has been issued). Once a transaction is committed, it cannot be rolled back.

General Syntax:

```
ROLLBACK;
```

This statement undoes all changes performed by INSERT, UPDATE, and DELETE statements since the last COMMIT (or since the beginning of the current session if no COMMIT has been issued). In other words, it takes the database back to the state it was in at the time of the last COMMIT. There is no facility available for going back to a state that existed *prior* to the last COMMIT.

General Syntax:

```
SAVEPOINT name;
ROLLBACK TO name;
```

where name follows standard naming conventions.

Savepoints mark intermediate "bookmarks" that a rollback may go back to. Once a savepoint is named, then a ROLLBACK TO statement may be used to take the database back to the state it was in when that savepoint was created. If no SAVEPOINT is specified on the ROLLBACK command, then the database is rolled back to the previous COMMIT.

In general, when modifications are to be performed, a script file is used to perform the change and display the results. After viewing the changes, the user should determine whether or not the modifications are accurate. This can be accomplished by examining the table contents. If the changes made are not what were intended, then a ROLLBACK should be issued. Otherwise, a COMMIT should be issued. SAVEPOINTs can be used to mark intermediate steps in a file involving several changes. Then a rollback to a named savepoint can be used as needed.

Specific examples of the TCO statements will be included in conjunction with other statements throughout the rest of this chapter.

Section B: Insert

The INSERT command is used to add one new row to a table. This may include a value for each column in the table, or values only for specific columns.

Part 1: Complete Rows

The simplest format involves specifying a value for each column using the general syntax as follows:

INSERT INTO table-name

VALUES (value list);

where the following rules apply:

1. The value list consists of one value for each column.
2. The values are listed in the same order as the order in which the columns are displayed by the DESCRIBE command.
3. The values are separated by commas.
4. Character string values must be enclosed in single quotes.
5. Numeric values may contain digits and optionally, a sign and/or decimal point.
6. Date values entered as character strings must be converted using TO_DATE.
7. SYSDATE can be used to supply the current date.
8. NULL can be used to specify an empty column value.

Example 5.B.1

A new doctor has been hired. Add a row to the DOCTOR table with 807 for the ID, Malone for the name, the current date for the date hired, $10,000 for the monthly salary, neurology for the area, 289 for the supervisor, and $65 for the charge per appointment. No annual bonus is earned until a doctor has been on staff for five years. Verify the insertion.

Script File Contents

```
INSERT INTO doctor
VALUES (807, 'Malone', SYSDATE, 10000, 'Neurology', 289, 65, NULL);
SELECT *
FROM doctor
WHERE doc_id = 807;
```

Execution Results

```
1 row created.
```

DOC_ID	DOC_NAME	DATEHIRED	SALPERMON	AREA	SUPERVISOR_ID	CHGPERAPPT	ANNUAL_BONUS
807	Malone	03-JUL-03	10000	Neurology	289	65	

Reminder: The execution of each example in this chapter is followed by a rollback so that none of the modifications are reflected in subsequent examples. For each example, SQL and execution results are as follows:

```
SQL: ROLLBACK;
```

Execution Results

```
Rollback complete.
```

Example 5.B.2

A new doctor has been hired. Allow the user to enter each individual column value (with the exceptions of the date hired and the annual bonus). Verify the insertion.

Script File Contents

```
ACCEPT id PROMPT 'Enter doctor"s ID: '
ACCEPT name PROMPT 'Enter doctor"s name: '
ACCEPT salary PROMPT 'Enter salary per month: '
ACCEPT area PROMPT 'Enter area of specialization: '
ACCEPT s_id PROMPT 'Enter supervisor"s ID: '
ACCEPT chg PROMPT 'Enter charge per appointment: '
SET VERIFY OFF

INSERT INTO doctor
VALUES (&id, '&name', SYSDATE, &salary, '&area',
    &s_id, &chg, NULL);
SELECT *
FROM doctor
WHERE doc_id = &id;
SET VERIFY ON
```

Execution Results

```
Enter doctor's ID: 976
Enter doctor's name: Hartley
Enter salary per month: 8000
Enter area of specialization: Rehab
Enter supervisor's ID: 889
Enter charge per appointment: 60

1 row created.
```

DOC_ID	DOC_NAME	DATEHIRED	SALPERMON	AREA	SUPERVISOR_ID	CHGPERAPPT	ANNUAL_BONUS
976	Hartley	01-JUL-03	8000	Rehab	889	60	

Reminder: Two single quotes are used within some of the prompts in order to provide one quote within the prompt during execution.

Example 5.B.3

A new movie is available for rental. Allow the user to enter each individual column. Verify the insertion.

Script File Contents

```
ACCEPT m_id PROMPT 'Enter movie ID: '
ACCEPT fee PROMPT 'Enter movie fee: '
ACCEPT title PROMPT 'Enter movie title: '
ACCEPT category PROMPT 'Enter movie category: '
SET VERIFY OFF

INSERT INTO movie
VALUES (&m_id, &fee, '&title', '&category');
SELECT *
FROM movie
WHERE m_id = &m_id;
SET VERIFY ON
```

Execution Results

```
Enter movie ID:  356
Enter movie fee: 2.99
Enter movie title:  Thomas Crowne Affair
Enter movie category:  Action

1 row created.
```

M_ID	FEE	TITLE	CATEGORY
356	2.99	Thomas Crowne Affair	Action

```
1 row selected.
```

Part 2: Partial Rows

When only a subset of the new column values are known, a column list should be included on the INSERT command. General syntax is as follows:

```
INSERT INTO table-name (column-list)
VALUES (value-list);
```

where column-list consists of one or more column names separated by commas. The first column listed will receive the first value in the value list; the second column listed will receive the second value, and so on. The order does not have to match the order shown by the DESCRIBE command.

Example 5.B.4

An appointment has been made for a new patient for May 20, 2003, with doctor number 289. The patient's ID is 495, the name is Paul Young. No other data is known at this point. Add a row to the PATIENT table and verify the insertion.

Script File Contents

```
INSERT INTO patient (nextapptdate, doc_id, pt_id,  pt_fname, pt_lname)
VALUES(TO_DATE('May 20, 2003', 'Month DD, RRRR'), 289, 495, 'Paul', 'Young');
SELECT *
FROM patient
WHERE pt_id = 495;
```

Execution Results

```
1 row created.
```

PT_ID	PT_LNAME	PT_FNAME	PTDOB	DOC_ID	NEXTAPPTD	LASTAPPTD
495	Young	Paul		289	20-MAY-03	

Note: As with the previous example, substitution parameters could have been used for this example as well; their inclusion would provide a more versatile script file.

Example 5.B.5

Allow the user to specify values for the BILLING table for the patient added in the last example. There is no balance or due date yet, and all patients are Illinois residents.

Script File Contents

```
ACCEPT pt_id PROMPT 'Enter patient ID: '
ACCEPT phone PROMPT 'Enter phone number: '
ACCEPT addr PROMPT 'Enter street address: '
ACCEPT city PROMPT 'Enter city: '
ACCEPT zip PROMPT 'Enter zip code: '
ACCEPT pt_ins PROMPT 'Enter insurance provider: '
SET VERIFY OFF

INSERT INTO billing(pt_id, phone, addr, city, st, zip, pt_ins)
VALUES(&pt_id, '&phone', '&addr', '&city', 'il', '&zip', '&pt_ins');
SELECT *
FROM billing
WHERE pt_id = &pt_id;
```

Execution Results

```
Enter patient ID: 110
Enter phone number: 549-7227
Enter street address: 135 Throgmorton Road
Enter city: Anna
Enter ZIP code: 62906
Enter insurance provider: HealthCare

1 row created.
```

PT_ID	BALANCE	DUEDATE	PHONE	ADDR	CITY	ST	ZIP	PT_INS
110			549-7227	135 Throgmorton Road	Anna	IL	62906	HealthCare

```
1 row selected.
```

Part 3: Primary Key Constraints

By definition, a primary key is used to uniquely identify a row in a table, and therefore, no duplicate primary key values are allowed. The mechanism that prevents the undesirable duplication is called a constraint. Constraints can be defined on primary keys, foreign keys, and other columns for various purposes, and they will be examined in detail in the next chapter. For now, just be aware that when primary key constraints are specified on a table, any attempt to insert duplicate values should be blocked by the software.

Example 5.B.6

For illustration purposes only, attempt to add a row for patient number 264 (which already exists).

```
SQL: INSERT INTO patient (pt_id)
     VALUES (264);
```

Execution Results

```
INSERT INTO PATIENT (PT_ID)
              *
ERROR at line 1:
ORA-00001: unique constraint (LPREECE.PATIENT_PT_ID_PK) violated
```

This error indicates that a unique constraint would be violated if this insertion were to be allowed. Patient ID 264 already exists in the PATIENT table as a primary key, so the insertion would not be a unique value—it would be a duplicate. You do not need to concern yourself with the specifics of the constraint name enclosed in parentheses in the error message; naming conventions for constraints will be covered in the next chapter. Just be aware that an error referencing a unique constraint violation indicates the attempted insertion of a nonunique primary key value.

Part 4: Using Subqueries to Insert Rows from Other Tables

A subquery can be used in place of the VALUES clause on the INSERT statement to retrieve copies of rows from another table and insert them into the specified table. This can also be used to make copies of entire tables or copies of portions of tables.

Example 5.B.7

Foreign films are currently very popular, so their data is being moved to a separate table, and is being removed from the MOVIE table (eventually). Assuming that a new table named FOREIGNFILMS has been created with exactly the same columns as the MOVIE table (except for category), copy all of the data on foreign films to the new table. Verify the insertions.

Script File Contents

```
INSERT INTO foreignfilms
     SELECT m_id, fee, title
     FROM movie
     WHERE category = 'Foreign';
SELECT *
FROM foreignfilms;
```

Execution Results

```
3 rows created.

      M_ID        FEE TITLE
---------- ---------- --------------------
       255       2.99 Amelie
       315       2.99 Himalaya
       325       2.99 Beautiful Life

3 rows selected.

Commit completed.
```

Example 5.B.8

Dr. Vester's list of patients has expanded to the point that all patient data should be placed in a separate table. Assuming that a new table named VESTER_PATIENT has been created with exactly the same columns as the PATIENT table, copy all of his patients' data to the new table. An additional subquery will be needed to determine Dr. Vester's ID. Verify the insertions.

Script File Contents

```
INSERT INTO vester_patient
    SELECT *
    FROM patient
    WHERE doc_id =
        (SELECT doc_id
        FROM doctor
        WHERE doc_name = 'Vester');
SELECT *
FROM vester_patient;
```

Execution Results

```
3 rows created.
```

PT_ID	PT_LNAME	PT_FNAME	PTDOB	DOC_ID	NEXTAPPTD	LASTAPPTD
816	Smith	Jason	12-DEC-99	509	15-NOV-03	15-MAY-03
703	Davis	Linda	17-JUL-02	509	21-JUL-03	22-MAY-03
307	Jones	J.C.	17-JUL-02	509	21-JUL-03	22-MAY-03

Section C: The DELETE Statement

The DELETE statement is used to remove one or more rows from a table. General syntax is as follows:

DELETE FROM table-name

WHERE condition;

where the condition follows the same guidelines as those used on the WHERE clause of the SELECT statement.

Reminder: The execution of each example in this chapter is followed by a rollback so that none of the modifications are reflected in subsequent examples.

Part 1: All Rows

The WHERE clause is optional, and if omitted, all of the table contents will be deleted, but the table structure will remain.

Example 5.C.1

For illustration purposes only, remove all rows from the PATIENT table. Verify the deletions.

Script File Contents

```
DELETE FROM patient;
SELECT *
FROM patient;
```

Execution Results

```
22 rows deleted.

no rows selected
```

Example 5.C.2

For illustration purposes only, remove the contents of the RENTAL table, and verify the results. Then restore the database to the state it was in before the change. Verify the results.

Script File Contents

```
SAVEPOINT pre_delete;
DELETE FROM rental;
SELECT *
FROM rental;
ROLLBACK TO pre_delete;
SELECT *
FROM rental;
```

Execution Results

```
Savepoint created.

15 rows deleted.

no rows selected

Rollback complete.

      C_ID       M_ID DATE_OUT  DUE_DATE
---------- ---------- --------- ---------
       673        216 30-JUN-03 02-JUL-03
       673        249 30-JUN-03 01-JUL-03
       388        320 01-JUL-03 04-JUL-03
       400        354 29-JUN-03 30-JUN-03
       579        354 01-JUL-03 04-JUL-03
       673        304 29-JUN-03 01-JUL-03
       673        337 01-JUL-03 04-JUL-03
       388        216 30-JUN-03 02-JUL-03
       388        316 01-JUL-03 04-JUL-03
       388        236 01-JUL-03 04-JUL-03
       400        320 01-JUL-03 04-JUL-03
       400        255 29-JUN-03 01-JUL-03
       701        216 30-JUN-03 02-JUL-03
       701        278 29-JUN-03 01-JUL-03
       579        320 01-JUL-03 03-JUL-03

15 rows selected.
```

Part 2: Selected Rows

When the WHERE clause is included, only the rows that satisfy the specified condition will be deleted. The condition is of the same form as the condition used on the WHERE clause of the SELECT statement, and may include subqueries.

Example 5.C.3

Patient number 163 has changed clinics. Remove his data from the PATIENT table.

```
SQL: DELETE FROM patient
     WHERE pt_id = 163;
```

Execution Results

```
1 row deleted.
```

Example 5.C.4

The movie *Field of Dreams* is no longer being rented and has been taken out of inventory. Remove it from the database.

```
SQL: DELETE FROM movie
     WHERE title = 'Field of Dreams';
```

Execution Results

```
1 row deleted.
```

Example 5.C.5

Modify the previous example to allow the user to specify the movie name.

Script File Contents

```
ACCEPT title PROMPT 'Enter movie title: '
SET VERIFY OFF
DELETE FROM movie
WHERE UPPER(title) = UPPER('&title');
```

Execution Results

```
Enter movie title:  E.T.

1 row deleted.
```

Example 5.C.6

All of the cheap movies (in which the fee is under $1) not currently rented have been removed from inventory. Remove them from the database.

```
SQL: DELETE FROM movie
     WHERE fee < 1.00
         AND m_id NOT IN
             (SELECT DISTINCT m_id FROM rental);
```

Execution Results

```
1 row deleted.
```

Example 5.C.7

All patients that have no upcoming appointment and haven't had an appointment within the last two years should be removed from the database.

```
SQL: DELETE FROM patient
     WHERE nextapptdate IS NULL
         AND ADD_MONTHS (lastapptdate, -2 * 12) < SYSDATE;
```

Execution Results

```
3 rows deleted.
```

Note: The usage of the negative value on the ADD_MONTHS illustrates the versatility of this function. A positive value gives a date forward in time from the first argument, whereas a negative value gives a date backward in time.

Example 5.C.8

Write a script file that can be used to remove a row from the rental table when a movie is returned. Allow the user to enter the customer ID and movie ID.

Script File Contents

```
ACCEPT m_id PROMPT 'Enter ID of movie being returned: '
ACCEPT c_id PROMPT 'Enter customer ID: '
SET VERIFY OFF
DELETE FROM rental
WHERE c_id = &c_id
    AND m_id = &m_id;
```

Execution Results

```
Enter ID of movie being returned:   255
Enter customer ID:   400


1 row deleted.
```

Part 3: Foreign Key Constraints

As you may remember from your study of database design and implementation, a foreign key is used to represent a relationship between two tables. By definition, the value of a foreign key must either match the value of a primary key in the related table or be null. This maintains referential integrity. For example, the PATIENT table has a foreign key (DOC_ID) linking it to the DOCTOR table. Therefore, if a row in the patient table references doctor ID 234, then doctor ID 234 must appear in the DOCTOR table. If it did not, it would be a violation of referential integrity.

As with primary keys, constraints can be defined to enforce this rule. If a table has a foreign key constraint, referential integrity will be maintained. With such a constraint, if the primary key in a row being deleted appears as a foreign key in another table, the software will prevent the deletion.

Example 5.C.9

For illustration purposes only, attempt to delete the row for a doctor whose ID appears as a foreign key in the PATIENT table.

```
SQL: DELETE FROM doctor
     WHERE doc_id =235;
```

Execution Results

```
DELETE FROM DOCTOR
            *
ERROR at line 1:
ORA-02292: integrity constraint (LPREECE.PATIENT_DOC_ID_FK)
violated - child record found
```

This error indicates that a (referential) integrity constraint would be violated if this deletion were to be allowed. Doctor ID 235 is referenced as a foreign key in the PATIENT table as a primary key, so if the deletion were allowed, the foreign key would not have a matching row in the related table. The relationship represented by a foreign key is sometimes referred to as a parent-child relationship, with the table containing the foreign key being the child, and the related table being the parent, thus leading to the "child record found" reference in the error message.

Example 5.C.10

For illustration purposes only, attempt to delete a row for a movie whose ID appears as a foreign key in the RENTAL table.

```
SQL: DELETE FROM movie
     WHERE m_id IN
         (SELECT m_id
          FROM rental);
```

Execution Results

```
DELETE FROM MOVIE
*
ERROR at line 1:
ORA-02292: integrity constraint (LPREECE.RENTAL_M_ID_FK) violated -
child record found
```

These examples serve to illustrate the value of defining foreign key constraints. Violation of referential integrity will give an inconsistent database, yielding inaccurate retrievals. The database designer should always define foreign key constraints to force the software to maintain referential integrity.

Part 4: Using Subqueries

As with all other statements that involve a WHERE clause, a subquery can be included on the DELETE statement. Subqueries can be used to determine results that cannot be found in one step, but rather, require two or more steps. A single value, several columns of values, and/or several rows may be returned by a subquery. When subqueries are used, the inner-most query is evaluated before the outermost query.

Example 5.C.11

Assuming that all of Dr. Vester's patient data has been correctly moved to a new table named VESTER_PATIENT, delete the data from the PATIENT table.

```
SQL: DELETE FROM patient
    WHERE doc_id =
        (SELECT doc_id
        FROM doctor
        WHERE doc_name = 'Vester');
```

Execution Results

```
3 rows deleted.
```

Example 5.C.12

Ryan Baily has moved to another state. Remove his data from both the PATIENT table and the BILLING table.

```
SQL: DELETE FROM patient
    WHERE pt_lname = 'Baily'
        AND pt_fname = 'Ryan';

    DELETE FROM billing
    WHERE pt_id =
        (SELECT pt_id
        FROM patient
        WHERE pt_lname = 'Baily'
            AND pt_fname = 'Ryan');
```

Execution Results

```
1 row deleted.
```

```
1 row deleted.
```

Note: The subquery is needed in this case because only the patient name is known, not the patient ID.

Section D: The UPDATE Statement

The UPDATE statement is used to modify *existing* rows by placing new values in a column. The column may have had a value previously, or it may have been null. General syntax is as follows:

```
UPDATE table-name
SET column-name = expression
WHERE condition;
```

where the expression is of the format used for calculations on the SELECT clause and the condition is of the format used on the WHERE clause of the SELECT statement.

As mentioned previously, a rollback was completed after each of the examples in this chapter so that updates performed do not affect subsequent examples.

Part 1: All Rows

The WHERE clause is optional, and if omitted, all of the rows will be updated.

Example 5.D.1

All appointment charges are to be increased by 10 percent. Verify the changes by displaying doctor number 356's charge per appointment before and after the change.

Script File Contents

```
SELECT chgperappt
FROM doctor
WHERE doc_id = 356;

UPDATE doctor
SET chgperappt = chgperappt + chgperappt * .10;

SELECT chgperappt
FROM doctor
WHERE doc_id = 356;
```

Execution Results

```
CHGPERAPPT
----------
        80

12 rows updated.

CHGPERAPPT
----------
        88
```

Example 5.D.2

Increase all salaries by $500. Verify the changes by examining one row before and after.

Script File Contents

```
SELECT salpermon
FROM doctor
WHERE doc_id = 389;

UPDATE doctor
SET salpermon = salpermon + 500;

SELECT salpermon
FROM doctor
WHERE doc_id = 389;
```

Execution Results

```
SALPERMON
---------
    10000

12 rows updated.

SALPERMON
---------
    10500
```

Example 5.D.3

The clinic is growing, and patient ID numbers need to be expanded to four digits. Assuming that the column size has been correctly increased, add a "1" to the beginning of every patient ID number.

Script File Contents

```
UPDATE billing
SET pt_id = pt_id + 1000;

UPDATE patient
SET pt_id = pt_id + 1000;
```

Execution Results

```
22 rows updated.


22 rows updated.
```

Part 2: Selected Rows

When the WHERE clause is included, only the rows that satisfy the specified condition will be updated. The condition is of the same form as the condition used on the WHERE clause of the SELECT and DELETE statements and may include subqueries.

Example 5.D.4

On the first of each month, all patients with balances past due have a 5 percent fee added to their balance. Use a script file each month to update the PATIENT table. Verify the changes.

Script File Contents

```
SELECT balance "Old Balances"
FROM billing
WHERE duedate < SYSDATE AND balance > 0;

UPDATE billing
SET balance = balance * 1.05
WHERE duedate < SYSDATE AND balance > 0;

SELECT balance "New Balances"
FROM billing
WHERE duedate < SYSDATE AND balance > 0;
```

Execution Results

```
Old Balances
------------
         100
       35000
       98000


3 rows updated.


New Balances
------------
         105
       36750
      102900
```

Example 5.D.5

Customers frequently extend rentals by a day or two. Use a script file to prompt the user for the customer ID, movie ID, and number of days the rental is to be extended. Modify the database and verify the changes.

Script File Contents

```
ACCEPT c_id PROMPT 'Enter customer ID: '
ACCEPT m_id PROMPT 'Enter movie ID: '
ACCEPT days PROMPT 'Enter number of days for rental extension: '
SET VERIFY OFF

SELECT due_date "Old Due Date"
FROM rental
WHERE c_id = &c_id and m_id = &m_id;

UPDATE rental
SET due_date = due_date + &days
WHERE c_id = &c_id and m_id = &m_id;

SELECT due_date "New Due Date"
FROM rental
WHERE c_id = &c_id and m_id = &m_id
SET VERIFY ON
```

Execution Results

```
Enter customer ID:  673
Enter movie ID:  249
Enter number of days for rental extension:  3

OLD
---------
01-JUL-03

1 row selected.

1 row updated.

NEW
---------
04-JUL-03

1 row selected.
```

Example 5.D.6

When a payment is made, allow the user to enter the patient ID and the amount of the payment. Then update that patient's balance. Verify the change.

Script File Contents

```
ACCEPT id PROMPT 'Enter patient ID: '
ACCEPT pmt PROMPT 'Enter payment amount (digits only): '
SET VERIFY OFF

SELECT balance "Old Balance"
FROM billing
WHERE pt_id = &id;
```

```
UPDATE billing
SET balance = balance - &pmt
WHERE pt_id = &id;

SELECT balance "New Balance"
FROM billing
WHERE pt_id = &id;
```

Execution Results

```
Enter patient ID:  966
Enter payment amount (digits only):  1000

Old Balance
-----------
      98700

1 row updated.

New Balance
-----------
      97700
```

Example 5.D.7

Write a script file that can be used when customers get married and changes their last name and phone number.

Script File Contents

```
ACCEPT c_id PROMPT 'Enter customer ID: '
ACCEPT lasT PROMPT 'Enter new last name: '
ACCEPT phone PROMPT 'Enter new phone number: '
SET VERIFY OFF

SELECT lname "Old Last Name", phone "Old Phone #"
FROM customer
WHERE c_id = &c_id;

UPDATE customer
SET phone = '&phone', lname = '&last'
WHERE c_id = &c_id;
SELECT lname "New Last Name", phone "New Phone #"
FROM customer
WHERE c_id = &c_id;
```

Execution Results

```
Enter customer ID:  701
Enter new last name:  Padrosa
Enter new phone number:  529-8118

OLD         OLD
---------- --------
Williams   549-8840

1 row selected.

1 row updated.
```

```
NEW          NEW
----------   --------
Padrosa      529-8118

1 row selected.
```

Part 3: Primary Key and Foreign Key Constraints

Caution must be exercised if the UPDATE command is used to SET a new value in a primary key or foreign key column. If the new primary key is not unique, entity integrity would be violated, so the software prevents the update from occurring and displays a message regarding attempted violation of a unique constraint.

If the column on the SET clause is a foreign key column, then the value entered must match an existing primary key value in the related table. Otherwise, referential integrity would be violated. Hence, the software prevents the update from occurring and displays an error message regarding attempted violation of a (referential) integrity constraint due to the lack of a parent (related) row being present in the linked table.

Example 5.D.8

For illustration purposes, test the primary key constraint on the DOCTOR table by attempting to change a DOC_ID to a value that already exists.

```
SQL: UPDATE doctor
     SET doc_id = 239
     WHERE doc_id = 889;
```

Execution Results

```
UPDATE DOCTOR
       *
ERROR at line 1:
ORA-00001: unique constraint (LPREECE.DOCTOR_DOC_ID_PK) violated
```

This error indicates that a unique constraint would be violated if this update were to be allowed, because 239 already exists in the DOCTOR table as a primary key value.

Example 5.D.9

For illustration purposes, test the foreign key constraint on the PATIENT table by attempting to change a DOC_ID to a value that does not appear in the DOCTOR table.

```
SQL: UPDATE patient
     SET doc_id = 292
     WHERE pt_id =  331;
```

Execution Results

```
UPDATE PATIENT
       *
ERROR at line 1:
ORA-02291: integrity constraint (LPREECE.PATIENT_DOC_ID_FK)
violated - parent key not found
```

This error indicates that a (referential) integrity constraint would be violated if this update on the PATIENT table were to be allowed, because there is no existing primary key value of 292 in the DOCTOR table.

Part 4: Using Subqueries

As with all other statements that involve a WHERE clause, a subquery may be included on the UPDATE statement. Subqueries can be used to determine results that cannot be found in one step, but rather, require two or more steps. A single value, several columns of values, and/or several rows may be returned by a subquery. When subqueries are used, the inner-most query is evaluated before the outermost queries.

Example 5.D.10

A customer has just paid a fee to extend his or her movie rental by three days. Use a script file to allow the user to enter the customer's name and movie title, then adjust the rental due date accordingly.

Script File Contents

```
ACCEPT last PROMPT 'Enter customer"s last name: '
ACCEPT first PROMPT 'Enter customer"s first name: '
ACCEPT title PROMPT 'Enter movie title: '
SET VERIFY OFF

UPDATE rental
SET due_date = due_date + 3
WHERE c_id =
    (SELECT c_id
     FROM customer
     WHERE lname = '&last' AND fname = '&first')
AND m_id =
    (SELECT m_id
     FROM movie
     WHERE title = '&title');
SET VERIFY ON
```

Execution Results

```
Enter customer's last name: Woolard
Enter customer's first name: Jessica
Enter movie title: Ocean's Eleven

1 row updated.
```

Note: When there is a need to enter a single quote within a character string, two single quotes are used, similar to their use within an ACCEPT prompt.

Example 5.D.11

When a doctor leaves the clinic permanently, his or her patients are assigned to another doctor. Allow the user to enter the name of the doctor leaving and the ID of the doctor to whom the patients should be assigned. Update the PATIENT table and verify the changes.

Script File Contents

```
ACCEPT doctor_going PROMPT 'Enter name of departing doctor: '
ACCEPT new_doc_id PROMPT 'Enter new doctor"s ID: '
SET VERIFY OFF

SELECT pt_id, doc_id
FROM patient
WHERE doc_id =
    (SELECT doc_id
     FROM doctor
     WHERE doc_name = '&doctor_going');

UPDATE patient
SET doc_id = &new_doc_id
WHERE doc_id =
    (SELECT doc_id
     FROM doctor
     WHERE doc_name = '&doctor_going');
```

```
SELECT pt_id, doc_id
FROM patient
WHERE doc_id = &new_doc_id;
SET VERIFY ON
```

Note: It would be better for the user if the new doctor's name could have been entered (rather than the ID). However, there is no facility for using a subquery on the SET clause. This situation can be handled in PL/SQL, though, and will be covered in the last chapter.

Execution Results

```
Enter name of departing doctor: Lewis
Enter new doctor's ID:   432


    PT_ID     DOC_ID
--------- ---------
      103        389


1 row updated.

    PT_ID     DOC_ID
--------- ---------
      168        432
      103        432
```

Note: This doctor already had one patient, and one more was added with the change.

Example 5.D.12

For all films in the most popular category (the one with the largest number of titles), increase fees by $1.00.

Script File Contents

```
UPDATE movie
SET fee = fee + 1
WHERE category =
    (SELECT category
     FROM movie
     GROUP BY category
     HAVING COUNT(*) =
         (SELECT MAX(COUNT(*))
          FROM movie
          GROUP BY category));
```

Execution Results

```
7 rows updated.
```

Example 5.D.13

For all doctors who earn an annual bonus beneath the average bonus earned by either neurologists or pediatricians, increase their bonus by 10 percent. Verify the changes.

Script File Contents

```
SELECT annual_bonus "Old Bonuses"
FROM doctor
WHERE annual_bonus < ANY
    (SELECT AVG(annual_bonus)
     FROM doctor
     WHERE area IN ('Neurology', 'Pediatrics')
     GROUP BY area);
```

```
UPDATE doctor
SET annual_bonus = annual_bonus * 1.10
WHERE annual_bonus < ANY
    (SELECT AVG(annual_bonus)
    FROM doctor
    WHERE area IN ('Neurology', 'Pediatrics')
    GROUP BY area);

SELECT annual_bonus "New Bonuses"
FROM doctor
WHERE annual_bonus < ANY
    (SELECT AVG(annual_bonus)
    FROM doctor
    WHERE area IN ('Neurology', 'Pediatrics')
    GROUP BY area);
```

Execution Results

```
Old Bonuses
-----------
       4500
       2250
       2250
       6500
       3200
       6500

6 rows updated.

New Bonuses
-----------
       4950
       2475
       2475
       7150
       3520
       7150
```

Chapter Summary

Tables can be modified by using the INSERT statement to add new rows, the DELETE statement to remove existing rows, or the UPDATE statement to modify existing rows. On each of these statements, subqueries can be used to determine results requiring more than one step. On the INSERT command, subqueries can also be used to retrieve rows from other tables.

When modifications are made, the software will maintain entity integrity by requiring unique values for primary keys. The software will also maintain referential integrity by requiring values for foreign keys that match primary key values in the linked table, and by preventing the deletion of primary key values that appear as foreign key values in a linked table. Transaction control operations include COMMIT, ROLLBACK, and SAVEPOINT.

Exercises

Section A: Transaction Control Operations

1. Write the command used to save the changes made to the database.
2. Write the command used to undo the changes made since the last COMMIT.
3. Write the command used to mark a SAVEPOINT between commands named SVPT_X.
4. Write the command used to roll back the database to the SAVEPOINT created in exercise 3.

Section B: The INSERT Statement

1. You've just become a new customer at the movie rental place. Add a row for yourself to the table. Verify the change and make it permanent.
2. You've just rented your favorite movie. Add a row to the current rental table. Verify the change and make it permanent.
3. Due to a current two-for-one special, customers frequently rent two movies at a time. Write a script file that can be used to add two rows to the current rental table, allowing the user to enter all necessary values. Verify the additions and make them permanent.
4. Data on overdue rentals is copied to a new table at the beginning of each day, along with the customer's phone number so that calls can be made the next morning. Assuming that a table named OVERDUE exists with columns named C_ID, M_ID, DUE_DATE, and PHONE, write the script file that can be executed at the beginning of each day to copy the appropriate rows and display the additions.
5. Management has asked for a table named ASSIGNMENT that can be manipulated with "what-if" scenarios regarding patient assignments. Assuming that the new table has been created, fill it with patient IDs, insurance providers, doctor IDs, and areas. The new table has columns named the same as the source columns, but the order of their creation is unknown. Verify the additions.

Section C: The DELETE Statement

1. Mark a SAVEPOINT, remove the contents of the BILLING table, mark a second SAVE-POINT, and then remove the contents of the PATIENT table. Verify the deletions. Then restore only the PATIENT table, and verify the restoration. Then restore the BILLING table, and verify the restoration. Finally, make the restorations of both tables permanent.
2. A certain delinquent customer has finally paid his or her overdue balance, and the account has been closed. Permanently remove his or her data from the database. Allow the user to specify the customer's name.
3. A new branch is being opened, and records for patients living in that city have been copied over to new tables. Delete all records for patients living in the city whose name is entered by the user.
4. The pediatrics department is moving to another clinic, and is taking their patients with them. Remove all related data from the database, verify the change, and make it permanent. Consider the statement order that must be used to avoid a violation of referential integrity.
5. Test the referential integrity (foreign key constraint) of the DOCTOR table by trying to delete a row for one of the supervisors.

Section D: The UPDATE Statement

1. Movies are being discounted for a month of anniversary celebration. Decrease each fee by 5 percent, and verify the change by examining one row before and after.
2. The annual $20 fee for membership is being added to the balance of each customer. Modify the database accordingly.
3. Due to damage from a fire at a neighboring business, the movie rental business was closed for two days. Give all current rentals a two-day extension.
4. A patient is switching to a different doctor. Allow the user to enter the patient's name and the doctor's ID, and make the change.
5. Write a script file that can be used when a patient moves to a new address.

6. Test the entity integrity (primary key constraint) of the CUSTOMER table by attempting to change a C_ID to a value that already exists.

7. Test the referential integrity (foreign key constraint) of the RENTAL table by attempting to change a movie ID to a value that does not exist in the MOVIE table.

8. Test the referential integrity of the DOCTOR table by attempting to change a supervisor ID to a value that does not exist in the doctor ID column.

9. When a customer pays off his or her current balance, the balance is set to zero and the due date is cleared. Write a script file for this task.

10. A patient has just completed an appointment and has scheduled an appointment for one month from now. Allow the user to enter the patient's name and change the database accordingly.

11. Modify the previous problem to allow the user to specify the date of the next appointment.

12. Some appointment charges are being increased. For all areas whose average charge per appointment is at least $10 less than the average charge per appointment for all areas together, increase the charge per appointment by $20. Execute each subquery separately before adding an outer portion so that the results can be verified by examining the table printouts.

Chapter 6

Table Structures and Constraints

The two categories of commands covered thus far are DML (data manipulation language) and TCO (transaction control operations). This chapter examines a third category consisting of data definition language (DDL) commands. These statements are used to add, remove, and modify table *structures* rather than table contents. All DDL statements automatically issue a COMMIT statement upon completion; it does not need to be coded. The result is that DDL statements have an immediate effect on the database, and because of this, they should be executed with caution.

Note: As with Chapter 5, none of the table changes made in this chapter were made permanent, thereby allowing the printouts of the table contents shown in Appendix B to be used consistently throughout this book.

Section A: Fundamentals

Part 1: Data Dictionary Views

Since this chapter involves defining new objects in the database, it becomes necessary to examine various data dictionary views that are available to all database users. Their contents can be used to show details on various database objects (such as tables and users), and can also be used to verify the results of DDL commands.

These views can be treated like tables in that their structure can be displayed by using the DESCRIBE command, and their contents can be displayed by using the SELECT command (with or without a WHERE clause).

A naming convention that has been used for all data dictionary views is the inclusion of a name prefix. When a prefix of ALL_ is used, the data dictionary view displays data on all database objects in that category (regardless of owner) that are *accessible* to the user. Conversely, when a prefix of USER_ is used, the data dictionary view displays data on all database objects in that category that are *owned* specifically by the current user. Hence, ALL_TABLES displays data on all tables in the database that the user can access, while USER_TABLES displays data only on tables that the user owns.

Another naming convention used in data dictionary (DD) views is that view names are generally plural, whereas the column names in views are generally singular. There are a few exceptions, but this is still a good assumption to use when accessing DD views on the fly.

Although quick reference manuals usually include the names of the data dictionary views, the column names are rarely listed. Frequently, an individual DD view will have far more data than is needed, so the list of column names is sometimes quite lengthy. Hence, rather than selecting all columns and retrieving an unreadable, wrapped-around result, you should select only the columns that will be helpful. Additionally, to further avoid wrap-around, the column display size may need to be shortened with a COLUMN command (as covered in Chapter 4).

In general, the steps for using a DD view are as follows:

1. Describe the view to determine which columns will be helpful.
2. If necessary to avoid wraparound, use a COLUMN command to shorten the display size for the necessary column(s).
3. Select the necessary column(s) from the DD view.

Example 6.A.1

For illustration purposes, display everything in USER_TABLES.

```
SQL: SELECT *
     FROM user_tables;
```

Execution Results

```
TABLE_NAME                     TABLESPACE_NAME
------------------------------ ------------------------------
CLUSTER_NAME                   IOT_NAME                         PCT_FREE
------------------------------ ------------------------------ ----------
  PCT_USED  INI_TRANS  MAX_TRANS INITIAL_EXTENT NEXT_EXTENT MIN_EXTENTS
---------- ---------- ---------- -------------- ----------- -----------
MAX_EXTENTS PCT_INCREASE  FREELISTS FREELIST_GROUPS LOG B   NUM_ROWS     BLOCKS
----------- ------------ ---------- --------------- --- - ---------- ----------
EMPTY_BLOCKS  AVG_SPACE  CHAIN_CNT AVG_ROW_LEN AVG_SPACE_FREELIST_BLOCKS
----------- ---------- ---------- ---------- -------------------------
NUM_FREELIST_BLOCKS DEGREE     INSTANCES  CACHE TABLE_LO SAMPLE_SIZE LAST_ANAL
------------------- ---------- ---------- ----- -------- ----------- ---------
PAR IOT_TYPE     T S NES BUFFER_ ROW_MOVE GLO USE DURATION         SKIP_COR MON
--- ------------ - - --- ------- -------- --- --- -------------- -------- ---
CLUSTER_OWNER                  DEPENDEN
------------------------------ --------
BILLING                        SYSTEM

TABLE_NAME                     TABLESPACE_NAME
------------------------------ ------------------------------
CLUSTER_NAME                   IOT_NAME                         PCT_FREE
------------------------------ ------------------------------ ----------
  PCT_USED  INI_TRANS  MAX_TRANS INITIAL_EXTENT NEXT_EXTENT MIN_EXTENTS
---------- ---------- ---------- -------------- ----------- -----------
MAX_EXTENTS PCT_INCREASE  FREELISTS FREELIST_GROUPS LOG B   NUM_ROWS     BLOCKS
----------- ------------ ---------- --------------- --- - ---------- ----------
```

```
(and so on; remainder of execution results not printed)
```

Note: As you can see, this format is unreadable. A better solution is to follow the three steps listed previously, as illustrated by the next example.

Example 6.A.2

Display the names of the columns in USER_TABLES.

At the prompt:

```
DESCRIBE user_tables
```

Execution Results

Name	Null?	Type
TABLE_NAME	NOT NULL	VARCHAR2(30)
TABLESPACE_NAME		VARCHAR2(30)
CLUSTER_NAME		VARCHAR2(30)
IOT_NAME		VARCHAR2(30)
PCT_FREE		NUMBER
PCT_USED		NUMBER
INI_TRANS		NUMBER
MAX_TRANS		NUMBER
INITIAL_EXTENT		NUMBER
NEXT_EXTENT		NUMBER
MIN_EXTENTS		NUMBER
MAX_EXTENTS		NUMBER
PCT_INCREASE		NUMBER
FREELISTS		NUMBER
FREELIST_GROUPS		NUMBER
LOGGING		VARCHAR2(3)
BACKED_UP		VARCHAR2(1)
NUM_ROWS		NUMBER
BLOCKS		NUMBER
EMPTY_BLOCKS		NUMBER
AVG_SPACE		NUMBER
CHAIN_CNT		NUMBER
AVG_ROW_LEN		NUMBER
AVG_SPACE_FREELIST_BLOCKS		NUMBER
NUM_FREELIST_BLOCKS		NUMBER
DEGREE		VARCHAR2(10)
INSTANCES		VARCHAR2(10)
CACHE		VARCHAR2(5)
TABLE_LOCK		VARCHAR2(8)
SAMPLE_SIZE		NUMBER
LAST_ANALYZED		DATE
PARTITIONED		VARCHAR2(3)
IOT_TYPE		VARCHAR2(12)
TEMPORARY		VARCHAR2(1)
SECONDARY		VARCHAR2(1)
NESTED		VARCHAR2(3)
BUFFER_POOL		VARCHAR2(7)
ROW_MOVEMENT		VARCHAR2(8)
GLOBAL_STATS		VARCHAR2(3)
USER_STATS		VARCHAR2(3)
DURATION		VARCHAR2(15)
SKIP_CORRUPT		VARCHAR2(8)
MONITORING		VARCHAR2(3)
CLUSTER_OWNER		VARCHAR2(30)
DEPENDENCIES		VARCHAR2(8)

The column named TABLE_NAME is the only one of any use at this point, so the best thing to do is to display that column only. Since this display involves a total line size of less than 80, no COLUMN commands are needed (the previous DESC results show that the size of the TABLE_NAME column is 30 characters).

```
SQL: SELECT table_name
     FROM user_tables;
```

Execution Results

```
TABLE_NAME
--------------
BILLING
CUSTOMER
DOCTOR
MOVIE
PATIENT
RENTAL
```

Note: The names of tables and other database objects are stored in the DD views in all capital letters. Therefore, even though you can normally use any case when entering table names, if you refer to a specific table name from a view (on a WHERE clause, for example), you must use all capital letters and enclose it in single quotes.

Also note that the exact list of table names displayed by this statement will vary depending on the specific tables available on your system. This is also true for other DD view contents displayed throughout the rest of this book; system-to-system variability is to be expected.

Example 6.A.3

For the RENTAL table, what is the current setting for DEPENDENCIES, and is monitoring currently active (MONITORING)?

```
SQL: SELECT dependencies, monitoring
     FROM user_tables
     WHERE table_name = 'RENTAL';
```

Execution Results

```
DEPENDEN MON
-------- ---
DISABLED NO

1 row selected.
```

Note: This example is just intended to illustrate the display of DD view contents for a specific table; generally, only the DBA is interested in the current values of DEPENDENCIES and MONITORING.

As you add and/or remove tables from a database, the USER_TABLES DD view can be used to verify the results. Other DD views will be discussed later in this chapter as well as in upcoming chapters.

Part 2: Naming Guidelines

All names must follow the same guidelines, regardless of whether the name is used for a table, a view, or any other object. Rules are as follows:

1. Must begin with a letter.
2. Can contain only letters, digits, and underscores.
3. May be up to 30 characters in length.
4. Should be meaningful.
5. Cannot be a reserved word.
6. Are not case-sensitive (except on the WHERE clause of a DD view SELECT).

Examples of valid names are SALES_CONTACT, RATES_FOR_2003, and FORM_90A. Examples of invalid names are 2003_RATES (does not start with a letter), STREET ADDRESS (contains something other than letters, digits, and underscores), and E_DEP_SP (is not meaningful).

Part 3: Column Types

There are several data types available for columns, but only the four most common types will be covered in this book.

1. CHAR(length)
   - Specifies a character string of a constant length.
2. VARCHAR2(max-length)
   - Specifies a variable-length character string.
3. NUMBER(max-length, decimal-places)
   - Specifies a numeric value with a total number of digits no more than the max-length specified.
   - The decimal-places value indicates the number of digits to the right of the decimal.
4. DATE
   - Specifies a date value (no format is specified).
   - Includes storage for a full format including the year (four digits), day of the year, hours, minutes, and seconds. From these values, month, day, and day of the week can also be determined.

Section B: Table Creation

Part 1: The CREATE TABLE Statement

These fundamental concepts can now be brought together with the CREATE TABLE statement. General syntax is as follows:

```
CREATE TABLE table-name
    (column-name column-type,
    column-name column-type,...
    PRIMARY KEY (primary-key-column(s)),
    [, FOREIGN KEY (foreign-key column)
        REFERENCES linked-table-name
        ON DELETE CASCADE]);
```

Where the following applies:

1. The table name and column names follow the naming guidelines.
2. The column types are formatted as described in the previous section.
3. One PRIMARY KEY clause is included.
4. If a foreign key is present, then the FOREIGN KEY clause is required (including the REFERENCES and ON DELETE phrases). If two foreign keys are present, then two complete FOREIGN KEY clauses are required, and so on.

Example 6.B.1

Create the MOVIE table. Then display its structure. (*Note:* Some of the upcoming CREATE TABLE commands will have already been executed if you initially used the script files to build and fill the tables.)

```
SQL: CREATE TABLE movie
     (m_id      NUMBER(3),
      fee       NUMBER(3,2),
      title     VARCHAR2(20),
      category  VARCHAR2(10),
      PRIMARY KEY (m_id));
```

Execution Results

```
Table created.
```

Example 6.B.2

Assuming that the doctor table has already been created, create the PATIENT table. Then display its structure.

```
SQL: CREATE TABLE patient
     (pt_id        NUMBER (3),
      pt_lname     VARCHAR2 (15),
      pt_fname     VARCHAR2 (25),
      pt_dob       DATE,
      doc_id       NUMBER(3),
      nextapptdate DATE,
      lastapptdate DATE,
      PRIMARY KEY (pt_id),
      FOREIGN KEY(doc_id)
          REFERENCES doctor
          ON DELETE CASCADE);
```

Execution Results

```
Table created.
```

Example 6.B.3

Create a table that can be used to store data on nurses, including their ID, first name, last name, monthly salary, and preferred work area. Then display its structure.

```
SQL: CREATE TABLE nurse
     (n_id           NUMBER (3),
      n_fname        VARCHAR2 (10),
      n_lname        VARCHAR2 (20),
      monthly_salary NUMBER (5,0),
      area           VARCHAR2 (15),
      PRIMARY KEY (n_id));
```

Execution Results

```
Table created.
```

Example 6.B.4

Assuming that the patient and doctor tables have already been created, create a table that can be used to store appointment information. Include the patient ID, doctor ID, and date.

```
SQL: CREATE TABLE appt
     (appt_date  DATE,
      pt_id      NUMBER (3),
      doc_id     NUMBER (3),
      PRIMARY KEY (pt_id, doc_id),
      FOREIGN KEY (pt_id)
          REFERENCES patient
          ON DELETE CASCADE,
```

```
            FOREIGN KEY (doc_id)
                REFERENCES doctor
                ON DELETE CASCADE);
```

Execution Results

```
Table created.
```

Note: The USER_TABLES view can be used to verify the creation of these tables.

```
SQL: SELECT TABLE_NAME
       FROM USER_TABLES;
```

Execution Results

```
TABLE_NAME
-----------------
APPT
BILLING
CUSTOMER
DOCTOR
MOVIE
NURSE
PATIENT
RENTAL
```

Note: The exact list of table names displayed by this statement will vary depending on the specific tables available on your system.

Part 2: Creation by Subquery

Some of the examples for the INSERT command illustrated a means for taking copies of existing rows and inserting them into a new table that had already been created. The two steps of table creation and insertion of rows from an existing table can be combined into one step by using a subquery (SELECT) on the CREATE TABLE command. When selected columns are being created based on another table, the column names must be listed following the new table name in a manner similar to that used on the INSERT statement. General syntax is as follows:

> CREATE TABLE table-name [(column-list)] AS subquery;
>
> where the column-list is required only when the column names in the source table do not match the column names in the (new) destination table
>
> and the subquery is a SELECT command that may *or may not* have its own subqueries.

Example 6.B.5

At the end of each day, all rental data on movies due the next day needs to be moved to a separate table named RENTALS_DUE. Create the table, move copies of the appropriate rows, then remove the rows from the RENTAL table.

Script File Contents

```
CREATE TABLE rentals_due AS
    SELECT *
    FROM rental
    WHERE due_date = SYSDATE + 1;

DESCRIBE rentals_due
```

```
SELECT *
FROM rentals_due;

DELETE FROM rental
WHERE due_date = SYSDATE + 1;
```

Execution Results

```
Table created.
```

Name	Null?	Type
C_ID		NUMBER(3)
M_ID		NUMBER(3)
DATE_OUT		DATE
DUE_DATE		DATE

C_ID	M_ID	DATE_OUT	DUE_DATE
673	216	30-JUN-03	02-JUL-03
388	216	30-JUN-03	02-JUL-03
701	216	30-JUN-03	02-JUL-03

```
3 rows selected.

3 rows deleted.
```

Example 6.B.6

The rehab department is moving to another clinic, and taking their patients with them. Assuming that all related patient data has already been moved, create a table of data on all former rehab doctors, and remove them from the DOCTOR table. Do not include the AREA column in the new table. Verify the changes.

Script File Contents

```
CREATE TABLE rehab_docs (doc_id, doc_name, datehired,
    salpermon, supervisor_id, chgperappt, annual_bonus) AS
        SELECT doc_id, doc_name, datehired, salpermon,
            supervisor_id, chgperappt, annual_bonus
        FROM doctor
        WHERE area = 'Rehab';

DESCRIBE rehab_docs

SELECT *
FROM rehab_docs;

DELETE FROM doctor
WHERE area = 'Rehab';
```

Execution Results

```
Table created.
```

Name	Null?	Type
DOC_ID		NUMBER(3)
DOC_NAME		VARCHAR2(9)
DATEHIRED		DATE
SALPERMON		NUMBER(12)

SUPERVISOR_ID	NUMBER(3)
CHGPERAPPT	NUMBER(3)
ANNUAL_BONUS	NUMBER(5)

DOC_ID	DOC_NAME	DATEHIRED	SALPERMON	SUPERVISOR_ID	CHGPERAPPT	ANNUAL_BONUS
889	Thompson	18-MAR-97	6500	100	65	3200
239	Pronger	18-DEC-99	3500	889	40	

```
2 rows selected.

2 rows deleted.
```

Note: The column list is required on both the CREATE TABLE clause on the SELECT clause because not all of the columns from the source table are being copied to the new table.

Example 6.B.7

All pediatrics patient data needs to be moved to a separate table named PED_PATIENT. Create the table, move copies of the appropriate rows, then remove the rows from the PATIENT table.

Script File Contents

```
CREATE TABLE ped_patient AS
    SELECT *
    FROM patient
    WHERE doc_id IN
        (SELECT doc_id
        FROM doctor
        WHERE area = 'Pediatrics');

DESCRIBE ped_patient

SELECT *
FROM ped_patient;

DELETE FROM patient
WHERE doc_id IN
    (SELECT doc_id
    FROM doctor
    WHERE area = 'Pediatrics');
```

Execution Results

```
Table created.
```

Name	Null?	Type
PT_ID		NUMBER(3)
PT_LNAME		VARCHAR2(15)
PT_FNAME		VARCHAR2(15)
PTDOB		DATE
DOC_ID		NUMBER(3)
NEXTAPPTDATE		DATE
LASTAPPTDATE		DATE

```
PT_ID PT_LNAME          PT_FNAME         PTDOB        DOC_ID NEXTAPPTD LASTAPPTD
------ ----------------  ---------------- ---------  --------- --------- ---------
   168 James             Paul             14-MAR-97       432 01-JUL-03 01-JUN-03
   816 Smith             Jason            12-DEC-99       509 15-NOV-03 15-MAY-03
   103 Poole             Jennifer         13-MAY-02       389 01-DEC-03 01-JUN-03
   703 Davis             Linda            17-JUL-02       509 21-JUL-03 22-MAY-03
   307 Jones             J.C.             17-JUL-02       509 21-JUL-03 22-MAY-03
```

5 rows deleted.

Note: The inner subqueries are needed to determine which doctors work in pediatrics, as there is no direct indication in the PATIENT table.

Section C: Table Structure Modification

New columns can be added to tables, and the data type for existing columns can be modified. Some versions also support dropping columns, and for those that do not, an alternative means for "dropping" columns will be presented.

Part 1: Add a New Column

The ALTER TABLE command with the ADD clause is used to add a new column to a table. General syntax is as follows:

ALTER TABLE table-name

ADD column-name column-type

[ADD column-name column-type . . .];

where the column-types available are the same as those used on the CREATE TABLE command.

Example 6.C.1

Add a column to the PATIENT table for emergency phone number. Verify the results.

Script File Contents

```
ALTER TABLE patient
ADD emergency_phone VARCHAR2(12);
DESCRIBE patient
```

Execution Results

```
Table altered.
```

Name	Null?	Type
PT_ID	NOT NULL	NUMBER(3)
PT_LNAME		VARCHAR2(15)
PT_FNAME		VARCHAR2(15)
PTDOB		DATE
DOC_ID		NUMBER(3)
NEXTAPPTDATE		DATE
LASTAPPTDATE		DATE
EMERGENCY_PHONE		VARCHAR2(12)

Example 6.C.2

Add columns to the customer table for amount and date of last payment. Verify the results.

Script File Contents

```
ALTER TABLE customer
ADD last_pmt_amt NUMBER(4,2)
ADD last_pmt_date DATE;
DESCRIBE customer
```

Execution Results

```
Table altered.
```

```
SQL> DESCRIBE CUSTOMER
```

Name	Null?	Type
C_ID	NOT NULL	NUMBER(3)
PHONE		VARCHAR2(8)
LNAME		VARCHAR2(10)
FNAME		VARCHAR2(10)
CURR_BAL		NUMBER(5,2)
DUEDATE		DATE
LAST_PMT_AMT		NUMBER(4,2)
LAST_PMT_DATE		DATE

Part 2: Modify an Existing Column

The ALTER TABLE command with the MODIFY clause is used to change the data type for a column. In this case, lengths are usually increased. Decreasing a column length may cause loss of data, and is therefore not allowed. General syntax is as follows:

> ALTER TABLE table-name
>
> MODIFY column-name column-type
>
> [MODIFY column-name column-type . . .];

Example 6.C.3

The last name field in the patient table needs to be increased to 25 characters.

```
SQL: ALTER TABLE patient
        MODIFY pt_lname VARCHAR2(25);
```

Execution Results

```
Table altered.
```

Example 6.C.4

For illustration purposes only, attempt to decrease the column size down to 10 characters.

```
SQL: ALTER TABLE patient
        MODIFY pt_lname VARCHAR2(10);
```

Execution Results

```
    MODIFY pt_lname VARCHAR2(5)
            *
ERROR at line 2:
ORA-01441: cannot decrease column length because some value is too big
```

Example 6.C.5

Due to the arrival of some collector's sets of movies, the FEE column needs to be increased to support fees of $11.99.

```
SQL: ALTER TABLE movie
        MODIFY fee NUMBER(4,2);
```

Execution Results

```
Table altered.
```

Part 3: Remove a Column

Depending on which software version is being used, the DROP COLUMN option may or may not be supported. For those installations in which it is not supported, an alternative means of removing a column will be presented after the next example.

General Syntax

> ALTER TABLE table-name
> DROP (column-name);

Note: Repetition of the DROP clause is not allowed (unlike the ADD and MODIFY clauses).

Example 6.C.6

Remove the new emergency phone column from the PATIENT table.

```
SQL: ALTER TABLE patient
     DROP (emergency_phone);
```

Execution Results

```
Table altered.
```

In situations where the drop column clause is not available, an alternative method may be used. Another means of "removing" a column from a table is by creating a new table that contains all of the columns except the one to be removed. Then the old table can be dropped and the new table renamed to match the old table. Commands for dropping and renaming tables will be covered in the next section of this chapter.

Example 6.C.7

Annual bonuses will now be determined by area rather than on an individual doctor basis. Move all other columns of the DOCTOR table to a new table named TEMP_DOC.

```
SQL: CREATE TABLE temp_doc(doc_id, doc_name, datehired, salpermon, area, supervisor_id)
         AS SELECT doc_id, doc_name, datehired, salpermon, area, supervisor_id
            FROM doctor;

     DESCRIBE temp_doc

     SELECT *
     FROM temp_doc;
```

Execution Results

```
Table created.
```

Name	Null?	Type
DOC_ID		NUMBER(3)
DOC_NAME		VARCHAR2(9)
DATEHIRED		DATE
SALPERMON		NUMBER(12)
AREA		VARCHAR2(20)
SUPERVISOR_ID		NUMBER(3)

DOC_ID	DOC_NAME	DATEHIRED	SALPERMON	AREA	SUPERVISOR_ID
432	Harrison	05-DEC-94	12000	Pediatrics	100
509	Vester	09-JAN-02	8100	Pediatrics	432
389	Lewis	21-JAN-96	10000	Pediatrics	432
504	Cotner	16-JUN-98	11500	Neurology	289
235	Smith	22-JUN-98	4550	Family Practice	100

```
356 James      01-AUG-98    7950 Neurology              289
558 James      02-MAY-95    9800 Orthopedics            876
876 Robertson  02-MAR-95   10500 Orthopedics            100
889 Thompson   18-MAR-97    6500 Rehab                  100
239 Pronger    18-DEC-99    3500 Rehab                  889
289 Borque     30-JUN-89   16500 Neurology              100
100 Stevenson  30-JUN-79   23500 Director
```

```
12 rows selected.
```

Note: At this point, the DOCTOR table can be removed, and the TEMP_DOC table can be renamed as DOCTOR, thus giving the effect of removing the ANNUAL_BONUS column from the DOCTOR table.

Also note that on the CREATE TABLE command, the column names must be listed following the new table name because only selected columns are being copied from the source table.

Section D: Other Table Commands

DROP TABLE

This command is used to remove a table. Both the table contents and the table structure will be deleted. General syntax is DROP TABLE table-name. Caution should be exercised, though, because the effects of issuing this command are permanent. As with all other DDL commands, a COMMIT is automatically executed.

Example 6.D.1

Remove the NURSE table from the database.

```
SQL: DROP TABLE nurse;
```

Execution Results

```
Table dropped.
```

Example 6.D.2

Remove the RENTALS_DUE table from the database.

```
SQL: DROP TABLE rentals_due;
```

Execution Results

```
Table dropped.
```

TRUNCATE TABLE

This command removes all of the rows from the table, but the table structure remains intact. A COMMIT is automatically executed, so ROLLBACK is not an option. If a ROLLBACK may be needed, then the DELETE command should be used instead of TRUNCATE. TRUNCATE has the additional effect of releasing the storage space used by the deleted rows, while DELETE does not. General syntax is TRUNCATE TABLE table-name.

Example 6.D.3

For illustration purposes only, permanently remove all rows from the TEMP_DOC table, and verify the results.

Script File Contents

```
TRUNCATE TABLE temp_doc;

SELECT *
FROM temp_doc;
```

Execution Results

```
Table truncated.

no rows selected
```

RENAME

The name of a table can be changed by using the RENAME command. General syntax is as follows: RENAME old-name TO new-name

Example 6.D.4

Change the name of the PATIENT table to CLIENT.

```
SQL: RENAME patient TO client;
```

Execution Results

```
Table renamed.
```

Example 6.D.5

At the end of example number 6.C.7, it was noted that after the new temporary table was created, the DOCTOR table could be removed, and the TEMP_DOC table can be renamed as DOCTOR, thus giving the effect of removing the ANNUAL_BONUS column from the DOCTOR table. Those commands can now be illustrated. Verify the results by examining a DD view.

Script File Contents

```
DROP TABLE doctor;

RENAME temp_doc TO doctor;

SELECT table_name
FROM user_tables;
```

Execution Results

```
Table dropped.

Table renamed.

TABLE_NAME
-----------------
APPT
BILLING
CUSTOMER
DOCTOR
MOVIE
NURSE
PATIENT
RENTAL
```

Note: The exact list of table names displayed by this statement will vary depending on the specific tables available on your system.

COMMENT ON

Comments can be added to both tables and columns using the COMMENT ON statement. This provides a facility for storing table and column descriptions that may have been specified in a data dictionary during the design phase. These comments will be stored in various data dictionary views, such as USER_TAB_COMMENTS and USER_COL_COMMENTS.

General Syntax

```
COMMENT ON TABLE table-name IS 'character string';
```

or:

```
COMMENT ON COLUMN table-name.column-name IS 'character string';
```

Example 6.D.6

Add a comment to the BILLING table, and verify the results.

Script File Contents

```
COMMENT ON TABLE billing IS 'Data used for patient billing';

SELECT comments
FROM user_tab_comments
WHERE table_name = 'BILLING';
```

Execution Results

```
Comment created.


COMMENTS
----------------------------------------
Data used for patient billing
```

Example 6.D.7

Add a comment to the RENTALS table, and verify the results.

Script File Contents

```
COMMENT ON TABLE rental
    IS 'RECORDS OF MOVIES CURRENTLY DUE';
SELECT comments
FROM user_tab_comments
WHERE table_name = 'RENTAL';
```

Execution Results

```
Comment created.


COMMENTS
-----------------------------------------
RECORDS OF MOVIES CURRENTLY DUE
```

Example 6.D.8

Add a comment to the AREA column of the DOCTOR table, and verify the results.

Script File Contents

```
COMMENT ON COLUMN doctor.area IS 'Area of Specialization';
SELECT comments
FROM user_col_comments
WHERE table_name = 'DOCTOR'
AND column_name = 'AREA';
```

Execution Results

```
Comment created.


COMMENTS
--------------------------------------------
Area of Specialization
```

Note: As with table names, when a column name is stored in a DD view, it is in all capital letters.

<table>
<tr><td>

Example 6.D.9

</td><td>

Add a comment to the CURR_BAL column of the CUSTOMER table.

</td></tr>
</table>

Script File Contents

```
COMMENT ON COLUMN customer.curr_bal
    IS 'Current balance owed by customer';
SELECT comments
FROM user_col_comments
WHERE table_name = 'CUSTOMER'
AND column_name = 'CURR_BAL';
```

Execution Results

```
Comment created.


COMMENTS
-------------------------------------------------------
Current balance owed by customer
```

Section E: Constraint Specification

Constraints can be used to ensure that entity integrity and referential integrity are maintained. Specifically, a primary key constraint will prevent the insertion of primary key values that already exist, thus ensuring uniqueness and entity integrity. Without a primary key constraint, duplicate values could be stored, thus making it impossible to consistently retrieve exactly one row of data based on the intended primary key value.

Similarly, foreign key constraints should be used to enforce referential integrity. A foreign key constraint will prevent the appearance of foreign key value that does not have a corresponding matching primary key value in the related table. For example, a rental may refer to movie ID 400 when there is no such movie, thus violating referential integrity. Foreign key constraints are an easy-to-use mechanism that will prevent that type of situation.

Additionally, constraints can be defined to ensure that certain business rules are followed, such as requiring that all employee hourly rates be within a certain range, or that all product size codes come from a specific set of allowed sizes. These are called check constraints, and some people refer to these as a means of maintaining database integrity in general.

All constraints can be specified either when the table is created or at a later time by using the ALTER TABLE command.

Part 1: Naming Conventions

Constraints should be named by the user. If this is not done, then the software will provide a unique constraint name such as SYS_C2002698. As this is not a very descriptive name, the user should provide a name and follow standard industry naming conventions. Parts of the constraint name are as follows:

1. The table name
2. An underscore
3. The column name
4. An underscore
5. The constraint type (PK for primary key, FK for foreign key, NN for Not Null, CK for check)

Example 6.E.1

Give a constraint name for the primary key constraint for the BILLING table's PT_ID.

Solution

```
BILLING_PT_ID_PK
```

Part 2: Primary and Foreign Key Constraints

During Table Creation

Examples of constraints have already been illustrated with the CREATE TABLE commands, but they did not include specification of appropriate constraint names. Hence, when example 6.B.3 was executed by the author, the primary key constraint was named by the software as SYS_C002725. A better version of the CREATE TABLE statement for that table follows:

```
SQL: CREATE TABLE nurse
     (n_id          NUMBER (3),
     n_fname        VARCHAR2 (10),
     n_lname        VARCHAR2 (20),
     monthly_salary NUMBER (5,0),
     area           VARCHAR2 (15),
     CONSTRAINT nurse_n_id_pk
         PRIMARY KEY (n_id));
```

Note: If you wanted to type and execute this statement, it would need to be preceded with a DROP TABLE statement (see Section D of this chapter), as the table already exists.

Also note that the only modification included in this example is the addition of the keyword CONSTRAINT followed by the constraint name before the primary key specification.

Similar modifications can be made for the CREATE TABLE statement used in example 6.B.4, as follows:

```
SQL: CREATE TABLE appt
     (appt_date  DATE,
     pt_id       NUMBER (3),
     doc_id      NUMBER (3),
     CONSTRAINT appt_pt_id_doc_id_pk
         PRIMARY KEY (pt_id, doc_id),
     CONSTRAINT appt_pt_id_fk
         FOREIGN KEY (pt_id)
             REFERENCES patient
             ON DELETE CASCADE,
     CONSTRAINT appt_doc_id_fk
         FOREIGN KEY (doc_id)
             REFERENCES doctor
             ON DELETE CASCADE);
```

Constraints may be viewed by examining the DD view USER_CONSTRAINTS. This is when it is most helpful to have used better names than those generated by the system.

Example 6.E.2

Display data on currently defined constraints for the APPT and NURSE tables.

Steps Required

```
DESCRIBE user_constraints

SELECT constraint_name, constraint_type, table_name
FROM user_constraints
WHERE table_name IN ('APPT', 'NURSE');
```

Execution Results

```
Name                            Null?    Type
------------------------------- -------- ----
OWNER                           NOT NULL VARCHAR2(30)
CONSTRAINT_NAME                 NOT NULL VARCHAR2(30)
CONSTRAINT_TYPE                          VARCHAR2(1)
TABLE_NAME                      NOT NULL VARCHAR2(30)
SEARCH_CONDITION                         LONG
R_OWNER                                  VARCHAR2(30)
R_CONSTRAINT_NAME                        VARCHAR2(30)
DELETE_RULE                              VARCHAR2(9)
STATUS                                   VARCHAR2(8)
DEFERRABLE                               VARCHAR2(14)
DEFERRED                                 VARCHAR2(9)
VALIDATED                                VARCHAR2(13)
GENERATED                                VARCHAR2(14)
BAD                                      VARCHAR2(3)
LAST_CHANGE                              DATE


CONSTRAINT_NAME                 C TABLE_NAME
------------------------------- - --------------------
APPT_PT_ID_DOC_ID_PK            P APPT
APPT_PT_ID_FK                   R APPT
APPT_DOC_ID_FK                  R APPT
NURSE_N_ID_PK                   P NURSE
```

Note: The column with heading C is the constraint type (with the heading truncated due to a column size of one character). A type of P indicates a primary key, while a type of R indicates a reference, such as a foreign key that references another column.

Both the primary key and foreign key constraints illustrated thus far were specified as table constraints following all column specifications. These particular constraints could have instead been specified as column constraints by including the CONSTRAINT keyword, the constraint name, and constraint type following specification of the column name and type. Yet another possible version of the CREATE TABLE statement for the NURSE table is as follows:

```
SQL: CREATE TABLE nurse
     (n_id          NUMBER (3)
          CONSTRAINT nurse_n_id_pk PRIMARY KEY,
     n_fname        VARCHAR2 (10),
     n_lname        VARCHAR2 (20),
     monthly_salary NUMBER (5,0),
     area           VARCHAR2 (15));
```

Similarly, for the APPT table, the two foreign key constraints could have been specified at the column level. However, since the primary key is a composite key, the corresponding primary key constraint can be specified only at the table level. This third version of the CREATE TABLE statement for the APPT table is as follows:

```
SQL: CREATE TABLE appt
     (appt_date DATE,
     pt_id NUMBER (3) CONSTRAINT appt_pt_id_fk
          FOREIGN KEY
              REFERENCES patient
              ON DELETE CASCADE,
```

```
doc_id NUMBER (3) CONSTRAINT appt_doc_id_fk
        FOREIGN KEY
                REFERENCES doctor
                ON DELETE CASCADE,
    CONSTRAINT appt_pt_id_doc_id_pk
        PRIMARY KEY (pt_id, doc_id));
```

After Table Creation

Constraints may also be specified after table creation by using the ALTER TABLE statement with the ADD CONSTRAINT option. This is especially useful for a table that contains a foreign key link to itself (such as with the "supervises" or "manages" relationship).
Such a foreign key cannot be defined during table creation because the table being referenced has not been completely created yet.

Example 6.E.3

Add the foreign key constraint to the DOCTOR table, as it could not be defined during table
creation. Verify the results.

```
SQL: ALTER TABLE doctor
    ADD CONSTRAINT doctor_supervisor_id_fk
        FOREIGN KEY(supervisor_id)
        REFERENCES doctor;
    SELECT constraint_name, constraint_type
    FROM user_constraints
    WHERE table_name = 'DOCTOR';
```

Execution Results

```
Table altered.


CONSTRAINT_NAME                 C
------------------------------- -
DOCTOR_DOC_ID_PK                P
DOCTOR_SUPERVISOR_ID_FK         R
```

Example 6.E.4

Test the foreign key constraint by attempting to change one of the supervisor IDs (the
foreign key) to one that does not exist as a doctor ID (primary key) in the DOCTOR
table.

```
SQL: UPDATE doctor
    SET supervisor_id = 111
    WHERE doc_id = 432;
```

Execution Results

```
UPDATE DOCTOR
*
ERROR at line 1:
ORA-02291: integrity constraint (LPREECE.DOCTOR_SUPERVISOR_ID_FK)
violated - parent key not found
```

As expected, the error message indicates an attempted violation of the constraint, as the
foreign key value (111) is not present in the table as a primary key value.

Example 6.E.5

For illustration purposes, test the primary key constraint by attempting to add a new row
with a primary key value that already exists in the table.

```
SQL: INSERT INTO doctor (doc_id)
    VALUES (432);
```

Execution Results

```
INSERT INTO doctor (doc_id)
*
ERROR at line 1:
ORA-00001: unique constraint (LPREECE.DOCTOR_DOC_ID_PK) violated
```

Note: A similar error message would have been generated by an UPDATE command that attempts to place a duplicate primary key value in the table.

Part 3: Check Constraints

CHECK constraints can be used to enforce various business rules and/or range restrictions (also known as attribute domains). For example, a business may require that all hourly pay rates be in the range $5.75 through $10.25, or that values for marital status be 'S', 'M', 'D', or 'W'. These fall under the category of CHECK constraints. General syntax for a column level CHECK constraint is as follows:

> CONSTRAINT constraint-name CHECK (condition)

where the condition is similar to conditions specified on a WHERE clause with the following exceptions:

1. SYSDATE may not be used.
2. Subqueries may not be used.

As with the other types of constraints, CHECK constraints can be defined during table creation or added later. They may be defined at the column level or at the table level.

Example 6.E.6	Add a constraint to guarantee that the only insurance types that can be entered into the BILLING table are SIH, BCBS, Military, MediSupplA, HealthCare, and QualityCare. Verify the results.

```
SQL: ALTER TABLE billing
     ADD CONSTRAINT billing_pt_ins_ck
     CHECK(pt_ins IN('SIH','BCBS','Military','MediSupplA','HealthCare','QualityCare'));

     COLUMN constraint_name FORMAT A17
     COLUMN search_condition FORMAT A75

     SELECT constraint_name, constraint_type, search_condition
     FROM user_constraints
     WHERE table_name = 'BILLING';
```

Execution Results

```
Table altered.

CONSTRAINT_NAME    C SEARCH_CONDITION
----------------   - ----------------------------------------------------------------------------
BILLING_PT_INS_CK  C PT_INS IN('SIH','BCBS','Military','MediSupplA','HealthCare','QualityCare')
BILLING_PT_ID_PK   P
```

Note: In the constraint type column (with a heading of C), the check constraint has a type of C, and the primary key constraint has a type of P.

Example 6.E.7 Add a constraint to guarantee that all charges per appointment are at least $25 and no more than $100. Verify the results.

```
SQL: ALTER TABLE doctor
        ADD CONSTRAINT doctor_chgperappt_ck
        CHECK (chgperappt BETWEEN 25 AND 100);

        SELECT constraint_name, constraint_type, search_condition
        FROM user_constraints
        WHERE table_name = 'DOCTOR';
```

Execution Results

```
Table altered.

CONSTRAINT_NAME              C SEARCH_CONDITION
------------------------     - ----------------------------
DOCTOR_DOC_ID_PK            P
DOCTOR_SUPERVISOR_ID_FK     R
DOCTOR_CHGPERAPPT_CK        C CHGPERAPPT BETWEEN 25 AND 100
```

Part 4: Other Constraint Options

Using the ALTER TABLE command, a constraint can be removed with the DROP clause, disabled with the DISABLE clause, or enabled with the ENABLE clause. Disabling/ enabling can be used on an as-needed basis, while dropping a constraint causes permanent removal. All three options are of the form option-name constraint-name.

Example 6.E.8 Equicor needs to be added as another insurance company in the BILLING table. Verify the modification.

```
SQL: ALTER TABLE billing
        DROP CONSTRAINT billing_pt_ins_ck;
        ALTER TABLE billing
        ADD CONSTRAINT billing_pt_ins_ck
            CHECK(pt_ins IN ('SIH','BCBS','Military','MediSupplA', 'HealthCare',
                'QualityCare','Equicor'));

        COLUMN constraint_name FORMAT A17
        COLUMN search_condition FORMAT A50

        SELECT constraint_name, constraint_type, search_condition
        FROM user_constraints
        WHERE table_name = 'BILLING';
```

Execution Results

```
Table altered.

CONSTRAINT_NAME   C SEARCH_CONDITION
----------------- - -----------------------------------------------
BILLING_PT_INS_CK C PT_INS IN ('SIH','BCBS','Military','MediSupplA',
                    'HealthCare','QualityCare','Equicor')
```

Chapter Summary

Data dictionary views can be used to examine data regarding various database objects and specifications. Two of the more commonly used DD views include USER_TABLES and USER_CONSTRAINTS. When using a DD view, you should DESCRIBE the view and SELECT the desired columns, formatting columns as needed to avoid wraparound.

Tables are created by using the CREATE TABLE statement. A subquery may be used within this statement to allow copying all or part of one table to a new table. Individual columns can be changed by using the ALTER TABLE statement's MODIFY option, and new columns can be added by using the ALTER TABLE statement's ADD option. Other table commands include DROP TABLE, TRUNCATE TABLE, RENAME, and COMMENT ON.

Constraints provide a means for having the software guarantee entity integrity, referential integrity, and the enforcement of business rules and/or domain restrictions. Constraints can be specified during table creation or at a later time, and may be defined at either the table level or the column level. The three main types of constraints are PRIMARY KEY, FOREIGN KEY, and CHECK. Constraints may be dropped, disabled, or enabled by using the ALTER TABLE command.

Exercises

Section A: Fundamentals

1. Use the steps listed in Part 1 of Section A of this chapter to use the ALL_TABLES DD view. Display the names of the tables that you have access to.
2. Display the names of the tables to which you have access that are owned by someone other than SYS.
3. Display the names of the tables that you have access to that are owned by someone other than a user with the string SYS anywhere in their user ID.

Section B: Table Creation

1. Create the DOCTOR table, omitting the foreign key specification on SUPERVISOR_ID for now. Display its structure.
2. Create the CUSTOMER table and display its structure.
3. Assuming that the customer and movie tables have already been created, create the RENTAL table, and display its structure.
4. Consider an example of a one-to-many relationship between two entities not covered thus far in the book. Create two tables for these two entities. Define at least three columns per table, and include specification of the foreign key. In a one-to-many relationship, the entity on which side (one or many) always gets the foreign key?
5. Create and fill a table consisting of customer data for those customers whose balance of over $20 is overdue. Verify the results.
6. Create and fill a table to be used for patient mailing labels. Include last name, first name, address, city, state, and ZIP. Store all city names in initial cap form. Verify the results.
7. All patients who have no upcoming appointment and haven't had an appointment within the last two years should be removed from the PATIENT and BILLING tables. Create the two new tables, move copies of the appropriate rows, then remove the rows from the PATIENT and BILLING tables. Eliminate the NEXTAPPTDATE column from the new table.

Section C: Table Structure Modification

1. Add a column to the DOCTOR table for cell phone number. Verify the results.
2. Add columns to the MOVIE table for rating (G, PG, etc.), number of copies in inventory, and release date.
3. Increase the size of the ZIP column in the BILLING table to allow for nine digits.
4. Five digits (instead of three) will be used for patient IDs. Increase the size of the column, and then add a "10" to the front of the IDs of each of the patients under 21 years of age, and add a "20" to each of the IDs of patients of age 21 or above.

5. Assuming that your installation supports the DROP column clause, remove the state (ST) column from the BILLING table.

6. Assuming that your installation does not support the DROP column clause, create a new table consisting of all columns from the BILLING table except the state column.

Section D: Other Table Commands

1. Remove the table you created for problem 5 in Section B.

2. Remove both of the tables you created for problem 7 in Section B.

3. Change the name of the DOCTOR table to PHYSICIAN.

4. Review your work for problem 6 of Section C. Now complete the task of dropping a column by removing the original table from the database, and changing the name of the newly created table to that of the old table.

5. Add comments to each of the new tables that you created for problem 4 of Section B. Verify the results.

6. For any one of the new tables you created for this chapter, specify a comment for each column. Verify the results.

Section E: Constraint Specification

1. Write the CREATE TABLE command for the MOVIE table. Include specification of the primary key constraint at the column level.

2. Assuming that the customer and movie tables have already been created, write the CREATE TABLE command for the RENTAL table. Include specification of the primary and foreign key constraints.

3. Verify the definition of the constraints from problems 1 and 2 by examining the appropriate DD view.

4. Add a primary key constraint to the CUSTOMER table. Verify. Test the constraint by attempting to add a new row with a primary key value that already exists in the table.

5. Add a foreign key constraint to the PATIENT table. Verify. Test the constraint by attempting to change one of the doctor IDs to one that does not exist in the DOCTOR table.

6. Add all primary and foreign key constraints to the tables created in your solution to problem 7 of Section B. Verify. Test all constraints.

7. Add a check constraint to the DOCTOR table for the AREA column. Areas should be in this list: Pediatrics, Neurology, Family Practice, Orthopedics, Rehab, Director. Verify and test.

8. Add a check constraint to the PATIENT table's NEXTAPPTDATE column. The next appointment date should always be later than the last appointment date. Verify and test.

9. Add check constraints to the CUSTOMER table. All balances should be under $200, and all due dates should be in June or July of 2003. Verify and test.

10. Two additional categories need to be included in the movie table, and they are "Classic" and "Special Interest." Increase the column size and modify the constraint. Verify and test.

11. Drop the check constraint on the DOCTOR table's CHGPERAPPT column, and add a new one. Allow the user to specify the lower and upper limits for the range of values to be allowed in this column. Verify and test.

12. Add appropriate constraints to each of the new tables that you created for problem 4 of Section B. Verify the results.

Chapter  7

Additional Objects

In addition to tables, many other database objects can be defined and used. These include views, sequences, indexes, and synonyms. Still other objects are available but will not be covered in this book.

Section A: Views

A view can be used to give other users access to a portion of a table (or tables) rather than the entire table. This allows the table owner to hide confidential information, or protect rows and/or columns as needed. Additionally, the view can be based on a fairly complex subquery, perhaps involving more than one table and/or additional subqueries. By defining this as a view, future access is greatly simplified, as the subquery needs to specified only once during view creation rather than repeatedly at each access.

Once created, a view can be treated like a table by using the SELECT statement. If the view involves only one table, then the INSERT, DELETE, and UPDATE statements can also be used on the view. It is important to be aware that such statements will actually modify the underlying base table, and not just the view. To prevent such modifications, a read-only option can be specified when the view is created.

Part 1: Creation

General syntax for view creation is as follows:

    CREATE VIEW view-name
    AS query;

where view-name should follow the naming convention of having a suffix of _VU.

Example 7.A.1

Create a view consisting of all doctor data except salary and bonus amounts. Then display the contents of the view.

Script File Contents

```
CREATE VIEW doctor_vu
AS SELECT doc_id, doc_name, datehired, area, supervisor_id
FROM doctor;

SELECT *
FROM doctor_vu;
```

Execution Results

```
View created.
```

DOC_ID	DOC_NAME	DATEHIRED	AREA	SUPERVISOR_ID
432	Harrison	05-DEC-94	Pediatrics	100
509	Vester	09-JAN-02	Pediatrics	432
389	Lewis	21-JAN-96	Pediatrics	432
504	Cotner	16-JUN-98	Neurology	289
235	Smith	22-JUN-98	Family Practice	100
356	James	01-AUG-98	Neurology	289
558	James	02-MAY-95	Orthopedics	876
876	Robertson	02-MAR-95	Orthopedics	100
889	Thompson	18-MAR-97	Rehab	100
239	Pronger	18-DEC-99	Rehab	889
289	Borque	30-JUN-89	Neurology	100
100	Stevenson	30-JUN-79	Director	

```
12 rows selected.
```

Example 7.A.2

Create a view consisting of all data on patients that use HealthCare insurance. Then display the contents of the view.

Script File Contents

```
CREATE VIEW healthcare_patient_vu
AS SELECT pt_id, balance, duedate, phone, addr, city, st, zip
FROM billing
WHERE pt_ins = 'HealthCare';


SELECT *
from healthcare_patient_vu;
```

Execution Results

```
View created.
```

PT_ID	BALANCE	DUEDATE	PHONE	ADDR	CITY	ST	ZIP
103	4500	01-JUL-03	833-5547	298 Murphy School Rd	Anna	IL	62906
108	0	01-JAN-05	833-5542	334 Pansie Hill Rd.	JONESBORO	IL	62952
703	225	31-AUG-03	529-8332	909 N. Brown St.	Carbondale	IL	62901
307	450	31-AUG-03	457-6967	234 N. Allen	Carbondale	IL	62901
719	0	01-JAN-04	549-7848	867 Henderson St.	Carbondale	IL	62901
315	5000	14-SEP-03	833-6272	404 Williford Rd.	JONESBORO	IL	62952
163	0	01-JAN-04	833-2133	129 Fountain St.	Anna	IL	62906

```
7 rows selected.
```

Example 7.A.3

Create a view consisting of names, phone numbers, and current balances of customers with balances due today. Then display the contents of the view.

Script File Contents

```
CREATE VIEW bal_due_today_vu
AS SELECT lname, fname, phone, curr_bal
```

```
FROM customer
WHERE duedate = SYSDATE;

SELECT *
FROM bal_due_today_vu;
```

Execution Results

```
View created.
```

```
LNAME          FNAME        PHONE        CURR_BAL
----------     ----------   --------     ----------
Ackers         John         549-6711         1.99
```

Example 7.A.4	Create a view consisting of names, phone numbers, and movie titles for customers with a movie or movies due today. Then display the contents of the view.

Script File Contents

```
CREATE VIEW movie_due_today_vu
AS SELECT lname, fname, phone, title
FROM customer c, movie m, rental r
WHERE c.c_id = r.c_id
    AND r.m_id = m.m_id
    AND r.due_date = SYSDATE;

SELECT *
FROM movie_due_today_vu;
```

Execution Results

```
View created.
```

```
LNAME          FNAME        PHONE        TITLE
----------     ----------   --------     --------------------
Akers          Janet        549-8400 U-571
Akers          Janet        549-8400 Wild, Wild West
Salyers        Loretta      549-8440 Amelie
Williams       Tisha        549-8840 Monster's Ball
```

Part 2: The Read-Only Option

If users need to be prevented from making any changes to the base table underlying the view, then the view should be created with the WITH READ-ONLY option. This option should be listed following the subquery.

Example 7.A.5	Create a read-only view of patient names and mailing addresses. Then display the contents of the view.

```
SQL: CREATE VIEW mailing_list_vu
    AS SELECT pt_lname, pt_fname, addr, city, st, zip
    FROM patient p, billing b
    WHERE p.pt_id = b.pt_id
    WITH READ ONLY;
    SELECT *
    FROM mailing_list_vu;
```

Execution Results

```
View created.
```

PT_LNAME	PT_FNAME	ADDR	CITY	ST	ZIP
James	Paul	128 W. Apple #4	Jonesboro	IL	62952
Anderson	Brian	3434 Mulberry St.	Anna	IL	62906
James	Scott	334 Tailgate Ln	COBDEN	IL	62920
Smith	Jason	8814 W. Apple	JONESBORO	IL	62952
Porter	Susan	445 Oak St.	Carbondale	IL	62901
Walters	Stephanie	8898 Bighill Drive	HERRIN	IL	62948
Poole	Jennifer	298 Murphy School Rd	Anna	IL	62906
Baily	Ryan	334 Pansie Hill Rd.	JONESBORO	IL	62952
Crow	Lewis	456 E. Grand #14	Carbondale	IL	62901
Cochran	John	6543 W. Parkview Ln.	Carbondale	IL	62901
Jackson	John	6657 N. Allen	Carbondale	IL	62901
Kowalczyk	Paul	3345 Hwy 127 N.	Murphysboro	IL	62966
Davis	Linda	909 N. Brown St.	Carbondale	IL	62901
Vanderchuck	Keith	5546 W. James	Carbondale	IL	62901
Mcginnis	Allen	9009 Taylor Ave.	Anna	IL	62906
Westra	Lynn	6755 US Route 148	HERRIN	IL	62948
Jones	J.C.	234 N. Allen	Carbondale	IL	62901
Rogers	Anthony	867 Henderson St.	Carbondale	IL	62901
Wright	Chasity	4456 N. Springer	Anna	IL	62906
Saillez	Debbie	404 Williford Rd.	JONESBORO	IL	62952
Roach	Becky	129 Fountain St.	Anna	IL	62906
Sakic	Joe	353 Tin Bender Rd.	Jonesboro	IL	62952

```
22 rows selected.
```

Note: Any attempt to modify the underlying base table through the view should be prevented by the software (although this particular error message gives little help in determining the cause of the error, as shown below).

```
SQL: DELETE FROM mailing_list_vu;
```

Execution Results

```
DELETE FROM MAILING_LIST_VU
            *
ERROR at line 1:
ORA-03752: cannot delete from view without exactly one key-preserved table
```

Example 7.A.6

Allow other users to view but not change customer IDs, names, and phone numbers by creating a view. Then display the contents of the view.

Script File Contents

```
CREATE VIEW cust_phones_vu
AS SELECT c_id, lname, fname, phone
FROM customer
WITH READ ONLY;

SELECT *
FROM cust_phones_vu;
```

Execution Results

```
View created.
```

```
        C_ID LNAME      FNAME      PHONE
---------- ---------- ---------- --------
       388 Woolard    Jessica    549-6730
       402 St. James  Ellen      529-8420
       673 Akers      Janet      549-8400
       579 Poston     Blaine     549-1234
       799 Ackers     John       549-6711
       767 Ralston    Cheri      453-8228
       133 Akers      Leita      453-2271
       239 Macke      Greg       549-1235
       400 Salyers    Loretta    549-8440
       701 Williams   Tisha      549-8840
```

```
10 rows selected.
```

Part 3: The Check Option

If changes to the underlying base table are to be made through the view, then the WITH CHECK OPTION should be used to ensure that rows do not vanish from the definition of the view. For example, if an update were attempted that would cause a row to no longer appear in the view, then the WITH CHECK OPTION would prevent it. As with the read-only option, the check option is listed following the query.

Example 7.A.7

Create a view of patient data that can be used to update today's patient data after each appointment. The current date will eventually be placed in the last appointment date. Do not allow any rows to be removed from the view.

```
SQL: CREATE VIEW end_of_appt_vu
     AS SELECT *
     FROM patient
     WITH CHECK OPTION;
```

Execution Results

```
View created.
```

Example 7.A.8

Write a script file that will allow the user to enter the patient ID and update the last appointment date appropriately.

Script File Contents

```
SET VERIFY OFF
ACCEPT id PROMPT 'Enter patient ID: '

UPDATE end_of_appt_vu
SET lastapptdate = SYSDATE
WHERE pt_id = &id;

SELECT pt_id, lastapptdate
FROM end_of_appt_vu
WHERE pt_id = &id;

COMMIT;
SET VERIFY ON
```

Execution Results

```
Enter patient ID: 331

1 row updated.

    PT_ID LASTAPPTD
--------- ---------
      331 01-JUL-03

Commit complete.
```

Example 7.A.9

Attempt to change the doctor ID through the view (should be prevented due to the WITH CHECK OPTION).

```
SQL: UPDATE end_of_appt_vu
     SET doc_id = 509
     WHERE pt_id = 331;
```

Execution Results

```
UPDATE end_of_appt_vu
       *
ERROR at line 1:
ORA-01402: view WITH CHECK OPTION where-clause violation
```

Note: The DD view named USER_UPDATABLE_COLUMNS can be used to determine which columns in the view can be modified, the DD view named USER_VIEWS can be used to display details on all views owned by the user, and the DD view named ALL_VIEWS can be used to display details on all views that the user can access (including all of the DD views).

A common misconception is that the WITH CHECK OPTION will restrict access to columns in the underlying table, but that is not the case. If such a need arises, just list the allowed columns on the SELECT clause.

Example 7.A.10

Create a view that will allow the user to adjust the due date of a current rental, but not the date out.

```
SQL: CREATE VIEW rental_due_date_vu
     AS SELECT c_id, m_id, due_date
     FROM rental;
```

Execution Results

```
View created.
```

Example 7.A.11

Write a script file that will allow the user to enter the customer ID, movie ID, and number of days of rental extension, and update the row appropriately.

Script File Contents

```
SET VERIFY OFF
ACCEPT c_id PROMPT 'Enter customer ID: '
ACCEPT m_id PROMPT 'Enter movie ID: '
ACCEPT num_days PROMPT 'Enter number of days of extension: '
```

```
UPDATE rental_due_date_vu
SET due_date = due_date + &num_days
WHERE c_id = &c_id
    AND m_id = &m_id;

SET VERIFY ON
```

Execution Results

```
Enter customer ID: 400
Enter movie ID: 255
Enter number of days of extension: 3

1 rows updated.
```

Example 7.A.12

For illustration purposes only, attempt to change the date out through the view.

```
SQL: UPDATE rental_due_date_vu
    SET date_out = SYSDATE;
```

Execution Results

```
SET date_out = SYSDATE
        *
ERROR at line 2:
ORA-00904: "DATE_OUT": invalid identifier
```

Note: This message indicates that DATE_OUT is not defined as part of the view.

Part 4: Modification and Removal

A view can be modified by adding the clause OR REPLACE after the CREATE keyword on the CREATE VIEW statement. The remainder of the syntax is unchanged.

Example 7.A.13

Change the mailing list view so that it allows address corrections to be made.

```
SQL: CREATE OR REPLACE VIEW mailing_list_vu
    AS SELECT pt_lname, pt_fname, addr, city, st, zip
    FROM patient p, billing b
    WHERE p.pt_id = b.pt_id
    WITH CHECK OPTION;
```

Execution Results

```
View created.
```

Example 7.A.14

Modify the customer phone view (example 7.A.6) so that it allows new phone numbers to be recorded.

```
SQL: CREATE OR REPLACE VIEW cust_phones_vu
    AS SELECT c_id, lname, fname, phone
    FROM customer
    WITH READ ONLY;
```

Execution Results

```
View created.
```

A view can be deleted with the DROP VIEW statement. General syntax is DROP VIEW view-name.

Example 7.A.15	Remove the HealthCare patient view.

```
SQL: DROP VIEW healthcare_patient_vu;
```

Execution Results

```
View dropped.
```

Example 7.A.16	Delete the view of data on patients with balances due today.

```
SQL: DROP VIEW bal_due_today_vu;
```

Execution Results

```
View dropped.
```

Note: When changes to a view need to be made, it is better to use CREATE OR REPLACE rather than to drop the view and then create a new one, because CREATE OR REPLACE will preserve any object privileges that may have been granted on the view.

Section B: Sequences

Sequences are used to automatically generate increasing numeric values to be used in a column. This is especially useful for the generation of primary key values.

Part 1: Creation

Several clauses are available on the CREATE SEQUENCE command (note that all are optional; default values indicated below). Naming guidelines for sequence names specify a name format consisting of table name, underscore, column name, underscore, and SEQ. General syntax is as follows:

```
CREATE SEQUENCE sequence-name
     [INCREMENT BY value]
     [START WITH value]
     [CYCLE | NOCYCLE]
     [MAXVALUE value]
     [MINVALUE value]
     [CACHE value | NOCACHE];
```

where the following rules apply:

1. The START WITH value indicates the first number to be used (default is 1).
2. The INCREMENT BY value indicates the amount that will be added to the number generated each time (default is 1).
3. The MAXVALUE value indicates the highest number to be used (default is 1.0E27 or 1,000,000,000,000,000,000,000,000,000).
4. The CYCLE options indicate the sequence should start over at the beginning after reaching the MAXVALUE value (NOCYCLE is the default).
5. The MINVALUE value indicates the number that the sequence will start over with after reaching the MAXVALUE value if the CYCLE option is on (default is 1).
6. The CACHE value indicates the number of values that will be generated in advance and held in memory until needed (default is 20).

Example 7.B.1

Create a sequence that can be used for the primary key named N_ID in the new NURSE table (see example 6.B.3). Use the sequence 100, 110, 120, . . . , 990, and then have it start over with 100. Do not use caching.

```
SQL: CREATE SEQUENCE nurse_n_id_seq
        START WITH 100
        INCREMENT BY 10
        MAXVALUE 990
        CYCLE
        MINVALUE 100
        NOCACHE;
```

Execution Results

```
Sequence created.
```

Note: Even though START WITH is specified, MINVALUE is also required due to cycling. Otherwise, when the sequence starts over, it will go to the default MINVALUE of 1.

The DD view named USER_SEQUENCES can be used to verify the creation of the sequence or to view the current sequence specifications.

Example 7.B.2

Display the current specifications for the new sequence.

```
SQL: DESC user_sequences
```

Execution Results

Name	Null?	Type
SEQUENCE_NAME	NOT NULL	VARCHAR2(30)
MIN_VALUE		NUMBER
MAX_VALUE		NUMBER
INCREMENT_BY	NOT NULL	NUMBER
CYCLE_FLAG		VARCHAR2(1)
ORDER_FLAG		VARCHAR2(1)
CACHE_SIZE	NOT NULL	NUMBER
LAST_NUMBER	NOT NULL	NUMBER

```
SQL: SELECT *
     FROM user_sequences
     WHERE sequence_name = 'NURSE_N_ID_SEQ';
```

Execution Results

SEQUENCE_NAME	MIN_VALUE	MAX_VALUE	INCREMENT_BY	C	O	CACHE_SIZE	LAST_NUMBER
NURSE_N_ID_SEQ	100	990	10	Y	N	0	100

Example 7.B.3

Create a sequence that can be used for the primary key named DOC_ID in the new REHAB_DOCS table (see example 6.B.6). Use the sequence 10, 12, 14, . . . , 48, and then have it start over with 10. Do not use caching.

```
SQL: CREATE SEQUENCE rehab_docs_doc_id_seq
        START WITH 10
        INCREMENT BY 2
        MAXVALUE 48
        CYCLE
        MINVALUE 10
        NOCACHE;
```

Execution Results

```
Sequence created.
```

Part 2: Usage

Once the sequence is created, it can be used by referring to the NEXTVAL of the sequence. Each reference will automatically increment the current sequence value by the amount specified on the INCREMENT BY clause. Format is sequence-name.NEXTVAL. This can be used either on the INSERT command (for new rows) or the UPDATE command (for existing rows). The current value (CURRVAL) of the sequence can also be used or displayed anytime after the first value has been generated. The format is sequence-name.CURRVAL.

Example 7.B.4

A new nurse named Connie Carlton has been hired in the pediatrics department at a monthly salary of $2,500. Add this data to the NURSE table, and use the sequence to generate a primary key value for N_ID. Verify the results.

Script File Contents

```
INSERT INTO nurse
VALUES (nurse_n_id_seq.NEXTVAL, 'Connie', 'Carlton', 2500,
        'Pediatrics');
SELECT *
FROM nurse
WHERE n_lname = 'Carlton';
```

Execution Results

```
1 row created.
```

N_ID	N_FNAME	N_LNAME	MONTHLY_SALARY	AREA
100	Connie	Carlton	2500	Pediatrics

Example 7.B.5

Modify the previous example to work for any newly hired nurse by allowing the user to enter the necessary values.

Script File Contents

```
ACCEPT fname PROMPT 'Enter nurse"s first name: '
ACCEPT lname PROMPT 'Enter nurse"s last name: '
ACCEPT sal PROMPT 'Enter salary: '
ACCEPT area PROMPT 'Enter area: '
SET VERIFY OFF
INSERT INTO nurse
     VALUES (nurse_n_id_seq.NEXTVAL, '&fname',
             '&lname', &sal, '&area');
SELECT *
FROM nurse
WHERE n_lname = '&lname';
SET VERIFY ON
```

Execution Results

```
Enter nurse's first name: Janet
Enter nurse's last name: Akers
Enter salary: 2750
Enter area: Orthopedics

1 row created.
```

N_ID	N_FNAME	N_LNAME	MONTHLY_SALARY	AREA
110	Janet	Akers	2750	Orthopedics

Example 7.B.6

Assume that the sequence has been used for some time, and there is a need to know the value of the last value that was used. Display this value without generating a new value. (*Hint:* what table can be used to display a value that is not stored in a table?)

```
SQL: SELECT nurse_n_id_seq.CURRVAL
     FROM DUAL;
```

Execution Results

```
  CURRVAL
---------
      110
```

Example 7.B.7

A new rehab doctor was hired today, and a row should be added to the REHAB_DOCS table (see example 6.B.6). Allow the user to enter the doctor's name, monthly salary, supervisor ID, and charge per appointment. Use the sequence to generate a new ID, and leave the annual bonus empty. Add this data to the REHAB_DOCS table, and use the sequence to generate a primary key value for DOC_ID. Verify the results.

Script File Contents

```
ACCEPT name PROMPT 'Enter doctor"s last name: '
ACCEPT sal PROMPT 'Enter monthly salary: '
ACCEPT super_id PROMPT 'Enter supervisor ID: '
ACCEPT apptchg PROMPT 'Enter charge per appointment: '
SET VERIFY OFF

INSERT INTO rehab_docs
      VALUES (rehab_docs_doc_id_seq.NEXTVAL,
         '&name', SYSDATE, &sal, &super_id, &apptchg, NULL);

SELECT *
FROM rehab_docs
WHERE doc_name = '&name';

SET VERIFY ON
```

Execution Results

```
Enter doctor's last name: Garnett
Enter monthly salary: 5000
Enter supervisor ID: 889
Enter charge per appointment: 60

1 row created.
```

DOC_ID	DOC_NAME	DATEHIRED	SALPERMON	SUPERVISOR_ID	CHGPERAPPT	ANNUAL_BONUS
10	Garnett	01-JUL-03	5000	889	60	

Part 3: Modification and Removal

A sequence can be modified by using the ALTER SEQUENCE statement. Only the increment, maxvalue, cycling, and caching options can be changed. If other changes are needed, then the sequence should be dropped and a new one created. Changes made with the

ALTER SEQUENCE statement will affect only future values generated, and will have no impact on values that have already been generated and stored in tables. General syntax is the same as for the CREATE SEQUENCE command with the exception of the word ALTER instead of CREATE.

Example 7.B.8

Change the increment amount from 10 to 20 on the nurse ID sequence. Verify the results.

```
SQL: ALTER SEQUENCE nurse_n_id_seq
        INCREMENT BY 20;
    SELECT INCREMENT_BY
    FROM user_sequences
    WHERE sequence_name = 'NURSE_N_ID_SEQ';
```

Execution Results

```
INCREMENT_BY
------------
          20
```

A sequence can be removed by using the DROP SEQUENCE statement. This, too, has no effect on values that have already been generated by the sequence.

Example 7.B.9

Discontinue cycling on the rehab doctor ID sequence. Verify the results.

```
SQL: ALTER SEQUENCE rehab_docs_doc_id_seq
        NOCYCLE;
    SELECT cycle_flag
    FROM user_sequences
    WHERE sequence_name = 'REHAB_DOCS_DOC_ID_SEQ';
```

Execution Results

```
Sequence altered.

C
-
N
```

Note: Many of the DD views have column commands defined so that as many columns as possible can be displayed in as small a space as possible. Hence, the column heading "C" is used for the CYCLE_FLAG column. The value of "N" indicates that no cycling is currently being used for the sequence.

Example 7.B.10

Remove the nurse ID sequence. Verify the results.

```
SQL: DROP SEQUENCE nurse_n_id_seq;
    SELECT *
    FROM user_sequences
    WHERE sequence_name = 'NURSE_N _ID_SEQ';
```

Execution Results

```
Sequence dropped.

no rows selected
```

Section C: Indexes

An index is automatically created for each table's primary key, but users can also create indexes. Such indexes are used to speed data retrieval when a secondary key is commonly used. For example, a patient's last name may be used to retrieve a set of records on patients with the same last name, and from there, the patient ID can be used to narrow the retrieval down to the desired row. Similarly, date of birth or phone number could be used as secondary keys. If these types of retrievals are common and the table is large, an index should be created.

Part 1: Creation

General syntax for the creation of an index is as follows:

CREATE INDEX index-name
ON table-name (column-name[, column-name, . . .]);

where naming guidelines for index names specify a name format consisting of table name, underscore, column name(s), underscore, IDX

and up to 16 column names may be specified.

Example 7.C.1

Create an index on the patient's date of birth.

```
SQL: CREATE INDEX patient_ptdob_idx
     ON patient(ptdob);
```

Execution Results

```
Index created.
```

Note: This example is *for illustration purposes only*. Normally, an index would not be created for such a small table. "Small" depends on the particular application (and the developer's opinion), but usually refers to a table with fewer than 50 rows.

The DD view USER_INDEXES can be used to verify the creation of an index. Be careful of the spelling: it is indexes (not indices). If specific column names used by the index are needed, then the DD view USER_IND_COLUMNS can be used. Join these two DD views on the column named INDEX_NAME.

Example 7.C.2

Verify the creation of the patient date of birth index.

Script File Contents

```
DESC user_ind_columns

COLUMN column_name FORMAT A15

SELECT index_name, table_name, column_name
FROM user_ind_columns;
```

Execution Results

```
Name                               Null?    Type
--------------------------------- -------- ----
 INDEX_NAME                        NOT NULL VARCHAR2(30)
 TABLE_NAME                        NOT NULL VARCHAR2(30)
 COLUMN_NAME                                VARCHAR2(4000)
 COLUMN_POSITION                   NOT NULL NUMBER
 COLUMN_LENGTH                     NOT NULL NUMBER
```

```
INDEX_NAME                       TABLE_NAME                       COLUMN_NAME
-----------------------------    -----------------------------    ---------------
BILLING_PT_ID_PK                 BILLING                          PT_ID
CUST_C_ID_PK                     CUSTOMER                         C_ID
DOCTOR_DOC_ID_PK                 DOCTOR                           DOC_ID
MOVIE_M_ID_PK                    MOVIE                            M_ID
PATIENT_PT_ID_PK                 PATIENT                          PT_ID
PATIENT_PTDOB_IDX                PATIENT                          PTDOB
RENTAL_PK                        RENTAL                           C_ID
RENTAL_PK                        RENTAL                           M_ID

8 rows selected.
```

Note: Since the results of the describe command show that the COLUMN_NAME column is 4,000 characters in size, the COLUMN command is necessary to format the display to fewer characters to avoid wraparound.

Also, these results clearly show that an index is automatically associated with the primary key constraint created for each table; they do not need to be created by the user.

Example 7.C.3

Create an index on customer phone, and verify its creation.

Script File Contents

```
CREATE INDEX cust_phone_idx
ON customer(phone);

COLUMN column_name FORMAT A15

SELECT index_name, table_name, column_name
FROM user_ind_columns;
```

Execution Results

```
Index created.

INDEX_NAME                       TABLE_NAME                       COLUMN_NAME
-----------------------------    -----------------------------    ---------------
BILLING_PT_ID_PK                 BILLING                          PT_ID
CUST_C_ID_PK                     CUSTOMER                         C_ID
CUST_PHONE_IDX                   CUSTOMER                         PHONE
DOCTOR_DOC_ID_PK                 DOCTOR                           DOC_ID
MOVIE_M_ID_PK                    MOVIE                            M_ID
PATIENT_PT_ID_PK                 PATIENT                          PT_ID
PATIENT_PTDOB_IDX                PATIENT                          PTDOB
RENTAL_PK                        RENTAL                           C_ID
RENTAL_PK                        RENTAL                           M_ID

9 rows selected.
```

Part 2: Usage

Using an index is quite simple, as it is automatically used as needed. Once it is created, no other commands are needed. It operates in a manner similar to the index in the back of a book, keeping track of each column value (like the keyword in a book's index) and the row IDs of the rows that contain that value in the indexed column (like the page numbers in a book's index). When modifications are made to the table contents, the index is automatically updated as well. Due to this continual automatic updating process, caution should be exercised when creating a new index, as each index adds overhead and processing time.

Part 3: Removal

The DROP INDEX statement is used to remove an index from the database. This has no effect on the table on which the index was created.

Example 7.C.4

Remove the patient date of birth index. Verify the results.

Script File Contents

```
DROP INDEX patient_ptdob_idx;

COLUMN column_name FORMAT A20

SELECT index_name, table_name, column_name
FROM user_ind_columns;
```

Execution Results

```
Index dropped.


INDEX_NAME                        TABLE_NAME                       COLUMN_NAME
------------------------------    -----------------------------    ----------------
BILLING_PT_ID_PK                  BILLING                          PT_ID
CUST_C_ID_PK                      CUSTOMER                         C_ID
CUST_PHONE_IDX                    CUSTOMER                         PHONE
DOCTOR_DOC_ID_PK                  DOCTOR                           DOC_ID
MOVIE_M_ID_PK                     MOVIE                            M_ID
PATIENT_PT_ID_PK                  PATIENT                          PT_ID
RENTAL_PK                         RENTAL                           C_ID
RENTAL_PK                         RENTAL                           M_ID


8 rows selected.
```

Example 7.C.5

Remove the customer phone index. Verify the results.

Script File Contents

```
DROP INDEX cust_phone_idx;

COLUMN column_name FORMAT A20

SELECT index_name, table_name, column_name
FROM user_ind_columns;
```

Execution Results

```
Index dropped.


INDEX_NAME                        TABLE_NAME                       COLUMN_NAME
------------------------------    -----------------------------    ----------------
BILLING_PT_ID_PK                  BILLING                          PT_ID
CUST_C_ID_PK                      CUSTOMER                         C_ID
DOCTOR_DOC_ID_PK                  DOCTOR                           DOC_ID
MOVIE_M_ID_PK                     MOVIE                            M_ID
PATIENT_PT_ID_PK                  PATIENT                          PT_ID
RENTAL_PK                         RENTAL                           C_ID
RENTAL_PK                         RENTAL                           M_ID


7 rows selected.
```

Note: Primary key indexes cannot be dropped, as they are used to facilitate the maintenance of entity integrity.

Section D: Synonyms

A synonym is used to give an additional name to a database table, view, or sequence. These are especially useful for long table names, or for referring to a table owned by another user (which would have to be qualified with the user name). They can also be used to provide shorter names for any of the DD views. Just be sure to prefix the DD view name with the qualifier SYS., because those views are owned by the SYS user ID.

Users may create private synonyms for any object they have access to. Additionally, users with database administrator privileges may create public synonyms that can be used by all users. However, it is assumed that students using this book do not have DBA privileges, so only private synonyms will be discussed here.

Part 1: Creation
General syntax is as follows:

    CREATE SYNONYM synonym-name
    FOR table-name;

The DD view named USER_SYNONYMS includes details on all synonyms created by the user.

Example 7.D.1

Create a short synonym for the PATIENT table. Verify the results.

The following steps are involved:

    CREATE SYNONYM p
    FOR patient;

    DESC user_synonyms

    SELECT synonym_name, table_name
    FROM user_synonyms;

Execution Results

```
Synonym created.
```

Name	Null?	Type
SYNONYM_NAME	NOT NULL	VARCHAR2(30)
TABLE_OWNER		VARCHAR2(30)
TABLE_NAME	NOT NULL	VARCHAR2(30)
DB_LINK		VARCHAR2(128)

SYNONYM_NAME	TABLE_NAME
P	PATIENT

Example 7.D.2

Create a short synonym for the REHAB_DOCS_DOC_ID_SEQ sequence. Verify.

Script File Contents

```
CREATE SYNONYM r_seq
FOR rehab_docs_doc_id_seq;
```

```
SELECT synonym_name, table_name
FROM user_synonyms;
```

Execution Results

```
Synonym created.


SYNONYM_NAME                              TABLE_NAME
------------------------------   ----------------------
P                                         PATIENT
R_SEQ                                     REHAB_DOCS_DOC_ID_SEQ
```

Part 2: Usage

Once created, the synonym can be used in any command or statement where the corresponding object name could be used.

Example 7.D.3

Display the names of patients with appointments today.

```
SQL: SELECT pt_fname, pt_lname
     FROM p
     WHERE nextapptdate = SYSDATE;
```

Execution Results

```
PT_FNAME         PT_LNAME
---------------  ---------------
Paul             James
Brian            Anderson
Debbie           Saillez
```

Example 7.D.4

Create synonyms for the USER_IND_COLUMNS DD view. Then use the synonym to display current index details.

Script File Contents

```
CREATE SYNONYM idx_cols
FOR sys.user_ind_columns;

SELECT index_name, table_name, column_name
FROM idx_cols;
```

Execution Results

```
Synonym created.

INDEX_NAME                       TABLE_NAME                        COLUMN_NAME
------------------------------   ------------------------------   ------------
BILLING_PT_ID_PK                 BILLING                           PT_ID
CUST_C_ID_PK                     CUSTOMER                          C_ID
DOCTOR_DOC_ID_PK                 DOCTOR                            DOC_ID
MOVIE_M_ID_PK                    MOVIE                             M_ID
PATIENT_PT_ID_PK                 PATIENT                           PT_ID
RENTAL_PK                        RENTAL                            C_ID
RENTAL_PK                        RENTAL                            M_ID

7 rows selected.
```

Note: Synonym names are similar to table aliases because they provide alternative means of referring to tables. The only difference is that they need to be defined only once (rather than once per SELECT statement as with table aliases).

Example 7.D.5

Chris Tinsley was hired yesterday as a new rehab doctor, working for supervisor number 889. Use the sequence synonym to add a new row to the table, leaving all unknown columns empty. Verify the change.

Script File Contents

```
INSERT INTO rehab_docs
VALUES(r_seq.NEXTVAL, 'Tinsley', SYSDATE - 1, NULL, 889, NULL, NULL);

SELECT *
FROM rehab_docs
WHERE doc_name = 'Tinsley';
```

Execution Results

```
1 row created.

   DOC_ID DOC_NAME   DATEHIRED   SALPERMON SUPERVISOR_ID CHGPERAPPT ANNUAL_BONUS
---------- --------- --------- ---------- ------------- ---------- ------------
       12 Tinsley    30-JUN-03                       889
```

Part 3: Removal

In keeping with the basic pattern followed for the removal of other database objects, the statement used to remove a synonym is DROP SYNONYM synonym-name.

Example 7.D.6

Remove the synonym created for the index columns view. Verify the results.

Script File Contents

```
DROP SYNONYM idx_cols;
SELECT synonym_name, table_name
FROM user_synonyms;
```

Execution Results

```
Synonym dropped.

SYNONYM_NAME                          TABLE_NAME
------------------------------- -----------------
P                               PATIENT
R_SEQ                           REHAB_DOCS_DOC_ID_SEQ
```

Example 7.D.7

Remove the two remaining synonyms. Verify the results.

Script File Contents

```
DROP SYNONYM r_seq;
DROP SYNONYM p;
SELECT synonym_name, table_name
FROM user_synonyms;
```

Execution Results

```
Synonym dropped.

Synonym dropped.

no rows selected
```

Overall, it may appear that table aliases, views, and synonyms are just several methods of accomplishing the same thing. However, there are differences between these three methods, as follows:

- Table aliases exist only during the execution of a specific query, whereas views and synonyms exist from the time they are created with a CREATE statement until the time they are dropped with a DROP statement.

- A table alias is another name for a table only, a synonym is another name for any database object (such as table, view, sequence, index, or user), and a view is another name for a query only.

- A table alias provides a shorter table name to use within that query, a synonym provides a shorter name to use for any database object, and a view provides a shorter name to use for a query.

- Of the three, table aliases are the most commonly used.

Chapter Summary

Database objects include tables, views, sequences, indexes, and synonyms. Views can be created to allow users to access tables or parts of tables by using the view name rather than running a more complicated query each time. Sequences can be used to automatically generate numeric values for insertion into a primary key column. Indexes can be created to speed up data retrieval when a secondary key is frequently used on a large table. Synonyms can be used to provide shorter names for long and/or qualified table names and other objects.

Exercises

Section A: Views

1. Create a view consisting of customer names and phone numbers only, and display the contents.

2. Create a view consisting of all data on movies costing $2 or less. Display the contents of the view.

3. Create a view consisting of the name and next appointment date for each patient with an appointment within the next week. Display the contents of the view with the date in the following format, for example: Monday, July 8

4. Create a view consisting of each doctor's name, salary per month, supervisor's name, and supervisor's salary per month. Display the contents of the view with the salaries formatted appropriately.

5. Create a view that will allow other users to view but not change all data on the patients of doctor number 432. Then display the contents of the view.

6. Modify problem 5 to work for all pediatric patients.

7. Create a view that can be used when a patient moves to change addresses and phone numbers. Do not allow modifications to cause rows to be removed from the view.

8. Using the view created in the previous problem, write a script file that can be used to allow the user to enter the patient ID, new phone number, and new address (street, city, and ZIP), and then change those column values.

9. Create a view that can be used to change patient balances and due dates when a payment is made. Do not allow modifications to cause rows to be removed from the view.

10. Using the view created in the previous problem, write a script file that can be used to allow the user to enter the patient ID and the amount of the payment, and then change the balance. Set the new due date to one month from the date of entry.

11. Write the command that will modify the view that you created for problem 6 of this section. Include both pediatric and family practice patients in the view.

12. Modify the view that you created for problem 1 so that no changes can be made to the underlying base table through the view.

13. Remove the view you created for problem 2.

14. Create an appropriate view for each of the tables you created for your solution to problem 4, Section B, Chapter 6.

Section B: Sequences

1. Create a sequence that can be used for future customers for the primary key C_ID in the CUSTOMER table. As none of the current customer numbers ends in zero, use the sequence 200, 210, 220, . . . , 500, and then have it start over with 200. Do not use caching.

2. Use the sequence that you created in the previous problem to add a new customer to the CUSTOMER table. Allow the user to specify phone number and name. Leave balance and due date empty.

3. Create a sequence that can be used for future new movies for the primary key M_ID in the MOVIE table. As all of the current movies have IDs lower than 400, use the sequence 400, 420, 440, . . . , 980, and then have it start over with 400. Do not use caching.

4. Use the sequence that you created in the previous problem to add a new movie to the MOVIE table. Allow the user to specify the fee, title, and category.

5. Write a command that will display the last value used by the sequence that you created for problem 3.

6. Write a script file that could be used when a new customer rents a movie. Allow the user to specify customer phone, last name, and first name. Use a balance of zero, and an empty due date. For the rental, allow the user to specify the movie ID. Date out is the current date, and due date is three days from the current date. Use the sequence for both C_ID entries (they should match).

7. Modify the customer ID sequence so that 10 values are cached in advance. Also, increase the max value to 600.

8. Remove the movie ID sequence from the database.

9. Consider the two tables you created for your solution to problem 4, Section B, Chapter 6. If either of them contains numeric primary keys, create an appropriate sequence that could be used to generate primary key values.

Section C: Indexes

1. Create an index on patient's doctor, and verify the results.

2. Create an index on doctor's area, and verify the results.

3. Remove the two indexes from the database, and verify the results.

4. Create an appropriate index for each of the two tables that you created for your solution to problem 4, Section B, Chapter 6.

Section D: Synonyms

1. Create a short synonym that could be used for the customer table.

2. Create a synonym that could be used for the customer ID sequence created in problem 1 of Section B.

3. Create short synonyms that could be used for the USER_TABLES and USER_OBJECTS DD views.

4. Use the synonym that you created in problem 1 to display all data on the customer whose ID is entered by the user.

5. Add a row for yourself to the customer table, using the synonym that you created in problems 1 and 2.

6. Use the synonym that you created in problem 3 to display the names of all of the tables that you own.

7. Create a synonym for one of the two tables that you created for your solution to problem 4, Section B, Chapter 6.

Chapter 8

User Privileges

The database administrator manages database users and system privileges. However, individual users can grant object privileges to other users. This chapter focuses on the statements that can be used by table owners to control the access to those tables by other users.

The individual user IDs referenced in this chapter are installation dependent; they don't exist on systems other than the one used by the author. You would need to have database administrator privileges on your system in order to create the user IDs shown in this chapter, and it is unlikely that such privileges have been granted to students using a client/server system. Therefore, if you want to test the commands, you must replace the specific user IDs shown here with actual user IDs that are available on your installation.

Another option is simply to study the examples and execution results carefully, and then write solutions for the exercises at the end of the chapter. While you won't be able to test those specific commands on the computer, you will most likely have a future opportunity to use the commands with user IDs that *are* available on your system as provided by your instructor.

Once again, this chapter focuses on the statements that can be used by table owners to control the access to those tables by other users. That includes granting and revoking object privileges as well as being able to exercise object privileges granted by other users.

Section A: Object Privileges

The owner of a particular object (such as a table, view, or sequence) has all of the object privileges for that object, and can grant those privileges to other users. There are many privileges that can be granted for individual objects, such as a table, or even just portions of tables, such as specific columns. Eight of the more commonly used object privileges are listed here.

1. ALTER—Allows modifications to be made to the table or sequence.
2. DELETE—Allows deletions to be made from the table or through the view.
3. EXECUTE—Allows execution of the stored procedure.
4. INDEX—Allows creation of an index on the table.
5. INSERT—Allows insertions to be made to the table or through the view.
6. REFERENCES—Allows the creation of a constraint that refers to the table.
7. SELECT—Allows the contents of the table or view to be examined, or allows the usage of NEXTVAL and/or CURRVAL for the sequence.
8. UPDATE—Allows modifications to be made to the table or through the view.

For all of these object privileges, granting the privilege on an existing synonym is the same as granting the privilege on the base object, and vice versa.

Section B: Granting Privileges

Object privileges can be given to other users by using the GRANT statement. General syntax is as follows:

GRANT object-privilege [(columns)]
ON object-name
TO {userID | PUBLIC}
[WITH GRANT OPTION];

where the following rules apply:

1. The object privilege is one (or more) of those listed in the previous section.
2. The user owns the object whose name is listed following the ON keyword.
3. The columns listed (if present) are part of the object.
4. The userID (if present) exists in the database.
5. The use of PUBLIC instead of a userID will grant the object privilege to all users.
6. The WITH GRANT OPTION will allow the user receiving the object privileges to grant the privileges on the object to other users.

The DD views USER_TAB_PRIVS_MADE and USER_COL_PRIVS_MADE can be used to view details on object privileges that have been granted by the user, and the DD views USER_TAB_PRIVS_RECD and USER_COL_PRIVS_RECD can be used to view details on object privileges that have been received by the user.

Example 8.B.1	Give the user with the ID *epeiper* select privileges on your PATIENT table. Verify the results.

The following steps are involved:

```
GRANT SELECT
ON patient
TO epeiper;

DESCRIBE user_tab_privs_made;

SELECT table_name, privilege
FROM user_tab_privs_made
WHERE grantee = 'EPEIPER';
```

Execution Results

```
Grant succeeded.
```

Name	Null?	Type
GRANTEE	NOT NULL	VARCHAR2(30)
TABLE_NAME	NOT NULL	VARCHAR2(30)
GRANTOR	NOT NULL	VARCHAR2(30)
PRIVILEGE	NOT NULL	VARCHAR2(40)
GRANTABLE		VARCHAR2(3)

TABLE_NAME	PRIVILEGE
PATIENT	SELECT

Note: As always, SQL statements can be entered in any combination of cases, so the userID on the TO clause of the GRANT statement was entered in lowercase in order to follow the conventions used throughout this book (keywords: uppercase; nonkeywords: lowercase). However, when an object name is stored in a DD view, it is in all capital letters, so the userID in quotes on the WHERE clause of the SELECT statement must be in all capital letters as well.

This applies to all identifiers referenced in DD views, and includes table names, view names, user IDs, and so on. If the command references a specific identifier within quotes, then that identifier must be in uppercase. Otherwise, no matching rows in the DD view will be found.

Example 8.B.2

Give the user with the ID *ypenny* select, insert, and update privileges on your DOCTOR table. Verify the results.

Script File Contents

```
GRANT SELECT, INSERT, UPDATE
ON doctor
TO ypenny;

SELECT table_name, privilege
FROM user_tab_privs_made
WHERE grantee = 'YPENNY';
```

Execution Results

```
Grant succeeded.


TABLE_NAME                         PRIVILEGE
------------------------------     -----------------
DOCTOR                             INSERT
DOCTOR                             SELECT
DOCTOR                             UPDATE
```

Example 8.B.3

Give all users the privilege of referencing your MOVIE table with a constraint. Allow them to pass the privilege on to any new users. Verify the results.

Script File Contents

```
GRANT REFERENCES
ON movie
TO PUBLIC
WITH GRANT OPTION;

SELECT table_name, privilege
FROM user_tab_privs_made
WHERE grantee = 'PUBLIC';
```

Execution Results

```
Grant succeeded.


TABLE_NAME                         PRIVILEGE
------------------------------     -----------
MOVIE                              REFERENCES
```

Example 8.B.4

Give cbarrall and rboucher the privileges needed to view your RENTAL table and make additions and deletions to it. Verify the results.

Script File Contents

```
GRANT SELECT, INSERT, DELETE
ON rental
TO cbarrall, rboucher;

SELECT table_name, privilege, grantee
FROM user_tab_privs_made
WHERE grantee IN ('CBARRALL', 'RBOUCHER');
```

Execution Results

```
Grant succeeded.
```

TABLE_NAME	PRIVILEGE	GRANTEE
RENTAL	DELETE	RBOUCHER
RENTAL	INSERT	RBOUCHER
RENTAL	SELECT	RBOUCHER
RENTAL	DELETE	CBARRALL
RENTAL	INSERT	CBARRALL
RENTAL	SELECT	CBARRALL

```
6 rows selected.
```

Section C: Exercising Privileges

Any object privileges that you receive from other users can be determined by examining one of these two DD views: USER_TAB_PRIVS_RECD and USER_COL_PRIVS_RECD. Each of these views contains grantor, table_name, and privilege columns. Other columns may be listed by using the DESCRIBE command on the specific view.

To refer to another user's object (assuming you have been granted privileges on it), you must prefix the object name with the user's ID and a period. For example, pmalone's invoice table would be referenced as PMALONE.INVOICE, and bwilke's assignment table would be referenced as BWILKE.ASSIGNMENT. The creation of synonyms could shorten these references considerably.

Example 8.C.1

Cindy Hanson is supposed to have given you some type of privileges on one of her tables. Determine what privileges you have and on what table. Her user ID is chanson. Then create a synonym for her table. (*Note:* Execution is broken into two parts, because the results from the first part would need to be viewed before the next part could be written.)

```
SQL: SELECT table_name, privilege
     FROM user_tab_privs_recd
     WHERE grantor = 'CHANSON';
```

Execution Results

TABLE_NAME	PRIVILEGE
INVENTORY	SELECT

```
SQL: CREATE SYNONYM inven
     FOR chanson.inventory;
```

Execution Results

```
Synonym created.
```

Example 8.C.2

Display the contents of Cindy's table.

```
SQL: SELECT *
     FROM inven;
```

Execution Results

```
SODA_ID SODA_NAME           QTY_ON_HAND COST_PER_CASE PRICE_PER_CASE
------- ------------------- ----------- ------------- --------------
    520 Diet Cola                    40         25.95          34.99
    560 Huckleberry Cream            45         19.99          24.96
    580 Bart's Root Beer             10         18.95          23.99
    600 Hilltop Dew                  20          22.8          24.99
```

Note: Without the synonym, the fully qualified name would be required as follows:

```
SQL: SELECT *
     FROM chanson.inventory;
```

Execution Results

```
SODA_ID SODA_NAME           QTY_ON_HAND COST_PER_CASE PRICE_PER_CASE
------- ------------------- ----------- ------------- --------------
    520 Diet Cola                    40         25.95          34.99
    560 Huckleberry Cream            45         19.99          24.96
    580 Bart's Root Beer             10         18.95          23.99
    600 Hilltop Dew                  20          22.8          24.99
```

Example 8.C.3

Cindy has given you more privileges so that you can add rows to her table using her sequence. Verify the granting of these new privileges, and then add a row to the table using her sequence. Verify the addition (again, execution is broken into parts).

```
SQL: SELECT table_name, privilege
     FROM user_tab_privs_recd
     WHERE grantor = 'CHANSON';
```

Execution Results

```
TABLE_NAME                      PRIVILEGE
------------------------------- -----------
INVENTORY                       SELECT
INVENTORY                       INSERT
INVENTORY_INV_ID_SEQ            SELECT
```

Note: Even though the DD view uses a column name of TABLE_NAME, sequence and view names may be included there as well.

```
SQL: CREATE SYNONYM inven_inv_id_seq
     FOR chanson.inventory_inv_id_seq;
```

Execution Results

```
Synonym created.
```

```
SQL: INSERT INTO inven
     VALUES (inven_inv_id_seq.NEXTVAL, 'Grapefruit Diet Rite',
          60, 20.50, 29.95);
```

```
SELECT *
FROM inven
WHERE inven_name = 'Grapefruit Diet Rite';
```

Execution Results

1 row created.

```
  SODA_ID INVEN_NAME              QTY_ON_HAND COST_PER_CASE PRICE_PER_CASE
--------- --------------------- ----------- ------------- --------------
      900 Grapefruit Diet Rite           60          20.5          29.95
```

Section D: Revoking Privileges

You may revoke any or all object privileges that you have granted by using the REVOKE statement. General syntax is as follows:

```
REVOKE {privilege(s) | ALL}
ON object-name
FROM {userID | PUBLIC};
```

The results can be verified by examining the appropriate DD view.

Example 8.D.1

Revoke ypenny's INSERT and UPDATE privileges on your DOCTOR table, but allow him to keep SELECT privileges. Verify the results.

Script File Contents

```
REVOKE INSERT, UPDATE
ON doctor
FROM ypenny;

SELECT privilege, table_name
FROM user_tab_privs_made
WHERE grantee = 'YPENNY';
```

Execution Results

Revoke succeeded.

```
PRIVILEGE          TABLE_NAME
------------------ -----------
SELECT             DOCTOR
```

Example 8.D.2

Revoke everyone's access of any kind to your DOCTOR table. Verify the results.

Script File Contents

```
REVOKE ALL
ON doctor
FROM PUBLIC;

SELECT privilege, table_name
FROM user_tab_privs_made
WHERE table_name = 'DOCTOR';
```

Execution Results

```
Revoke succeeded.

PRIVILEGE          TABLE_NAME
------------------ -----------
SELECT             DOCTOR
```

Note: This does not affect ypenny's SELECT access to the table, as that was granted separately from PUBLIC. If his access is to be removed as well, then an additional REVOKE statement is needed.

Example 8.D.3

Revoke cbarrall's INSERT access and rboucher's INSERT and DELETE access to your RENTAL table. Verify the results.

Script File Contents

```
REVOKE INSERT
ON rental
FROM cbarrall, rboucher;

REVOKE DELETE
ON rental
FROM rboucher;

SELECT privilege, table_name, grantee
FROM user_tab_privs_made
WHERE table_name = 'RENTAL;
```

Execution Results

```
Revoke succeeded.

Revoke succeeded.

PRIVILEGE   TABLE_NAME                          GRANTEE
----------  ------------------------------      ------------
DELETE      RENTAL                              CBARRALL
SELECT      RENTAL                              CBARRALL
SELECT      RENTAL                              RBOUCHER
```

Chapter Summary

Various object privileges on the objects that you own can be granted to other users. These include ALTER, DELETE, INDEX, INSERT, REFERENCES, SELECT, UPDATE, and EXECUTE. Privileges can be granted using the GRANT statement and removed using the REVOKE statement. The DD view named USER_TAB_PRIVS_MADE gives details on privileges granted by the user, whereas the DD view named USER_TAB_PRIVS_RECD gives details on privileges received by the user. Privileges received can be exercised by qualifying the object name with the user ID of the person granting the privilege. The use of synonyms is recommended to avoid having to repeatedly use long qualified names.

Exercises

Reminder (for this chapter only): When you write solutions for these exercises, you won't be able to test the specific commands on the computer, as the user IDs listed don't necessarily exist on your system. However, your instructor will most likely provide you with an opportunity to use the commands with user IDs that *are* available on your system.

Section A and B: Granting Object Privileges

1. Give the user jferguson alter privileges on your RENTAL and MOVIE tables. Verify the results.

2. Give users mreid and nferry privileges to use your CUSTOMER_C_ID_SEQ sequence. Verify the results.

3. Give all users privileges for viewing your MAILING_LABELS table. Verify the results.

4. Allow user jstillman to have all privileges on your CUSTOMER table. Verify the results.

Section C: Exercising Privileges

1. Check the appropriate DD view to see user objects to which you have been granted access.

2. User jbrune has granted you SELECT access to his MUTUAL_FUNDS table. Display the contents of his table.

3. Create a short synonym for the table described in problem 2, and again display the contents of the table.

4. User dyoung has given you delete privileges on his TEMP_STUDENT table. Write a script file that can be used to delete a row from this table for the student whose S_ID is entered by the user.

5. User mpatinkin has given you ALTER privileges on his SONG_LIST table. Expand the storage available for the SONG_TITLE column to 25 characters. Verify the change.

Section D: Revoking Privileges

1. Revoke jferguson's privileges on your MOVIE table (see Section B, problem 1). Verify the results.

2. Revoke mreid and nferry's privileges on your CUST_C_ID_SEQ sequence (see Section B, problem 2). Verify the results.

3. Revoke everyone's access to your MAILING_LABELs table (see Section B, problem 3). Verify the results.

4. Revoke all of jstillman's privileges on your CUSTOMER table (see Section B, problem 4). Verify the results.

Chapter 9

Introductory PL/SQL

SQL is an example of a fourth-generation language: The user specifies what is to be done, but doesn't have to indicate how it is to be done. For example, consider finding the names of all patients with appointments today. In SQL, a SELECT statement is used with a WHERE clause that restricts the results to rows with NEXTAPPTDATE equal to the current SYSDATE. However, there is no specification as to how these rows will actually be determined by the DBMS; the "how" is not specified by the user in a fourth-generation language. Of course, we can guess that some type of loop will be used, and it will most likely include an if-then statement to determine which rows satisfy the condition.

Conversely, third-generation languages are procedural languages, and include statements for iteration (looping) and conditional execution (if-then-else statements), among other things. Therefore, the coding of the solution for the "patients with appointments today" example would include specification of how the results were to be found, that is, the required looping and if-then-else statements would have to be written. In general, the programmer can do more with a third-generation language than they can with a fourth-generation language.

PL/SQL, Procedural Language SQL, is the third-generation language version of SQL. It includes the procedural capabilities of third-generation languages in addition to the fourth-generation language features of SQL, and because of this, PL/SQL is a much more powerful language than SQL. Mindset changes fairly dramatically for the last two chapters, so expect things to be a bit different than they've been in the rest of the book.

Section A: Fundamentals

PL/SQL statements are put together in blocks. This has the advantage of providing the ability to submit a block of several statements to the DBMS all at once rather than one at a time as with SQL. If network traffic is heavy, the amount of time saved can be significant.

Blocks may be either anonymous or named. Anonymous blocks can be stored in script files and executed as needed. Named blocks are database objects that can be referenced by other users, and can involve parameters. As the coverage of PL/SQL in this book is introductory in nature, only anonymous blocks will be presented.

The statements used in Section A of this chapter do not involve any interaction with the tables in the database; those statements will be covered in the next sections and chapter. Therefore, it may be difficult to see the point of these early examples, but the idea is to first focus on these basic concepts before including the additional statements needed for database interaction. Section B will reveal "the point of it all."

Part 1: Basic Anonymous Block Structure

There are three main sections within each anonymous block.

1. Declaration
    a. Optional section
    b. Starts with the keyword DECLARE
    c. Used for declaring variables, constants, and other identifiers
2. Executable statements
    a. Mandatory section
    b. Starts with the keyword BEGIN
    c. Contains executable PL/SQL statements, such as SELECT INTO, UPDATE, INSERT, DELETE, loops, and if-then-else's
    d. Ends with the keyword END
3. Exceptions
    a. Optional section
    b. Starts with the keyword EXCEPTION
    c. Coded immediately before the END keyword, after all other executable statements
    d. Is used to trap errors raised in PL/SQL blocks

All statements are terminated with a semicolon. There is no semicolon after the keywords DECLARE, BEGIN, and EXCEPTION, but a semicolon is used after the keyword END.

A forward slash must be included in the first column of the line following the END; of the procedure in order to cause the block to be executed. If an attempt is made to execute a script file containing a PL/SQL block and nothing happens, it's probably due to the missing slash at the end of the file. Additionally, execution will not occur if there are any spaces before the slash. If you think you might be stuck in a nonexecuting mode like this, try pressing slash and enter to cause execution of the block.

Comments may be included by starting the comment with a double dash, either inline or on a separate line. Readability is improved by including comments, and blank lines are useful for this purpose, as well. At a minimum, comments should be included for the main block sections. Additionally, any complex sections of code should be explained with comments as needed.

Part 2: Variable Declarations

Following the keyword DECLARE, each variable declaration includes a variable name and a type. There is no facility for combining variable declarations; each one must specify exactly one variable name and one type.

Variable names should follow the standard identifier naming conventions (see Chapter 6). Additionally, within blocks, naming conventions dictate that each variable should begin with a V and an underscore. Thus, a variable used to store an hourly wage might be named V_HOURLY_WAGE. This naming convention can be especially helpful when debugging blocks of code, as the V_ prefix indicates a block variable, while the & indicates a substitution parameter. These two categories of variables are similar in that both are used within PL/SQL blocks. They are different in that substitution variables receive their values only from user input outside of the block, while block variables receive their values only from within the block.

The available variable types are similar to the column types that are used when creating tables. Some of the more commonly used types are as follows:

1. VARCHAR2(max length)
2. CHAR(length)
3. NUMBER(max digits, decimal positions)—default decimal positions is zero
4. DATE

Additionally, %TYPE can be used to define a variable's type to be the same as that of a specific column from a table. This allows the variable type to match that of the column even when the specific type is unknown when the block is written.

The %TYPE should be prefixed with the fully qualified column name. Hence, a variable used to hold a value from the ITEM table's QUANTITY column would appear as ITEM.QUANTITY%TYPE Further qualification is needed if the table is owned by another user, assuming that the required privileges have been granted. For example, if the ITEM table was owned by a user with the user ID mreid, then the reference would be MREID.ITEM.QUANTITY%TYPE

Example 9.A.1

Give the variable declaration section for the following:

A. A variable used to store an annual salary between $25,000 and $50,000.
B. A variable used to store a department name up to 20 characters long.
C. A variable used to hold a value from the CUSTOMER table's STYLE column.

```
PL/SQL: DECLARE
            v_salary       NUMBER(5);
            v_dept_name    VARCHAR2(20);
            v_cust_style   CUSTOMER.STYLE%TYPE;
```

Following the indentation guidelines shown in this example is strongly suggested (though it makes no difference to the software). These guidelines include placing the DECLARE, BEGIN, END, and EXCEPTION keywords in column 1, and then indenting and aligning each of the other statements at the next tab setting. If a statement must be continued over a second line, then indent the second line an additional amount.

Part 3: Assignment Statements

Each assignment statement is used to assign a value to a block variable. This value may be a literal value (such as 25.95 or 'Sales'), a substitution parameter value, the result of an SQL function call, the value stored in another block variable (assuming that it already has a value), or an expression involving a combination of these items using arithmetic or string operators. The type of the expression must match the variable's type. General syntax is as follows:

variable-name := expression;

where the variable-name is one that has already been declared in the declaration section.

Example 9.A.2

Give assignment statements for each of the following:

A. Initialize the variable V_COUNT to zero.
B. Assign your first name to the variable V_NAME.
C. Assign a tax rate of 6.75% to the variable V_TAXRATE.
D. Assign the value of the substitution parameter DEPT_NAME to the variable V_DNAME.
E. Assign May 20, 2003, to the date variable V_CLOSING_DAY.
F. Calculate gross pay as V_HOURLY_RATE times V_HOURS_WORKED (assuming that both variables have values), and store the result in the variable named V_GROSS_PAY.
G. Calculate amount due as V_SUBTOTAL less the value of the substitution parameter DISCOUNT_RATE times V_SUBTOTAL (assuming that both variables have values), and store the result in the variable named V_TOTAL.

```
PL/SQL: v_count := 0;
        v_name := 'Linda';
        v_taxrate := .0675;
```

```
v_dname := '&dept_name';
v_closing_day := TO_DATE('20-MAY-03');
v_gross_pay :=  v_hourly_rate * v_hours_worked;
v_total := v_subtotal - &discount_rate * v_subtotal;
```

The precedence rules for evaluating operators in expressions within PL/SQL statements are the same as those for evaluating operators in expressions in SQL statements. Multiplication and division are evaluated before addition and subtraction. These rules can be overridden by using parentheses.

Example 9.A.3

Put it all together now. Write an anonymous block that can be used to calculate the amount of a payment due using three values: the amount of the loan ($4,000), the amount of interest to be paid ($900), and the number of payments (12).

```
PL/SQL: DECLARE
            v_loan_amt       NUMBER(6,2);
            v_interest_amt NUMBER(5,2);
            v_num_pmts       NUMBER(2);
            v_pmt_amt        NUMBER(6,2);
        BEGIN
            v_loan_amt := 4000;
            v_interest_amt := 500;
            v_num_pmts := 12;
            v_pmt_amt := (v_loan_amt + v_interest_amt)
                              / v_num_pmts;
        END;
        /
```

Note: The parentheses are required in the calculation of the payment amount in order to force evaluation of the addition before the division.

Also note that the slash *must* be placed in column 1 to cause execution of the block.

Example 9.A.4

Write an anonymous block that can be used to determine the total cost for a group of friends to go see a movie together. Use 10 for the number of people, $5.00 for the cost per ticket, and 10 percent for the group discount rate.

```
PL/SQL: DECLARE
            v_num_tickets            NUMBER(2);
            v_cost_per_ticket        NUMBER(4,2);
            v_discount_rate          NUMBER(2,2);
            v_subtotal               NUMBER(6,2);
            v_total_cost             NUMBER(6,2);
        BEGIN
            v_num_tickets := 10;
            v_cost_per_ticket := 5.00;
            v_discount_rate := .10;
            v_subtotal := v_num_tickets * v_cost_per_ticket;
            v_total_cost :=  v_subtotal
                                    - v_subtotal * v_discount_rate;
        END;
        /
```

No execution results have been shown for this chapter's examples so far because no output has been produced. This just happens to lead to the next topic.

Part 4: Output

In order to display values within a PL/SQL block, the DBMS_OUTPUT.PUT_LINE procedure is used. The steps are as follows:

1. Before the block is executed, SET SERVEROUTPUT ON (either at the SQL prompt or through the Environment menu).
2. Use the statement DBMS_OUTPUT.PUT_LINE (character-string); for each line of output to be displayed.

Note: This will print character strings ONLY. To print date or numeric values, convert them to character values by using the TO_CHAR function. You can also build strings consisting of combinations of strings by using the concatenation operator ||.

Example 9.A.5

Write output statements for each of the following:

A. Display the title Payroll Report.
B. Display the value of the V_NAME variable, appropriately labeled in sentence form.
C. Display the value of V_TAXRATE (stored in decimal form), appropriately labeled and formatted as a percentage.

```
PL/SQL:  DBMS_OUTPUT.PUT_LINE('Payroll Report');

         DBMS_OUTPUT.PUT_LINE('Employee name is ' || v_name || '.');

         DBMS_OUTPUT.PUT_LINE('Tax rate: ' ||
              TO_CHAR(v_taxrate * 100, '999.99')  || '%');
```

Execution Results

```
Payroll Report
Employee name is Linda.
Tax rate:    6.75%
```

Example 9.A.6

Using total monthly expenses of $1,500 and total monthly income of $2,000, calculate and display annual expenses, annual income, and annual savings/loss.

Script File Contents

```
SET SERVEROUTPUT ON

DECLARE
    v_mon_exp             NUMBER(6,2);
    v_mon_inc             NUMBER(6,2);
    v_ann_exp             NUMBER(7,2);
    v_ann_inc             NUMBER(7,2);
    v_savings_or_loss     NUMBER(6,2);

BEGIN
    v_mon_exp := 1500;
    v_mon_inc := 2000;

    v_ann_exp := v_mon_exp * 12;
    v_ann_inc := v_mon_inc * 12;
    v_savings_or_loss := v_ann_inc - v_ann_exp;

    DBMS_OUTPUT.PUT_LINE(' Annual income: ' ||
         TO_CHAR(v_ann_inc, 'fm$99,999.00'));
```

```
          DBMS_OUTPUT.PUT_LINE(' Annual expenses: ' ||
             TO_CHAR(v_ann_exp, 'fm$99,999.00'));
          DBMS_OUTPUT.PUT_LINE('Annual savings (or loss if negative): ' ||
             TO_CHAR(v_savings_or_loss, 'fm$99,999.00'));
      END;
      /


      SET SERVEROUTPUT OFF
```

Execution Results

```
Annual income:   $24,000.00
Annual expenses:  $18,000.00
Annual savings (or loss if negative):  $6,000.00

PL/SQL procedure successfully completed.
```

Note: As with the other system variables that were presented in Chapter 4, it is a good programming practice to reset SERVEROUTPUT at the end of the script file.

Common Error: Forgetting to turn on SERVEROUTPUT. If a procedure completes successfully but no output was produced, it is most likely that the SET SERVEROUTPUT ON command was mistakenly omitted.

Example 9.A.7

Calculate and display the total cost for carpeting a room. Use $15 for the carpet cost per square yard, 14 feet for the length of the room, 12 feet for the width of the room, and $250 for the installation charge.

Script File Contents

```
SET SERVEROUTPUT ON

DECLARE
      v_sq_yd_price        NUMBER(4,2);
      v_length             NUMBER(3,1);
      v_width              NUMBER(3,1);
      v_inst_chg           NUMBER(3,0);
      v_sq_footage         NUMBER(6,2);
      v_sq_yards_needed    NUMBER(4,2);
      v_total_cost         NUMBER(6,2);
BEGIN
      v_sq_yd_price:= 15;
      v_length := 14;
      v_width := 12;
      v_inst_chg := 250;
      v_sq_footage := v_length * v_width;
      v_sq_yards_needed := v_sq_footage / 9;
      v_total_cost := v_inst_chg +
          v_sq_yards_needed * v_sq_yd_price;
      DBMS_OUTPUT.PUT_LINE(' Number of square yards of carpet : '
          || TO_CHAR(v_sq_yards_needed, 'fm99.99'));
      DBMS_OUTPUT.PUT_LINE(' Total carpet cost: ' ||
          TO_CHAR(v_total_cost, 'fm$9,999.00'));
END;
/


SET SERVEROUTPUT OFF
```

Execution Results

```
Number of square yards of carpet:  18.67
Total carpet cost:  $530.05


PL/SQL procedure successfully completed.
```

Part 5: Inclusion of Substitution Parameters

Many of the previous examples could be improved by adding the use of substitution parameters instead of the literal values in the initial assignment statements. Specifically, for example 9.A.6 involving the calculation of annual savings/loss, the two additional lines at the beginning of the script file would be written as follows:

```
ACCEPT mon_exp PROMPT 'Enter total monthly expenses: '
ACCEPT mon_inc PROMPT 'Enter total monthly income: '
```

Then the first two assignment statements would be modified as follows:

```
v_mon_exp := &mon_exp;
v_mon_inc := &mon_inc;
```

It is also best to turn VERIFY off at the beginning of the script file (and back on at the end) so as to not clutter the output with old/new lines involving substitutions.

Example 9.A.8	Allow the user to enter the total restaurant dinner bill and the desired tip percentage. Calculate and display the tip amount.

Script File Contents

```
SET VERIFY OFF
SET SERVEROUTPUT ON
ACCEPT total PROMPT 'How much was the bill? '
ACCEPT tip_percent PROMPT -
   'What percentage should be used for the tip (enter a whole number)? '
DECLARE
     v_total          NUMBER(5,2);
     v_tip_percent    NUMBER(4,2);
     v_tip_amount     NUMBER(4,2);
BEGIN
     v_total := &total;
     v_tip_percent := &tip_percent;
     -- Next statement converts decimal value to true percentage
     v_tip_percent := v_tip_percent / 100;
     v_tip_amount := v_total * v_tip_percent;
     DBMS_OUTPUT.PUT_LINE('Tip amount is ' ||
          TO_CHAR( v_tip_amount, 'fm$99.99'));
END;
/
SET VERIFY ON
SET SERVEROUTPUT OFF
```

Execution Results

```
How much was the bill?  20.00
What percentage should be used for the tip (enter as a whole number)?  15
Tip amount is $3.


PL/SQL procedure successfully completed.
```

Note: When an SQL Plus command extends over more than one line, a dash is used at the end of the line that needs to be continued. This continuation character is used in the next example.

Example 9.A.9

Use the same specifications as in example 9.A.7, but allow the user to enter the cost per square yard of carpet, the length and width of the room, and the amount of the installation charge.

Script File Contents

```
SET VERIFY OFF
SET SERVEROUTPUT ON
ACCEPT sq_yd_price PROMPT -
     'What is the cost per square yard of carpet? '
ACCEPT length PROMPT 'Enter room length (in feet): '
ACCEPT width PROMPT 'Enter room width (in feet): '
ACCEPT Inst_chg PROMPT 'How much is the installation charge? '

DECLARE
     v_sq_yd_price          NUMBER(4,2);
     v_length               NUMBER(3,1);
     v_width                NUMBER(3,1);
     v_inst_chg             NUMBER(3,0);
     v_sq_footage           NUMBER(6,2);
     v_sq_yards_needed      NUMBER(4,2);
     v_total_cost           NUMBER(6,2);

BEGIN
     v_sq_yd_price := &sq_yd_price;
     v_length := &length;
     v_width := &width;
     v_inst_chg := &inst_chg;

     v_sq_footage := v_length * v_width;
     v_sq_yards_needed := v_sq_footage / 9;
     v_total_cost := v_inst_chg +
               v_sq_yards_needed * v_sq_yd_price;

     DBMS_OUTPUT.PUT_LINE(' Number of square yards of carpet : '
          || TO_CHAR(v_sq_yards_needed, 'fm99.99'));
     DBMS_OUTPUT.PUT_LINE(' Total carpet cost: ' ||
          TO_CHAR(v_total_cost, 'fm$9,999.00'));
END;
/

SET VERIFY ON
SET SERVEROUTPUT OFF
```

Execution Results

```
What is the cost per square yard of carpet?  15.99
Enter room length (in feet): 10
Enter room width (in feet): 15
How much is the installation charge? 100
Number of square yards of carpet:  16.67
Total carpet cost:  $366.55

PL/SQL procedure successfully completed.
```

Note: An alternative method of allowing the user to provide input involves the use of a named block with parameters, but such techniques are beyond the scope of this book.

Section B: DML Statements in PL/SQL Blocks

Now that the fundamentals have been covered, the more useful applications of anonymous blocks can be presented. In particular, anonymous blocks generally involve interaction with the database through the use of DML statements such as SELECT . . . INTO, INSERT, UPDATE, and DELETE.

Part 1: SELECT . . . INTO

The general syntax of the SELECT . . . INTO statement is as follows:

```
SELECT list
INTO variable(s)
FROM table(s)
[WHERE condition];
```

The SELECT . . . INTO statement works exactly like the SELECT statement with the following exceptions:

1. The items listed on the SELECT clause are stored in the variables listed on the INTO clause (rather than being displayed as with a regular SELECT).

2. Due to the limitation of exception 1 above, one and only one row (or set of values) can be retrieved.

3. Similarly, an empty retrieval is not allowed (as in no rows match the criteria on the WHERE clause).

4. The types of the variables used on the INTO clause should match the types of the values retrieved on the SELECT clause.

Note: The possible occurrence of the situations described in points 2 and 3 can be handled through the usage of exceptions, to be discussed in the next chapter.

Example 9.B.1

Use an anonymous block to retrieve and display the name of the customer whose phone number is entered by the user.

Script File Contents

```
SET VERIFY OFF
SET SERVEROUTPUT ON
ACCEPT phone PROMPT 'What is the customer"s phone number? '

DECLARE
    v_lname        customer.lname%TYPE;
    v_fname        customer.fname%TYPE;

BEGIN
    SELECT lname, fname
    INTO v_lname, v_fname
    FROM customer
    WHERE phone = '&phone';
```

```
                    DBMS_OUTPUT.PUT_LINE('Customer name is ' ||
                 v_fname || ' ' || v_lname);
END;
/

SET VERIFY ON
SET SERVEROUTPUT OFF
```

Execution Results

```
What is the customer's phone number?   549-1235
Customer name is Greg Macke

PL/SQL procedure successfully completed.
```

Example 9.B.2

Use an anonymous block to retrieve and display the next appointment date for the patient whose ID is entered by the user.

Script File Contents

```
SET VERIFY OFF
SET SERVEROUTPUT ON
ACCEPT id PROMPT 'Please enter patient ID: '

DECLARE
     v_nextappt DATE;
BEGIN
     SELECT nextapptdate
     INTO v_nextappt
     FROM patient
     WHERE pt_id = &id;
     DBMS_OUTPUT.PUT_LINE('Next appointment date is ' ||
          TO_CHAR(v_nextappt, 'fmMonth DD, RRRR'));
END;
/

SET VERIFY ON
SET SERVEROUTPUT OFF
```

Execution Results

```
Please enter patient ID:   264
Next appointment date is December 12, 2003

PL/SQL procedure successfully completed.
```

Note: An exception (error) will be raised if the query returns no rows, as illustrated by running the script file with a nonexistent ID.

Execution Results

```
Please enter patient ID:   263
                    DECLARE
*
ERROR at line 1:
ORA-01403: no data found
ORA-06512: at line 4
```

Additionally, an exception will be raised if the query returns more than one row, as illustrated by the following example:

Example 9.B.3

Use an anonymous block to retrieve and display the current balance for the customer whose last name is entered by the user.

Script File Contents

```
SET SERVEROUTPUT ON
ACCEPT lname PROMPT 'Enter customer"s last name: '
DECLARE
     v_balance          customer.curr_bal%TYPE;
BEGIN
     SELECT curr_bal
     INTO v_balance
     FROM customer
     WHERE lname = '&lname';
     DBMS_OUTPUT.PUT_LINE('Current balance: ' ||
          TO_CHAR(v_balance, 'fm$999.99'));
END;
/
SET SERVEROUTPUT OFF
```

Execution Results

```
Enter customer's last name:  Akers
old   7:                         WHERE lname = '&lname';
new   7:                         WHERE lname = 'Akers';
              DECLARE
*
ERROR at line 1:
ORA-01422: exact fetch returns more than requested number of rows
ORA-06512: at line 4
```

Note: You will learn how to trap this type of exception in the next chapter, thereby allowing the anonymous block to continue execution in this situation rather than ending abnormally.

By itself, the SELECT . . . INTO does not necessarily offer any advantages over the non-PL/SQL SELECT statement. All three of the previous examples could certainly have been completed more quickly and easily without the usage of an anonymous block. However, the intent of this part of the chapter is merely to provide coverage of the new statement by itself. As you will see throughout the rest of this chapter, the SELECT . . . INTO statement is actually quite useful when combined with other PL/SQL statements. In particular, when used in conjunction with other DML statements (such as UPDATE, DELETE, and INSERT), the value of the SELECT . . . INTO statement becomes more apparent, as illustrated by the next several examples.

Part 2: UPDATE

The syntax of the PL/SQL version of the UPDATE statement is exactly the same as the syntax of the SQL version presented in Chapter 4. The only difference is that block variables may be used on the SET and/or WHERE clauses of the UPDATE statement within an anonymous block.

Example 9.B.4

A customer complained that the video she rented did not work correctly, so her account needs to be credited for the cost of the rental. Allow the user to enter the movie title and customer ID.

Script File Contents

```
SET VERIFY OFF
ACCEPT id PROMPT 'Enter customer ID: '
ACCEPT title PROMPT 'Enter movie title: '

DECLARE
     v_fee                    movie.fee%TYPE;
BEGIN
     -- Get the movie fee
     SELECT fee
     INTO v_fee
     FROM movie
     WHERE title = '&title';

     --  Credit the customer's account
     UPDATE customer
     SET balance = NVL(balance,0) - v_fee
     WHERE c_id = &id;
END;
/
SET VERIFY ON
```

Execution Results

```
Enter customer ID:  388
Enter movie title:  Monsters, Inc.

PL/SQL procedure successfully completed.
```

Note: NVL was used to handle empty balances, because any calculation involving a null will yield a null result. Hence, in the case of a customer that has no balance, the fee would not be credited. NVL gets around this potential problem by supplying a value of zero to be used in the calculation if the customer has no balance.

Example 9.B.5

Allow the user to enter the ID of the patient whose appointment is over. Add his or her doctor's charge per appointment to their balance.

Script File Contents

```
SET VERIFY OFF
SET SERVEROUTPUT ON
ACCEPT id PROMPT 'Enter patient ID: '

DECLARE
     v_doc_id      patient.doc_id%TYPE;
     v_appt_chg    doctor.chgperappt%TYPE;
     v_balance     billing.balance%TYPE;

BEGIN
     -- Get the patient's doctor ID
     SELECT doc_id
     INTO v_doc_id
     FROM patient
     WHERE pt_id = &id;

     -- Get the doctor's charge per appointment
     SELECT chgperappt
```

```
        INTO v_appt_chg
        FROM doctor
        WHERE doc_id = v_doc_id;

        -- Display balance prior to update.
        SELECT balance
        INTO v_balance
        FROM billing
        WHERE pt_id = &id;
        DBMS_OUTPUT.PUT_LINE('Prior balance: ' ||
            TO_CHAR(v_balance, '$99,999.00'));

        -- Increase the patient's balance
        UPDATE billing
        SET balance = balance + v_appt_chg
        WHERE pt_id = &id;

        -- Display balance after update.
        DBMS_OUTPUT.PUT_LINE('New balance: ' ||
            TO_CHAR(v_balance + v_appt_chg, '$99,999.00'));
END;
/
SET VERIFY ON
SET SERVEROUTPUT OFF
```

Execution Results

```
Enter patient ID:  315
Prior balance:  $5,000.00
New balance:  $5,045.00

PL/SQL procedure successfully completed.
```

Note: After a professional database application developer has thoroughly debugged code such as that shown in this example, a COMMIT statement would normally be included at the end of the block. The other TCO statements, ROLLBACK and SAVEPOINT, may also be used within anonymous blocks as needed.

For purposes of this course, however, you should not include a COMMIT statement within a block. This will allow you to avoid permanently saving potentially erroneous modifications.

Also note that both of the previous examples could not have been completed using only the UPDATE statement. A two-step process was required; use a SELECT . . . INTO in order to retrieve information regarding the row to be updated, and then use an UPDATE to change the table contents. This two-step process can be completed only with a PL/SQL block; it cannot be done with just SQL. Hence, the SELECT . . . INTO is illustrated in a more useful light than in the earlier part of this section.

Part 3: INSERT

When used within a PL/SQL block by itself, the INSERT statement seems to be another case where the task could be completed more efficiently without a block. However, when included as part of a larger application, it is quite useful, as shown in the next two examples.

| **Example 9.B.6** | Use an anonymous block to handle a movie rental transaction. Allow the user to enter the movie title and customer phone number. The movie is due in five days. |

Script File Contents

```
SET VERIFY OFF
ACCEPT title PROMPT 'What is the movie title? '
ACCEPT phone PROMPT 'What is the customer"s phone number? '
DECLARE
        v_m_id       movie.m_id%TYPE;
        v_fee        movie.fee%TYPE;
        v_c_id       customer.c_id%TYPE;
BEGIN
        -- Determine customer ID.
        SELECT c_id
        INTO v_c_id
        FROM customer
        WHERE phone = '&phone';

        -- Determine movie ID.
        SELECT m_id, fee
        INTO v_m_id, v_fee
        FROM movie
        WHERE title = '&title';

        -- Add new rental data
        INSERT INTO rental
        VALUES (v_c_id, v_m_iD, SYSDATE, SYSDATE + 5);

        -- Update customer balance
        UPDATE customer
        SET balance = balance + v_fee
        WHERE c_id = v_c_id;
END;
/
SET VERIFY ON
```

Execution Results

```
What is the movie title?  A Beautiful Mind
What is the customer's phone number?   549-1235


PL/SQL procedure successfully completed.
```

Example 9.B.7

A new patient needs to be assigned to a doctor. The standard clinic policy is that a new patient in a given area is assigned to the doctor that has the fewest patients. Use an anonymous block that allows the user to enter all necessary data for the PATIENT table.

Script File Contents

```
SET VERIFY OFF
ACCEPT area PROMPT 'What area of specialization? '
ACCEPT pt_id PROMPT 'Enter patient"s ID: '
ACCEPT pt_lname PROMPT 'Enter patient"s last name: '
ACCEPT pt_fname PROMPT 'Enter patient"s first name: '
ACCEPT ptdob PROMPT 'Enter patient"s date of birth (DD-MON-YYYY): '
ACCEPT nextapptdate PROMPT -
        'Enter patient"s next appointment date (DD-MON-YYYY): '
DECLARE
        v_min_count    NUMBER(3);
        v_doc_id       patient.doc_id%TYPE;
```

```
BEGIN
    -- Determine doctor with fewest patients in desired area
    SELECT d.doc_id
    INTO v_doc_id
    FROM patient p, (SELECT doc_id FROM doctor
                        WHERE area = '&area') d
    WHERE p.doc_id = d.doc_id AND ROWNUM = 1
    GROUP BY d.doc_id
    ORDER BY COUNT(*);
    -- Add new patient for that doctor
    INSERT INTO patient
    VALUES (&pt_id, '&pt_lname', '&pt_fname',
        TO_DATE('&ptdob', 'DD-MON-RRRR'), v_doc_id,
        TO_DATE('&nextapptdate', 'DD-MON-RRRR'), NULL);
END;
/
SET VERIFY ON
```

Note: The pseudocolumn ROWNUM is used to limit the query results to the first row only.

Execution Results

```
What area of specialization?  Pediatrics
Enter patient's ID:  388
Enter patient's last name:  Woolard
Enter patient's first name:  Jessica
Enter patient's date of birth (DD-MON-YYYY):  07-mar-1988
Enter patient's next appointment date (DD-MON-YYYY):  09-sep-2003

PL/SQL procedure successfully completed.
```

Part 4: DELETE

The third and last DML statement that can be included within a PL/SQL block is the DELETE statement. As with UPDATE and INSERT, syntax is identical to the SQL DELETE statement.

Example 9.B.8	Dr. James in orthopedics is opening his own office and taking his patients with him. Assuming that a table named FORMER_PATIENT exists (containing the same columns as the PATIENT table), use an anonymous block to remove all of Dr. James's patient data as well as his doctor data.

Script File Contents

```
DECLARE
    v_doc_id      patient.doc_id%TYPE;
    v_apptdate    DATE;

BEGIN
    -- Find the ID for Dr. James in Orthopedics.
    SELECT doc_id
    INTO v_doc_id
    FROM doctor
    WHERE doc_name = 'James'
        AND area = 'Orthopedics';
```

```
        -- Move patient data to former patient table.
        INSERT INTO former_patient
            SELECT *
            FROM patient
            WHERE doc_id = v_doc_id;

        -- Remove patient data from patient table.
        DELETE FROM patient
        WHERE doc_id = v_doc_id;

        -- Remove data for Dr. James in Orthopedics.
        DELETE FROM doctor
        WHERE doc_id = v_doc_id;

END;
/
```

Execution Results

```
PL/SQL procedure successfully completed.
```

Example 9.B.9

A patient with an upcoming appointment has no balance due and is switching to another clinic. Find another patient (patient B) that sees the same doctor and has a later appointment than the patient who is leaving the clinic (patient A). Give patient A's appointment to patient B, and then delete patient A from the database. Allow the user to enter patient A's patient ID.

Script File Contents

```
SET VERIFY OFF
SET SERVEROUTPUT ON
ACCEPT pt_id PROMPT 'Enter patient"s ID: '
DECLARE
        v_doc_id        patient.doc_id%TYPE;
        v_apptdate      DATE;
        v_pt_id         patient.pt_id%TYPE;
BEGIN
    -- Determine patient A's doctor and next appointment date.
    SELECT doc_id, nextapptdate
    INTO v_doc_id, v_apptdate
    FROM patient
    WHERE pt_id = &pt_id;

    -- Determine ID of first patient with same doctor and a
    -- later next appointment date (patient B).
    SELECT pt_id
    INTO v_pt_id
    FROM patient
    WHERE doc_id = v_doc_id
        AND nextapptdate > v_apptdate
        AND ROWNUM = 1;

    -- Give patient A's appointment to patient B.
    UPDATE patient
    SET nextapptdate = v_apptdate
    WHERE pt_id = v_pt_id;
```

```
        DBMS_OUTPUT.PUT_LINE('Patient #' || v_pt_id ||
            ' has been given a next appt. date of' ||
            TO_CHAR(v_apptdate, 'fmMonth dd, rrrr.'));

        -- Remove patient A's data from the database.
        DELETE FROM patient
        WHERE pt_id = &pt_id;
        DELETE FROM billing
        WHERE pt_id = &pt_id;
        DBMS_OUTPUT.PUT_LINE('Patient #' || &pt_id ||
            ' has been removed from the database.');
END;
/
SET VERIFY ON
SET SERVEROUTPUT OFF
```

Execution Results

```
Enter patient's ID:  504
Patient #314 has been given a next appt. date of July 21, 2003.
Patient #504 has been removed from the database.

PL/SQL procedure successfully completed.
```

Section C: Other Logic Structures

The logic structure used in all examples thus far has been "simple sequence," or in other words, all statements have been executed in order according to the sequence listed. This flow of execution can be modified by using other logic structures. If-then-else statements can be used to implement conditional execution, and loops can be used to repeat sections of code.

Part 1: IF-THEN

The IF-THEN statement specifies a condition under which a statement (or set of statements) will be executed. If the condition evaluates to true, the statement is executed. If the condition evaluates to false, the statement is skipped. General syntax is as follows:

> IF condition THEN
>   Statement(s);
> END IF;

where the condition may involve any of the operators allowed on the WHERE clause, and the statements may be any valid PL/SQL statements.

Example 9.C.1

Patients often call and ask for the date of their next appointment. Use a script file to retrieve this data, and if they have no appointment scheduled, display an appropriate message.

Script File Contents

```
SET VERIFY OFF
SET SERVEROUTPUT ON
ACCEPT pt_id PROMPT 'Enter patient"s ID: '
DECLARE
     v_nextappt  DATE;
```

```
BEGIN
     SELECT nextapptdate
     INTO v_nextappt
     FROM patient
     WHERE pt_id = &pt_id;
     IF v_nextappt IS NULL THEN
         DBMS_OUTPUT.PUT_LINE('No appointment is scheduled');
     END IF;
     DBMS_OUTPUT.PUT_LINE( TO_CHAR(v_nextappt,
  'fmMonth DD, RRRR'));
END;
/
SET VERIFY ON
SET SERVEROUTPUT OFF
```

Execution Results (First Test)

```
Enter patient's ID:  966
No appointment is scheduled

PL/SQL procedure successfully completed.
```

Execution Results (Second Test)

```
Enter patient's ID:  267
February 02, 2004

PL/SQL procedure successfully completed.
```

Note: If the next appointment date is null, then nothing (the null value) will be displayed by the second output statement. The descriptive label (such as 'Next appointment is on') was intentionally left out for this reason.

Example 9.C.2

When a customer wants to rent a movie, he or she must first pay any balance owed. Use a script file to retrieve this data using the customer's phone number, and if he or she has no balance due, display an appropriate message.

Script File Contents

```
SET VERIFY OFF
SET SERVEROUTPUT ON
ACCEPT phonE PROMPT 'Enter customer"s phone number: '
DECLARE
     v_balance    customer.curr_bal%TYPE;
BEGIN
     SELECT NVL(curr_bal,0)
     INTO v_balance
     FROM customer
     WHERE phone = '&phone';
     IF v_balance = 0 THEN
         DBMS_OUTPUT.PUT_LINE('The customer does not ' ||
                 'have a balance due.');
     END IF;
     DBMS_OUTPUT.PUT_LINE( TO_CHAR(v_balance,
  '$999.99'));
END;
/
SET VERIFY ON
SET SERVEROUTPUT OFF
```

Execution Results (First Test)

```
Enter customer's phone number:   453-2271
$20.18
PL/SQL procedure successfully completed.
```

Execution Results (Second Test)

```
Enter customer's phone number:   549-6730
The customer does not have a balance due.
$.00
PL/SQL procedure successfully completed.
```

Note: At times when the DBMS_OUTPUT message is too long to fit on one line, divide it into pieces and use concatenation to join them (as illustrated above).

Part 2: IF-THEN-ELSE

It is sometimes necessary to choose one of two paths for execution, and this is supported with the IF-THEN-ELSE statement. If the condition is true, then the first statement (or set of statements) is executed, and the second statement (or set of statements) is skipped. If the condition is false, the first statement is skipped and the second statement is executed. General syntax is as follows:

```
IF condition THEN
      statement(s);
ELSE
      statement(s);
END IF;
```

Example 9.C.3

Modify example 9.C.1 so that it either displays the message regarding no appointment or it displays the date of the next appointment.

Change needed (all other code remains the same):

```
IF v_nextappt IS NULL THEN
      DBMS_OUTPUT.PUT_LINE('No appointment is scheduled');
ELSE
      DBMS_OUTPUT.PUT_LINE('Next appointment is on ' ||
            TO_CHAR(v_nextappt, 'fmMonth DD, RRRR'));
END IF;
```

Execution Results (First Test)

```
Enter patient's ID:   966
No appointment is scheduled

PL/SQL procedure successfully completed.
```

Execution Results (Second Test)

```
Enter patient's ID:   267
Next appointment is on February 02, 2004

PL/SQL procedure successfully completed.
```

Example 9.C.4

When a patient arrives for an appointment, records are checked to see if there is a balance owed on the account. If the balance is past due, display an appropriate message. Otherwise, indicate that no payment is currently due.

Script File Contents

```
SET VERIFY OFF
SET SERVEROUTPUT ON
ACCEPT pt_id PROMPT 'Enter patient"s ID: '
DECLARE
     v_balance          billing.balance%TYPE;
     v_duedate          DATE;
BEGIN
     SELECT balance, duedate
     INTO v_balance, v_duedate
     FROM billing
     WHERE pt_id = &pt_id;

     IF v_balance > 0 and v_duedate < SYSDATE THEN
         DBMS_OUTPUT.PUT_LINE('BALANCE OF ' ||
            TO_CHAR(v_balance, 'FM$99,999,99') ||
            'IS PAST DUE DATE OF' || TO_CHAR(v_duedate,
            'fmMON. DD, RRRR'));
     ELSE
            DBMS_OUTPUT.PUT_LINE('No payment is due today');
     END IF;
END;
/
SET VERIFY ON
SET SERVEROUTPUT OFF
```

Execution Results (First Test)

```
Enter patient's ID:  264
BALANCE OF $35,000 IS PAST DUE DATE OF JAN. 11, 2003

PL/SQL procedure successfully completed.
```

Execution Results (Second Test)

```
Enter patient's ID:  315
No payment is due today

PL/SQL procedure successfully completed.
```

Example 9.C.5

Use an anonymous block to handle a movie rental transaction. Allow the user to enter the movie title and customer phone number. If the customer has a balance due, then the transaction cannot be completed. Otherwise, the movie is due in five days.

Script File Contents

```
SET VERIFY OFF
SET SERVEROUTPUT ON
ACCEPT title PROMPT 'What is the movie title? '
ACCEPT phone PROMPT 'What is the customer"s phone number? '

DECLARE
     v_m_id      movie.m_id%TYPE;
     v_fee       movie.fee%TYPE;
     v_c_id      customer.c_id%TYPE;
     v_balance   customer.curr_bal%TYPE;
```

```
BEGIN
    -- Determine customer ID and balance.
    SELECT c_id, NVL(curr_bal,0)
    INTO v_c_id, v_balance
    FROM customer
    WHERE phone = '&phone';

    -- Check for balance due.
    IF v_balance > 0 THEN
        DBMS_OUTPUT.PUT_LINE('Customer has balance due. ' ||
                             'No rentals allowed.');
    ELSE
        -- Determine movie ID.
        SELECT m_id, fee
        INTO v_m_id, v_fee
        FROM movie
        WHERE title = '&title';

        -- Add new rental data
        INSERT INTO rental
        VALUES (v_c_id, v_m_id, SYSDATE, SYSDATE + 5);

        -- Update customer balance
        UPDATE customer
        SET balance = balance + v_fee
        WHERE c_id = v_c_id;
    END IF;
END;
/
SET VERIFY ON
SET SERVEROUTPUT OFF
```

Execution Results (First Test)

```
What is the movie title?  A Knight"s Tale
What is the customer's phone number?  453-8228
Customer has balance due.  No rentals allowed.

PL/SQL procedure successfully completed.
```

Execution Results (Second Test)

```
What is the movie title? A Knight"s Tale
What is the customer's phone number?  549-1234

PL/SQL procedure successfully completed.
```

Part 3: IF-THEN-ELSIF

The IF provides one conditional path, the IF-THEN provides two conditional paths, and the IF-THEN-ELSIF provides more than two conditional paths. Therefore, if three or more options are needed, the IF-THEN-ELSIF should be used. General syntax is as follows:

IF condition THEN
    statement(s)
ELSIF condition THEN
    statement(s)   .

```
        ELSE
            statement(s)
        END IF;
```

where the ELSIF condition THEN statement(s) sequence may be repeated as many times as needed.

Example 9.C.6

Modify the previous example to handle three cases: no balance due, balance due but not past due, and balance past due.

Change needed is as follows (all other code remains the same):

```
IF v_balance > 0 AND v_duedate < SYSDATE THEN
        DBMS_OUTPUT.PUT_LINE('BALANCE OF' ||
            TO_CHAR(v_balance, 'fm$999,999.99') ||
            'IS PAST DUE DATE OF' ||
            TO_CHAR(v_duedate, 'fmMON. DD, RRRR'));
ELSIF v_balance > 0 AND v_duedate >= SYSDATE THEN
        DBMS_OUTPUT.PUT_LINE('BALANCE OF' ||
            TO_CHAR(v_balance, 'fm$999,999.99') ||
            'IS DUE ON ' ||
            TO_CHAR(v_duedate, 'fmMON. DD, RRRR'));
ELSE
        DBMS_OUTPUT.PUT_LINE('No balance is due.');
END IF;
```

Execution Results (First Test)

```
Enter patient's ID:  264
BALANCE OF $35,000 IS PAST DUE DATE OF JAN. 11, 2003
```

Execution Results (Second Test)

```
Enter patient's ID:  331
BALANCE OF $300 IS DUE ON SEP. 09, 2003
```

Execution Results (Third Test)

```
Enter patient's ID:  315
No balance is due.
```

Note: Rather than using the ELSIF clause, this could have been written with nested-ifs (giving exactly the same execution results) as follows:

```
IF v_balance > 0 THEN
        IF v_duedate < SYSDATE THEN
                DBMS_OUTPUT.PUT_LINE('BALANCE OF ' ||
                    TO_CHAR(v_balance, 'fm$999,999.99') ||
                    ' IS PAST DUE DATE OF ' ||
                    TO_CHAR(v_duedate, 'fmMON. DD, RRRR'));
        ELSE
                DBMS_OUTPUT.PUT_LINE('BALANCE OF' ||
                    TO_CHAR(v_balance, 'fm$999,999.99') ||
                    ' IS DUE ON ' ||
                    TO_CHAR(v_duedate, 'fmMON. DD, RRRR'));
        END IF;
ELSE
        DBMS_OUTPUT.PUT_LINE('No balance is due.');
END IF;
```

Note: The ELSE goes with the closest unmatched IF, as indicated by the indentation.

Example 9.C.7

The billing procedure is being changed. Balances should be modified as follows:

Number of Days Past Due	Late Fee Charged (%)
30–59	2
60–89	4
90–119	7
120 and above	10

Allow the user to enter the ID of the patient whose balance is to be adjusted.

Script File Contents

```
SET VERIFY OFF
SET SERVEROUTPUT ON
ACCEPT pt_id PROMPT 'Enter patient''s ID:  '
DECLARE
      v_balance           billing.balance%TYPE;
      v_duedate          DATE;
      v_rate             NUMBER(2,2);
BEGIN
      -- Retrieve patient's balance and duedate
      SELECT balance, duedate
      INTO v_balance, v_duedate
      FROM billing
      WHERE pt_id = &pt_id;
      -- Determine rate for late fee
      IF SYSDATE - v_duedate < 30 THEN
            v_rate := 0;
      ELSIF SYSDATE - v_duedate <= 59 THEN
            v_rate := .02;
      ELSIF SYSDATE - v_duedate <= 89 THEN
            v_rate := .04;
      ELSIF SYSDATE - v_duedate <= 119 THEN
            v_rate := .07;
      ELSE
            v_rate := .10;
      END IF;

      -- Add late fee to patient's balance
      UPDATE billing
      SET balance = balance + balance * v_rate
      WHERE pt_id = &&pt_id;
      DBMS_OUTPUT.PUT_LINE('Rate for patient #' || &&pt_id ||
            ' is ' || TO_CHAR(v_rate * 100, 'fm99') || '%');
END;
/
SET VERIFY ON
SET SERVEROUTPUT OFF
```

Execution Results

```
Enter patient's ID:  314
Rate for patient #314 is 7%
```

Note: This script file works for only one patient at a time. More realistically, a cursor loop would be used to modify every row in the table (to be covered in the next chapter).

Also note that a double ampersand is used on the second reference to the substitution parameter PT_ID in order to avoid having the user reenter the value. If only one ampersand is used, the user will be prompted to enter another value.

Part 4: Loops

Loops can be used to repeat sections of code. A conditional loop, or WHILE loop, has this general syntax:

```
WHILE condition LOOP
        statement(s);
END LOOP;
```

where the statement(s) will repeatedly execute as long as the condition is true.

A counted loop, or FOR loop, has this general syntax:

```
FOR counter IN start-value . . . end-value LOOP
        statement(s);
END LOOP;
```

where the following rules apply:

1. The counter is implicitly declared as an integer variable.
2. The start-value is an integer expression representing the first value for the counter.
3. The end-value is an integer expression representing the last valid value for the counter.
4. The counter is incremented by 1 after each pass through the loop.
5. The statement(s) will repeatedly execute until the counter exceeds the end-value.

These loops have limited application within a PL/SQL block, because each execution of a SELECT . . . INTO statement included within the loop can still retrieve only one row. However, cursor loops are available, and they are much more useful for handling statement repetition. They will be covered in the next chapter.

Chapter Summary

PL/SQL blocks are used to add procedural language capabilities to SQL statements. Variables can be declared, calculations can be performed, and output can be produced. DML statements such as SELECT . . . INTO, UPDATE, INSERT, and DELETE can be included within PL/SQL blocks. Additional logic structures are supported by statements such as IF-THEN, IF-THEN-ELSE, and IF-THEN-ELSIF. Although loops such as WHILE and FOR are available, the cursor loops are much more valuable, and will be covered in the next chapter.

Exercises

Section A: Fundamentals

1. Give the variable declaration section for the following:
    a. A variable used to store a client's first name.
    b. A variable used to store an inventory item's quantity on hand (max value of 150).
    c. A variable used to store the labor charge (ranges from 0 to $500.00).
    d. A variable used to store a value from the MOVIE table's TITLE column.
    e. A variable used to store a value from a CD table's SONG_TITLE column. The table is owned by the user with ID iarie, and you may assume that the required privileges have been granted.
2. Give assignment statements for each of the following:
    a. Assign the name of your hometown to the variable V_CITY.
    b. Assign your date of birth to the variable V_BIRTHDATE.

c. Assign your shoe size to the numeric variable V_SHOESIZE.

d. Initialize the variable V_SUM to zero.

e. Calculate annual expenses using V_MONTHLY_EXPENSE, and store the result in the variable named V_ANNUAL_EXPENSE.

f. Calculate a new balance as an old balance plus a 5 percent late fee, using the variables V_OLD_BAL and V_NEW_BAL.

g. Calculate a person's age in years using V_BIRTHDATE, and store the results in V_AGE.

h. Calculate average annual income using the annual income amounts in &INCOME1, &INCOME2, and &INCOME3. Store the result in V_AVG_INCOME.

i. Store a value in V_FULL_NAME based on &FIRST_NAME and &LAST_NAME in this format: Last, First (note letter case used).

3. Write output statements for each of the following:

a. Display the title MOVIES AVAILABLE.

b. Display the value of the V_TITLE variable, appropriately labeled.

c. Display the values of the V_MOVIE_ID and V_CATEGORY variables, appropriately labeled in sentence form.

d. Display the value of V_FEE, appropriately labeled and formatted.

4. Write an anonymous block that can be used to determine and display the user's age in years given that the user enters their date of birth. Also allow the user to enter their first name, and display the final results in sentence form.

5. Write an anonymous block that can be used to calculate and display the amount of a grocery bill using the following values entered by the user: quantity of the first item, cost per item for the first item, quantity of the second item, cost per item for the second item, and tax rate (as a percentage). Format and label the output appropriately.

6. Write an anonymous block that can be used to determine and display the number of new audio CDs that can be purchased with a given amount of money. Allow the user to enter the amount of money, the average price per CD, and the tax rate (as a percentage). Format and label the output appropriately.

7. Write an anonymous block that can be used to calculate and display the number of flats of plants required to fill a landscaping area. Allow the user to enter the square footage of the area, the number of plants required per square foot, and the number of plants per flat. Round up the result to the nearest whole number of flats of plants.

Section B: DML Statements in PL/SQL Blocks

1. Use an anonymous block to retrieve and display the fee for the movie whose title is entered by the user. Label and format the output.

2. Use an anonymous block to retrieve and display the due date for a particular movie rental. Allow the user to enter the movie ID and the customer ID.

3. Use an anonymous block to retrieve and display the complete address for the patient whose full name is entered by the user. Display the results in sentence form.

4. Use an anonymous block to handle a patient payment transaction. Allow the user to enter all required values.

5. A customer wants to rent a copy of the same movie that his neighbor is currently renting. Allow the user to enter the customer's ID and his neighbor's full name. Then use an anonymous block to process a rental transaction for the customer (assuming that the neighbor has only one movie currently rented). Use a due date of three days after the rental date.

6. A new doctor for Dr. Vester's area was hired today. This new doctor will earn the same bonus as Dr. Vester, and the charge per appointment will also be the same. Allow the user to enter the new doctor's name and salary, and then use an anonymous block to handle the addition. Use the DOCTOR_DOC_ID_SEQ sequence to generate a new ID number.

7. Write a script file that uses an anonymous block to process a movie rental return. Allow the user to enter the movie title and the customer phone number.

8. Due to newly discovered flaws, all copies of specific movies are removed from inventory. Write a script file that allows the user to enter the title of the flawed movie. Use an anonymous block to credit the movie fee to the account of all customers currently renting the movie, and then remove all related data from the database (both the MOVIE table and the RENTAL table).

Section C: Other Logic Structures

1. Modify your solution to problem 8 in Section B so that it displays an appropriate message if the movie is late.

2. Further modify your solution to problem 1 so that it also charges a late fee to the customer's account if the movie is returned late. The late fee should be equal to half of the movie fee.

3. Retrieve and display the fee for the movie whose title is entered by the user. Movies in the Kids category are always on a two-for-one special. If the movie is in that category, display an appropriate message.

4. Write a script file that will handle a customer payment transaction. Allow the user to enter all required values. If the amount of the payment exceeds the balance, then inform the user and discontinue transaction processing. Otherwise, credit the account and inform the user of the new balance.

5. Patients' deductible amounts are based on their insurance provider. Write a script file that will allow the user to enter a patient's name. Then display the patient's deductible amount based on the following chart:

Insurance provider	Deductible amount
BCBS and SIH	$250
QualityCare	$200
HealthCare	$150
All others	None

6. All doctors are to receive raises, and the percentage of the increase is dependent upon their current salary. Write a script file that will give a raise to the doctor whose ID is entered by the user (this should work for only one doctor at a time). Use the following guidelines:

Current salary range	Raise percentage (%)
Over $15,000	10
$10,000–$15,000	15
Under $10,000	20

7. Movies in the Kids category are five-day rentals, those in the Family category are three-day rentals, and all others are two-day rentals. Write a script file that will allow the user to enter the customer ID and movie ID, and then use an anonymous block to add a row to the rental table.

Chapter

10

Advanced PL/SQL Concepts

This final chapter presents some of the more advanced capabilities of PL/SQL blocks. Explicit cursors are used to move through rows of a table, one at a time, and exceptions are used to define and trap errors that may occur during execution.

Section A: Explicit Cursors

Cursors are used by all DML commands. In simple terms, a cursor is used to select rows from a table, and then advance through them one at a time while acting as a pointer to the current row. In reality, the mechanics of using cursors is much more complex, but the software handles the majority of that complexity.

The two types of cursors are implicit cursors and explicit cursors. Most cursors are implicit cursors, and the software automatically handles all statements involving their manipulation. Conversely, explicit cursors are user-defined and can be used to implement a wide range of solutions within PL/SQL blocks. The focus of this section is on the statements used for the manipulation of explicit cursors.

Part 1: Records

Explicit cursors usually involve the use of a record variable. Records can be used for a variety of tasks, such as holding a row of values from a SELECT . . . INTO statement, but this book will examine their usage only as it relates to explicit cursors.

A record is a type of variable that can be used to hold data from an entire row or just part of a row. In other words, the record consists of several storage locations (one for each column value) rather than just one storage location. Each of the storage locations within a record is called a field.

As with other variables, the record must be declared before it can be used. A suffix of _REC should be included on the record name. For the type, the %ROWTYPE specification is generally used, preceded by the table name. This has the advantage of defining fields as exact matches of the columns involved, both in type and name.

The FETCH statement places values from a row of the table into the fields of the record. After the values are stored in the record, they can be accessed by qualifying the field name (or column name) with the record name, as in record-name.field-name. This access can occur in an assignment statement, another DML statement, or an output statement.

Example 10.A.1

For illustration purposes only, use a record to store the values from one row of the patient table. Then display the patient's name.

Script File Contents

```
SET SERVEROUTPUT ON
SET VERIFY OFF
ACCEPT pt_id PROMPT 'Enter patient"s ID: '
DECLARE
     patient_rec  patient%ROWTYPE;
BEGIN
     SELECT *
     INTO patient_rec
     FROM patient
     WHERE pt_id = &pt_id;
     DBMS_OUTPUT.PUT_LINE('Patient"s name is ' ||
          patient_rec.pt_fname || '' ||
          patient_rec.pt_lname);
END;
/
SET SERVEROUTPUT OFF
SET VERIFY ON
```

Execution Results

```
Enter patient's ID:  108
Patient's name is Ryan Baily
```

Note: Once the row is stored in the record, then the value of any field can be accessed. In this case, the patient's first and last names are being accessed on the output statement by using the fully qualified field name (record name, period, field name). Again, the ROW-TYPE declaration defines field names as exact matches of the column names involved.

Example 10.A.2

Use a record to store the values from one row of the rental table. Allow the user to enter the customer and movie IDs. Then display the due date.

Script File Contents

```
SET SERVEROUTPUT ON
SET VERIFY OFF
ACCEPT c_id PROMPT 'Enter customer ID: '
ACCEPT m_id PROMPT 'Enter movie ID: '
DECLARE
     rental_rec   rental%ROWTYPE;
BEGIN
     SELECT *
     INTO rental_rec
     FROM rentaL
     WHERE m_id = &m_id
        AND c_id = &c_id;
     DBMS_OUTPUT.PUT_LINE('Due date: ' ||
          TO_CHAR(rental_rec.due_date,
              'fmDay, Month DD'));
END;
/
SET SERVEROUTPUT OFF
SET VERIFY ON
```

Execution Results

```
Enter customer ID:  388
Enter movie ID:  216
Due date: Wednesday, July 2

PL/SQL procedure successfully completed.
```

Example 10.A.3

Use a record to store a row from the doctor table. Increase the doctor's annual bonus by 10 times the charge per appointment.

Script File Contents

```
SET SERVEROUTPUT ON
SET VERIFY OFF
ACCEPT doc_id PROMPT 'Enter doctor"s ID: '
DECLARE
      doctor_rec    doctor%ROWTYPE;
      v_increase    NUMBER(4);
BEGIN
      -- Retrieve row into record
      SELECT *
      INTO doctor_rec
      FROM doctor
      WHERE doc_id = &doc_id;

      -- Calculate amount of bonus increase
      v_increase := doctor_rec.chgperappt * 10;

      -- Store new bonus amount in table
      UPDATE doctor
      SET annual_bonus = doctor_rec.annual_bonus
            + v_increase
      WHERE doc_id = doctor_rec.doc_id;

      -- Output old and new bonus amounts
      DBMS_OUTPUT.PUT_LINE('Old bonus: ' ||
          TO_CHAR(doctor_rec.annual_bonus, '$9,999'));
      DBMS_OUTPUT.PUT_LINE('New bonus: ' ||
          TO_CHAR(doctor_rec.annual_bonus +
                v_increase, '$9,999'));
END;
/
SET SERVEROUTPUT OFF
SET VERIFY ON
```

Execution Results

```
Enter doctor's ID:  889
Old bonus:  $3,200
New bonus:  $3,850
```

Part 2: Cursors

The use of cursors in PL/SQL is similar to the use of files in a third-generation language. The file identifier is declared, the file is opened, a loop is used to process the records in the file, and then the file is closed. Similarly, the cursor identifier is declared, the cursor is opened, a loop is used to process the rows in the table referenced by the cursor, and then the cursor is closed. The specific statements used are presented next.

Declaration

As with other variable identifiers, the cursor declaration creates a named area of memory for the data used by the cursor. Among other things, this data includes the SELECT statement that is linked to the cursor. When processed, the cursor will then act as a pointer as it moves through the rows retrieved by the linked SELECT statement. General syntax is as follows:

> CURSOR cursor-name IS select-statement;
> where naming conventions include using a suffix of _CURSOR on the cursor-name
> and the select-statement is any valid SQL SELECT statement (no INTO clause included).

Example 10.A.4

Declare a cursor that can be used to move through the DOCTOR table.

```
PL/SQL: DECLARE
             CURSOR doc_cursor IS
             SELECT *
             FROM doctor;
```

Example 10.A.5

Declare a cursor that can be used to move through the titles and fees of movies.

```
PL/SQL: DECLARE
             CURSOR movie_cursor IS
             SELECT title, fee
             FROM movie;
```

Example 10.A.6

Declare a cursor that can be used to move through the rows of rentals that are due today.

```
PL/SQL: DECLARE
             CURSOR rental_cursor IS
             SELECT *
             FROM rental
             WHERE due_date = sysdate;
```

Example 10.A.7

Declare a cursor that can be used to move through the IDs, due dates, and balances of the patients who see the doctor whose ID is entered by the user.

```
PL/SQL: DECLARE
             CURSOR bills_cursor IS
             SELECT pt_id, duedate, balance
             FROM billing
             WHERE doc_id = &doc_id;
```

Open

Once declared, the OPEN statement is used to open the cursor. This causes the query linked to the cursor name to be executed. The data retrieved by the query is called the "active set," and it is this active set whose rows will be fetched one at a time with the FETCH statement. OPEN statements are usually the first statements written after the BEGIN statement of a block. General syntax is as follows:

```
OPEN cursor-name;
```

Example 10.A.8	Open the cursor that was declared in the previous example.

```
PL/SQL: BEGIN
            OPEN bills_cursor;
```

Example 10.A.9	Open the cursors that were declared in examples 10.A.5 and 10.A.6.

```
PL/SQL: BEGIN
            OPEN movie_cursor;
            OPEN rental_cursor;
```

Example 10.A.10	Put it together: declare and open a cursor that can be used to move through the customer name, movie ID, and due date for each current rental.

```
PL/SQL: DECLARE
            CURSOR cust_rent_cursor IS
            SELECT lname, fname, m_id, duedate
            FROM customer c, rental r
            WHERE c.c_id = r.c_id;
        BEGIN
            OPEN cust_rent_cursor;
```

Note: As illustrated in this example, the SELECT statement used on the cursor declaration may involve a join. In general, any clauses and/or functions allowed on a regular SELECT statement may be used on a cursor declaration (including subqueries).

Fetch

The FETCH statement retrieves the next row from the active set and stores it in the variables or record listed. Values can then be accessed by using the variable names or the fully qualified field names from the record. In addition to fetching values, the FETCH statement moves the cursor up so that it points to the next row in the active set.

General syntax is as follows:

FETCH cursor-name INTO { variables | record-name };

where the braces indicate that one of the items is used (either variables or a record); the braces are not a part of the syntax.

Example 10.A.11	Fetch the first row specified by the cursor that was declared and opened in the previous example (assuming that an appropriate record variable was also declared).

```
PL/SQL: FETCH cust_rent_cursor INTO cust_rent_rec;
```

Example 10.A.12	Declare a cursor and record that can be used to move through rows of the billing table. Then open the cursor and fetch the first row of values into the record.

```
PL/SQL: DECLARE
            CURSOR billing_cursor IS
            SELECT *
            FROM billing;
            billing_rec  billing%ROWTYPE;
        BEGIN
            OPEN billing_doc_cursor;
            FETCH billing_cursor INTO billing_rec;
```

Example 10.A.13

Declare a cursor and record that can be used to move through the rows of the DOCTOR table that pertain to doctors in pediatrics. Then open the cursor and fetch the first record. For purposes of illustrating a reference to a value fetched by the cursor, display the first doctor's name.

Script File Contents

```
SET SERVEROUTPUT ON
DECLARE
     CURSOR ped_doc_cursor IS
     SELECT *
     FROM doctor
     WHERE area = 'Pediatrics';
     doc_rec      doctor%ROWTYPE;
BEGIN
     OPEN ped_doc_cursor;
     FETCH ped_doc_cursor INTO doc_rec;
     DBMS_OUTPUT.PUT_LINE('First doctor"s name is ' ||
          doc_rec.doc_name);
END;
/
SET SERVEROUTPUT OFF
```

Execution Results

```
First doctor's name is Harrison
```

More realistically, the FETCH will be repeatedly executed so that each record in the active set is retrieved. Cursor loops will be covered in the next part of this section.

Example 10.A.14

Declare a cursor and record that can be used to move through the customer and movie IDs of yesterday's rentals. Then open the cursor and fetch the first record. For purposes of illustrating a reference to a value fetched by the cursor, display the first pair of IDs.

Script File Contents

```
SET SERVEROUTPUT ON
DECLARE
     CURSOR rental_cursor IS
     SELECT c_id, m_id
     FROM rental
     WHERE date_out = SYSDATE - 1;
     v_c_id      rental.c_id%TYPE;
     v_m_id      rental.m_id%TYPE;
BEGIN
     OPEN rental_cursor;
     FETCH rental_cursor INTO v_c_id, v_m_id;
     DBMS_OUTPUT.PUT_LINE('First customer: ' ||v_c_id
          || '    First movie: ' || v_m_id);
END;
/
SET SERVEROUTPUT OFF
```

Execution Results

```
First customer: 673    First movie:  216

PL/SQL procedure successfully completed.
```

Close

The CLOSE statement is used when the cursor's active set is no longer needed. General syntax is CLOSE cursor-name. An implicit CLOSE is executed when the anonymous block terminates, and therefore, this statement may not always be required within the block. However, it is a good exercise in self-documentation to specifically include it for each cursor anyway.

Example 10.A.15	Close the cursor used in the previous example.

```
PL/SQL: CLOSE ped_doc_cursor;
```

Note: This statement would be included immediately before the END; statement of the block.

Example 10.A.16	Close the cursors used in example 10.A.9.

```
PL/SQL: CLOSE movie_cursor;
        CLOSE rental_cursor;
```

Part 3: Cursor Loops

A loop is used to repeatedly fetch rows from the active set linked to a cursor. This loop is of the simple form LOOP – END LOOP. The loop will repeatedly execute until a condition is met with an EXIT statement.

The condition on the EXIT statement includes a reference to one of four cursor attributes, %NOTFOUND. Other cursor attributes are %FOUND, %ROWCOUNT, and %ISOPEN. The method used for referencing these cursor attributes is to precede the attribute with the desired cursor name, such as PED_DOC_CURSOR%NOTFOUND. This particular attribute returns a true value when there are no more rows left in the active set, and false otherwise.

General syntax of this loop structure is as follows:

```
LOOP
    FETCH cursor-name INTO record-name;
    EXIT WHEN cursor-name%NOTFOUND;
    -- Include statements needed to process 1 row of values here
END LOOP;
```

Example 10.A.17	Increase each doctor's annual bonus according to the following table:

Area	Amount of Increase
Neurology	15 times ChgPerAppt
Pediatrics	10 times ChgPerAppt
Rehab	10 times ChgPerAppt
Family Practice	8 times ChgPerAppt
Orthopedics	5 times ChgPerAppt

Script File Contents

```
DECLARE
    doc_rec         doctor%ROWTYPE;
    v_increase      NUMBER(4);
    CURSOR doc_cursor IS
    SELECT *
    FROM doctor;
```

```
BEGIN
      OPEN doc_cursor;
      LOOP
            -- Retrieve row from active set
            FETCH doc_cursor INTO doc_rec;
            -- Leave loop if no rows were left to retrieve
            EXIT WHEN doc_cursor%NOTFOUND;

            -- Calculate amount of bonus increase
            IF doc_rec.area = 'Neurology' THEN
                  v_increase := doc_rec.chgperappt * 15;
            ELSIF doc_rec.area IN ('Pediatrics', 'Rehab') THEN
                  v_increase := doc_rec.chgperappt * 10;
            ELSIF doc_rec.area = 'Family Practice' THEN
                  v_increase := doc_rec.chgperappt * 8;
            ELSE
                  v_increase := doc_rec.chgperappt * 5;
            END IF;

            -- Store new bonus amount in table
            UPDATE doctor
            SET annual_bonus = doc_rec.annual_bonus + v_increase
            WHERE doc_id = doc_rec.doc_id;

      END LOOP;
      CLOSE doc_cursor;
END;
/
```

Selected doctor IDs, areas, and bonuses before increase and after increase are shown here to illustrate the execution effects of this block. Be aware that this is not a complete list.

```
    DOC_ID AREA                    BEFORE    AFTER
 --------- -------------------- --------- ---------
       235 Family Practice         2610      2970
       289 Neurology               7925      9350
       389 Pediatrics              2850      3450
```

Example 10.A.18

The billing procedure has changed (as originally presented in example 9.C.7). All balances should be modified as follows:

Number of Days Past Due	Late Fee Charged (%)
30–59	2
60–89	4
90–119	7
120 and above	10

Script File Contents

```
DECLARE
      pt_rec    billing%ROWTYPE;
      v_rate    NUMBER(2,2);
      CURSOR pt_cursor IS
```

```
            SELECT *
            FROM billing;
     BEGIN
            OPEN pt_cursor;
            LOOP
                  -- Retrieve row from active set
                  FETCH pt_cursor INTO pt_rec;
                  -- Leave loop if no rows were left to retrieve
                  EXIT WHEN pt_cursor%NOTFOUND;

                  -- Determine rate for late fee
                  IF SYSDATE - pt_rec.duedate < 30 THEN
                        v_rate := 0;
                  ELSIF SYSDATE - pt_rec.duedate <= 59 THEN
                        v_rate := .02;
                  ELSIF SYSDATE - pt_rec. duedate <= 89 THEN
                        v_rate := .04;
                  ELSIF SYSDATE - pt_rec.duedate <= 119 THEN
                        v_rate := .07;
                  ELSE
                        v_rate := .10;
                  END IF;

                  -- Add late fee to patient's balance
                  UPDATE billing
                  SET balance = balance + balance * v_rate
                  WHERE pt_id = pt_rec.pt_id;

            END LOOP;
            CLOSE pt_cursor;
     END;
     /
```

Again, before and after values for balances are shown for selected rows.

PT_ID	DUEDATE	BEFORE	AFTER
168	21-AUG-03	15650	15650
331	09-SEP-03	300	300
313	01-JAN-04	0	0
314	31-MAR-03	100	107
264	11-JAN-03	35000	38500
103	01-JUL-03	4500	4500
847	31-JAN-02	98000	107800
504	01-JAN-03	0	0

Another type of loop that can be used with cursors is the cursor FOR loop. This loop implicitly handles the following tasks:

1. Declaring the record variable to be used with the cursor
2. Opening the cursor
3. Repeatedly fetching a row from the active set
4. Exiting the loop when %FOUND returns false
5. Closing the cursor

As the loop takes care of all of these, no statements need to be written for these tasks. Hence, the cursor FOR loop is a good shortcut statement. General syntax is as follows:

```
FOR record-name IN cursor-name LOOP
        -- Include various statements to process 1 row of values here
END LOOP;
```

Example 10.A.19

Modify example 10.A.17 so that a cursor FOR loop is used instead of explicit record declaration, OPEN, FETCH, EXIT, and CLOSE.

Script File Contents

```
DECLARE
     v_increase    NUMBER(4);
     CURSOR doc_cursor IS
     SELECT *
     FROM doctor;
BEGIN
     FOR doc_rec IN doc_cursor LOOP
          IF doc_rec.area = 'Neurology' THEN
               v_increase := doc_rec.chgperappt * 15;
          ELSIF doc_rec.area IN ('Pediatrics', 'Rehab') THEN
               v_increase := doc_rec.chgperappt * 10;
          ELSIF doc_rec.area = 'Family Practice' THEN
               v_increase := doc_rec.chgperappt * 8;
          ELSE
               V_increase := doc_rec.chgperappt * 5;
          END IF;

          UPDATE doctor
          SET annual_bonus = doc_rec.annual_bonus + v_increase
          WHERE doc_id = doc_rec.doc_id;
     END LOOP;
END;
```

Example 10.A.20

Modify example 10.A.18 so that a cursor FOR loop is used instead of explicit record declaration, OPEN, FETCH, EXIT, and CLOSE.

Script File Contents

```
DECLARE
     v_rate   NUMBER(2,2);
     CURSOR pt_cursor IS
     SELECT *
     FROM Billing;
BEGIN

     FOR pt_rec IN pt_cursor loop

          IF SYSDATE - pt_rec.duedate < 30 THEN
               v_rate := 0;
          ELSIF SYSDATE - pt_rec.duedate <= 59 THEN
               v_rate := .02;
          ELSIF SYSDATE - pt_rec. duedate <= 89 THEN
               v_rate := .04;
          ELSIF SYSDATE - pt_rec.duedate <= 119 THEN
               v_rate := .07;
```

```
          ELSE
                v_rate := .10;
          END IF;

          UPDATE billing
          SET balance = balance + balance * v_rate
          WHERE pt_id = pt_rec.pt_id;

     END LOOP;

END;
```

Section B: Exceptions

An exception is a facility provided for error handling. When a run-time error occurs, an exception is "raised." It can then be "trapped" with code written in the EXCEPTION section of the block. Trapping exceptions allows you to choose the course of action to be taken when an error occurs. If an error occurs and it is *not* trapped, then the procedure will crash. Therefore, in the interest of robust programming, PL/SQL blocks that will be used repeatedly should always contain an exception section.

The two types of exceptions are those that are predefined by the software, and those that are defined by the user. Predefined exceptions exist for the more common error situations, and user-defined exceptions can be used for application-specific errors. Both types of exceptions are used within PL/SQL blocks.

Part 1: Predefined Exceptions

Names

This category includes exception names for errors that usually arise during execution of PL/SQL blocks. The following table lists some of the more commonly used predefined exception names and the errors that cause them to be raised.

Error	Exception Raised by Error
1. More than one row returned by a SELECT . . . INTO statement	TOO_MANY_ROWS
2. Less than one row returned by a SELECT . . . INTO statement	NO_DATA_FOUND
3. Attempted division by zero	ZERO_DIVIDE
4. Attempted an illegal cursor operation	INVALID_CURSOR

Trapping

When one of these four errors occurs, the specified exception name is raised. If code is included in the EXCEPTION section for that exception name, then the exception is trapped and the code is executed. If no code is included for the exception, then the procedure will crash, ending abnormally. Such a crash can be avoided simply by coding an EXCEPTION section.

The EXCEPTION section is included after the main section of executable statements and just before the END of the block. General syntax is as follows:

```
EXCEPTION
     WHEN exception-name THEN
          statement(s);
```

```
[WHEN exception-name THEN
    statement(s);]
...
[WHEN OTHERS THEN
    statement(s);]
```

When an exception is raised, the flow of execution moves to the EXCEPTION section, and there is no facility available for returning to the main block of executable statements. Thus, execution will end after an exception is handled.

Within the EXCEPTION section, each exception name is examined until the name of the raised exception is found. The statements listed there are executed, and all other parts of the section are skipped. If the name of the raised exception is not found, then the statements listed following the WHEN OTHERS THEN clause are executed (if it is included). If there is no WHEN clause available to trap the exception, then the procedure crashes, ending abnormally.

The following example illustrates the use of two of the four most common predefined exceptions.

Example 10.B.1

Use an anonymous block to retrieve and display the current balance for the customer whose last name is entered by the user. Use exceptions to handle possible errors of zero rows retrieved and more than one row retrieved.

Script File Contents

```
SET SERVEROUTPUT ON
SET VERIFY OFF
ACCEPT lname PROMPT 'Customer last name? '
DECLARE
      v_balance customer.curr_bal%TYPE;

BEGIN
      SELECT curr_bal
      INTO v_balance
      FROM customer
      WHERE lname = '&lname';
      DBMS_OUTPUT.PUT_LINE('Current balance: ' ||
          TO_CHAR(v_balance,'fm$999.00'));

EXCEPTION
      WHEN NO_DATA_FOUND THEN
          DBMS_OUTPUT.PUT_LINE('There is no customer with ' ||
              'a last name of ' || '&lname');
      WHEN TOO_MANY_ROWS THEN
          DBMS_OUTPUT.PUT_LINE('There is more than one' ||
          ' customer with a last name of' || '&lname');
      WHEN OTHERS THEN
          DBMS_OUTPUT.PUT_LINE('An unknown error occurred');
END;
/
SET SERVEROUTPUT OFF
SET VERIFY ON
```

Execution Results (First Case)

```
Customer last name?  Sinclair
There is no customer with a last name of Sinclair

PL/SQL procedure successfully completed.
```

Execution Results (Second Case)

```
Customer last name? Akers
There is more than one customer with a last name of Akers

PL/SQL procedure successfully completed.
```

Execution Results (Third Case)

```
Customer last name?  Williams
Current balance:  $20.00

PL/SQL procedure successfully completed.
```

Example 10.B.2

Use an anonymous block to retrieve and display the next appointment date for the patient whose last name is entered by the user. Use exceptions to handle possible errors of zero rows retrieved and more than one row retrieved.

Script File Contents

```
SET SERVEROUTPUT ON
SET VERIFY OFF
ACCEPT phone PROMPT 'Enter patient"s phone number: '
DECLARE
    v_nextapptdate DATE;
BEGIN
    SELECT nextapptdate
    INTO v_nextapptdate
    FROM patient
    WHERE pt_id IN
       (SELECT pt_id
        FROM billing
        WHERE phone = '&phone');
    DBMS_OUTPUT.PUT_LINE('Next appointment date is ' ||
        TO_CHAR(v_nextapptdate,'fmMonth DD, RRRR'));

EXCEPTION
    WHEN NO_DATA_FOUND THEN
        DBMS_OUTPUT.PUT_LINE('No patients have ' ||
            'a phone number of ' || '&phone');
    WHEN TOO_MANY_ROWS THEN
        DBMS_OUTPUT.PUT_LINE('There is more than one' ||
        ' patient with a phone number of ' || '&phone ');
    WHEN OTHERS THEN
        DBMS_OUTPUT.PUT_LINE('An unknown error occurred');
END;
/
SET SERVEROUTPUT OFF
SET VERIFY ON
```

Note: The IN operator is used before the subquery on the SELECT to allow for the possibility of there being more than one patient with the same phone number. If the equal to operator was used instead, then multiple occurrences of the same phone number would raise the OTHERS exception rather than the TOO_MANY_ROWS exception.

Execution Results (First Case)

```
Enter patient's phone number: 453-7227
No patients have a phone number of 453-7227

PL/SQL procedure successfully completed.
```

Execution Results (Second Case)

```
Enter patient's phone number: 833-6654
There is more than one patient with a phone number of 833-6654

PL/SQL procedure successfully completed.
```

Execution Results (Third Case)

```
Enter patient's phone number: 549-7848
Next appointment date is November 01, 2003

PL/SQL procedure successfully completed.
```

Note: For this example, there is no need for the WHEN OTHERS THEN clause, because there is no other exception that could be caused by this particular block. It is included here only for illustration purposes.

Part 2: User-defined Exceptions

For errors other than those listed above, the user can define, raise, and trap other exceptions. For example, if an attempt is made to modify a row for a patient resulting in a next appointment date that is to occur BEFORE the previous appointment date, then an exception could be raised and trapped. Or perhaps an attempt is made to add a due date that precedes the current system date. In such a case, an exception could be raised and trapped.

There is no limit to the number of user-defined exceptions that can be used. The variety between applications is tremendous. Therefore, you should define exceptions to raise and trap as many potential errors as possible.

Declare

A user-defined exception name is declared by listing an identifier with a type of EXCEPTION. Naming conventions include the use of the prefix E_ on the name.

Example 10.B.3	Declare a user-defined exception for an error of salaries below $3,000.

```
PL/SQL: DECLARE
              e_sal_too_low  EXCEPTION;
```

Example 10.B.4	Declare a user-defined exception for an error of a doctor's date of hire being later than the current date.

```
PL/SQL: DECLARE
              e_invalid_datehired  EXCEPTION;
```

Example 10.B.5	Declare a user-defined exception for an error of a movie category other than Kids, Family, Adventure, Drama, Comedy, and Foreign.

```
PL/SQL: DECLARE
              e_wrong_category  EXCEPTION;
```

Raise

Within the executable statement section, an IF-THEN can be used to test for the error condition. Then the RAISE statement is used to raise the exception and pass control down to the EXCEPTION section of the block. General syntax is RAISE exception-name;

Example 10.B.6

Write the code needed to raise the exception declared in example 10.B.3.

```
PL/SQL: IF &sal < 3000 THEN
              RAISE e_sal_too_low;
        END IF;
```

Example 10.B.7

Write the code needed to raise the exception declared in example 10.B.4.

```
PL/SQL: IF TO_DATE('&datehired', 'DD-MON-RR') > SYSDATE THEN
              RAISE e_invalid_datehired;
        END IF;
```

Example 10.B.8

Write the code needed to raise the exception declared in example 10.B.5.

```
PL/SQL: IF '&Category' NOT IN
            ('Kids', 'Family', 'Adventure', 'Drama', 'Comedy', 'Foreign') THEN
                RAISE e_wrong_category;
        END IF;
```

Trap

Once the user-defined exception is raised, it can be trapped in the EXCEPTION section in exactly the same manner as predefined exceptions.

Example 10.B.9

Print an appropriate message when the movie category exception is raised.

```
PL/SQL: EXCEPTION
           WHEN e_wrong_category THEN
           DBMS_OUTPUT.PUT_LINE('A category of ' ||
              '&category' || 'does not exist in this database.' );
```

Example 10.B.10

Print an appropriate message when one of the two doctor-related exceptions are raised.

```
PL/SQL: EXCEPTION
           WHEN e_sal_too_low THEN
           DBMS_OUTPUT.PUT_LINE('Salary entered is ' ||
              TO_CHAR(&sal, 'fm$9,999.99'));
           DBMS_OUTPUT.PUT_LINE('This is below the current ' ||
              ' limit of $3,000');
           WHEN e_invalid_datehired THEN
           DBMS_OUTPUT.PUT_LINE('Hire date entered is ' ||
              '&datehired');
           DBMS_OUTPUT.PUT_LINE('This is later than ' ||
              'the current date of' || TO_CHAR(SYSDATE));
```

Of course, all of these steps would be put together in one block, as illustrated by the following examples:

Example 10.B.11

Write a script file that can be used to display the number of movies in the category entered by the user. If a nonexistent category is entered, trap the error and display an error message.

Script File Contents

```
SET SERVEROUTPUT ON
SET VERIFY OFF
ACCEPT category PROMPT 'What is the movie category? '
```

```
DECLARE
     e_wrong_category          EXCEPTION;
     v_num_movies              NUMBER(3);

BEGIN
     IF '&category' NOT IN
             ('Kids', 'Family', 'Adventure', 'Drama', 'Comedy', 'Foreign') THEN
                      RAISE e_wrong_category;
     ELSE
          SELECT COUNT(*)
          INTO v_num_movies
          FROM movie
          WHERE category = '&category';
          DBMS_OUTPUT.PUT_LINE('There are ' ||
               TO_CHAR(v_num_movies, 'fm999') || ' movies in the ' ||
               '&category' || ' category');
     END IF;
EXCEPTION
     WHEN e_wrong_category THEN
          DBMS_OUTPUT.PUT_LINE('A category of ' ||
               '&category' || ' does not exist in this database.' );
WHEN OTHERS THEN
          DBMS_OUTPUT.PUT_LINE ('An unknown error occurred');
END;
/
SET SERVEROUTPUT OFF
SET VERIFY ON
```

Execution Results (First Case)

```
What is the movie category?  Horror
A category of Horror does not exist in this database.

PL/SQL procedure successfully completed.
```

Execution Results (Second Case)

```
What is the movie category?  Drama
There are 7 movies in the Drama category

PL/SQL procedure successfully completed.
```

Example 10.B.12

Use an anonymous block to add a row for a new doctor to the DOCTOR table. Allow the user to enter all values except the supervisor ID, which should be determined by a query, and the annual bonus, which should be null. Use exceptions to trap the following errors:

1. The hire date is later than the current date.
2. The salary per month is under $3,000.
3. The area is something other than Pediatrics, Neurology, Rehab, Family Practice, or Orthopedics.
4. The charge per appointment is under $25 or over $100.

Script File Contents

```
SET SERVEROUTPUT ON
SET VERIFY OFF
ACCEPT id PROMPT 'Enter doctor"s ID: '
```

```
ACCEPT name PROMPT 'Enter doctor"s name: '
ACCEPT sal PROMPT 'Enter salary per month: '
ACCEPT area PROMPT 'Enter area of specialization: '
ACCEPT datehired PROMPT 'Enter date hired (DD-MON-YYYY): '
ACCEPT chg PROMPT 'Enter charge per appointment: '
DECLARE
      e_invalid_datehired      EXCEPTION;
      e_sal_too_low EXCEPTION;
      e_invalid_area EXCEPTION;
      e_chgperappt_out_of_range EXCEPTION;
      v_supervisor_id doctor.doc_id%TYPE;

BEGIN
      DBMS_OUTPUT.PUT_LINE('PROCEDURE RESULTS');

      IF TO_DATE('&datehired', 'DD-MON-RRRR') > SYSDATE THEN
            RAISE e_invalid_datehired;

      ELSIF &sal < 3000 THEN
            RAISE e_sal_too_low;

      ELSIF '&area' NOT IN ('Pediatrics', 'Neurology', 'Rehab', 'Family Practice',
                        'Orthopedics') THEN
            RAISE e_invalid_area;

      ELSIF &chg NOT BETWEEN 25 AND 100 THEN
            RAISE e_chgperappt_out_of_range;

      ELSE
            SELECT doc_id
            INTO v_supervisor_id
            FROM doctor
            WHERE area = '&area'
            AND supervisor_id = 100;

            INSERT INTO doctor
            VALUES (&id, '&name', TO_DATE('&datehired', 'DD-MON-RR'),
                  &sal, '&area', v_supervisor_id, &chg, NULL);

            DBMS_OUTPUT.PUT_LINE('New row added to table');
      END IF;

EXCEPTION

      WHEN e_invalid_datehired THEN
            DBMS_OUTPUT.PUT_LINE('Hire date entered is ' ||
                  '&datehired');
            DBMS_OUTPUT.PUT_LINE('This is later than ' ||
                  'the current date of ' || TO_CHAR(SYSDATE));

      WHEN e_sal_too_low THEN
            DBMS_OUTPUT.PUT_LINE('Salary entered is ' ||
                  TO_CHAR(&sal, 'fm$9,999.99'));
            DBMS_OUTPUT.PUT_LINE('This is below the current' ||
                  ' limit of $3,000');
```

```
      WHEN e_invalid_area THEN
            DBMS_OUTPUT.PUT_LINE('Area of specialization (' || '&area'
                || ') does not exist in the table');

      WHEN e_chgperappt_out_of_range THEN
            DBMS_OUTPUT.PUT_LINE ('Charge per appointment of' ||
                TO_CHAR(&chg, '$999') || ' is not between 25 and 100');

      WHEN OTHERS THEN
            DBMS_OUTPUT.PUT_LINE ('An unknown error occurred');

END;
/
SET SERVEROUTPUT OFF
SET VERIFY ON
```

Execution Results (First Case)

```
Enter doctor's ID:  506
Enter doctor's name:  Ledger
Enter salary per month:  10000
Enter area of specialization:  Orthopedics
Enter date hired (DD-MON-YYYY):  01-aug-2003
Enter charge per appointment:  50
PROCEDURE RESULTS
Hire date entered is 01-aug-2003
This is later than the current date of 01-JUL-03
PL/SQL procedure successfully completed.
```

Execution Results (Second Case)

```
Enter doctor's ID:  506
Enter doctor's name:  Ledger
Enter salary per month:  1000
Enter area of specialization:  Orthopedics
Enter date hired (DD-MON-YYYY):  01-jul-03
Enter charge per appointment:  50
PROCEDURE RESULTS
Salary entered is $1,000.
This is below the current limit of $3,000
PL/SQL procedure successfully completed.
```

Execution Results (Third Case)

```
Enter doctor's ID:  506
Enter doctor's name:  Ledger
Enter salary per month:  10000
Enter area of specialization:  Obstetrics
Enter date hired (DD-MON-YYYY):  01-jul-03
Enter charge per appointment:  50
PROCEDURE RESULTS
Area of specialization (Obstetrics) does not exist in the table
PL/SQL procedure successfully completed.
```

Execution Results (Fourth Case)

```
Enter doctor's ID:  506
Enter doctor's name:  Ledger
Enter salary per month:  10000
```

```
Enter area of specialization:  Orthopedics
Enter date hired (DD-MON-YYYY):  01-jul-03
Enter charge per appointment:  150
PROCEDURE RESULTS
Charge per appointment of $150 is not between 25 and 100
PL/SQL procedure successfully completed.
```

Execution Results (Fifth Case)

```
Enter doctor's ID:  506
Enter doctor's name:  Ledger
Enter salary per month:  10000
Enter area of specialization:  Orthopedics
Enter date hired (DD-MON-YYYY):  01-jul-03
Enter charge per appointment:  50
PROCEDURE RESULTS
New row added to table
PL/SQL procedure successfully completed.
```

Chapter Summary

Explicit cursors can be used to move through the rows of a table one at a time. A cursor is declared with a SELECT statement to define the active set of rows to be used, a record is declared to hold the row, the cursor is opened, a loop is used to repeatedly fetch a row from the cursor's active set, and then the cursor is closed. With the exception of the cursor declaration, all of these tasks can be handled implicitly through the use of the cursor FOR loop.

Exceptions are used to trap errors rather than to allow the errors to cause a block to crash, ending abnormally. The two categories of exceptions are predefined, such as NO_DATA_FOUND and TOO_MANY_ROWS, and user-defined, such as testing to see that certain business rules are followed when a new row is added to a table. Exceptions are declared in the DECLARE section, raised with the RAISE statement in the executable statement section, and then trapped in the EXCEPTION section.

Exercises

Section A: Explicit Cursors

1. Use a record to store a row from the movie table. Allow the user to specify the movie ID for the row to be retrieved. Then display all movie data in sentence form.

2. Use a record to store a row from the billing table, allowing the user to specify the patient ID. Display the patient's phone number and insurance provider. If the insurance provider is HealthCare, then change it to Equicor. No other providers are to be changed.

3. Declare a cursor that can be used to move through the customer table.

4. Declare a cursor that can be used to move through the names and balances of customers.

5. Declare a cursor that can be used to move through the rows for customers with a 549 phone prefix.

6. Declare a cursor that can be used to move through the IDs, balances, and due dates of customers with past due balances over $20.

7. Declare a cursor that can be used to move through the rows of data on doctors that are also supervisors.

8. Open the cursor that you declared in your solution for problem 3.

9. Open the cursors that you declared in your solutions for problems 6 and 7.

10. Declare and open a cursor that can be used to move through IDs and balances of patients that owe at least $300 and no more than $500.

11. Declare and open a cursor that can be used to move through the IDs, balances, and due dates for customers with balances due in April.

12. Fetch the first row specified by the cursor that was declared and opened in problem 11 (assuming that an appropriate record variable was also declared).

13. Declare a cursor and record that can be used to move through rows of the movie table. Then open the cursor and fetch the first row of values into the record.

14. Declare a cursor and record that can be used to move through the rows of movies with a fee of $1.99 or less. Then open the cursor and fetch the first record. Display the first movie's title.

15. Close the cursor used in the problem 14.

16. Close the cursors used in problems 10 and 11.

17. Movie prices are being increased according to the following guidelines:

Category	Percent of Increase
Kids	5
Family	5
Adventure	10
Drama	10
All others	No increase

Use a cursor to process these changes. Include explicit declaration, OPEN, FETCH, EXIT, and CLOSE statements.

18. Modify the previous problem so that it uses a cursor FOR loop.

19. Charges for past due customer balances are added on the first of each month. Calculations are based on the following chart:

Whole Weeks Past Due	Charge
Less than 2	None
2 to 4	$5
More than 4	$10

Use a cursor to process these changes. Include explicit declaration, OPEN, FETCH, EXIT, and CLOSE statements.

20. Modify the previous problem so that it uses a cursor FOR loop.

Section B: Exceptions

1. Use an anonymous block to retrieve and display the due date for the current rental by the customer whose ID is entered by the user. Use exceptions to handle possible errors of zero rows retrieved and more than one row retrieved.

2. A customer has rented several movies at different times, and needs to know which one is due on a certain day. Use an anonymous block to retrieve and display the title of the movie that is due on the date entered by the user. Also allow the user to enter the customer ID. Use exceptions to handle possible errors of zero rows retrieved and more than one row retrieved.

3. Declare a user-defined exception for an error of a user-entered movie fee below $0.99 or over $3.99.

4. Declare a user-defined exception for an error of a user-entered customer's balance exceeding $150.

5. Raise the exception you declared in problem 3.

6. Raise the exception you declared in problem 4.

7. Trap the exception you declared in problem 3, and print an appropriate error message.

8. Trap the exception you declared in problem 4, and print an appropriate error message.

9. Put it all together: write a script file that allows the user to enter a movie fee. Display the number of movies available for that fee. Use an exception to trap the error of a movie fee below $0.99 or over $3.99.

10. Use an anonymous block to add a row for a new patient to the BILLING table. Allow the user to enter all values. Use exceptions to trap the following errors:

    a. The patient ID is under 100 or over 999.

    b. The patient ID already exists in the BILLING table.

    c. The balance is below zero.

    d. The insurance provider is something other than SIH, BCBS, Military, MediSupplA, HealthCare, or QualityCare.

General Syntax

SQL Statements

```
SELECT [DISTINCT]expression,...
FROM table-name [table-alias],...
[WHERE condition]
[GROUP BY column,...]
[HAVING condition]
[ORDER BY expression [DESC],...];
```

Note—Conditions may involve subqueries

```
INSERT INTO table-name [(column-list)]
VALUES (value-list);

INSERT INTO table-name [(column-list)]
subquery;

DELETE FROM table-name
WHERE condition;
```

Note—Condition may involve subqueries

```
UPDATE table-name
SET column-name = expression
WHERE condition;
```

Note—Condition may involve subqueries

```
COMMIT;
SAVEPOINT name;
ROLLBACK [TO name];

CREATE TABLE table-name
(column-name column-type,...
        PRIMARY KEY (primary-key-column(s)),
        [ FOREIGN KEY (foreign-key column)
                REFERENCES linked-table-name
                ON DELETE CASCADE ] );

CREATE TABLE table-name AS
                subquery;

ALTER TABLE table-name
        ADD column-name column-type;
```

```
ALTER TABLE table-name
        MODIFY column-name column-type;
DROP TABLE table-name;

TRUNCATE TABLE table-name;

RENAME old-name TO new-name;

COMMENT ON TABLE table-name IS 'character string';

Constraints on CREATE TABLE and ALTER TABLE
        CONSTRAINT constraint-name
        PRIMARY KEY(primary-key-column(s))

        CONSTRAINT constraint-name
        FOREIGN KEY(foreign-key-column(s))

        CONSTRAINT constraint-name
        CHECK (condition)

CREATE [OR REPLACE] VIEW view-name
        AS subquery
        [ WITH READ ONLY |
                WITH CHECK OPTION ];

DROP VIEW view-name;

CREATE SEQUENCE sequence-name
        [INCREMENT BY value]
        [START WITH value]
        [CYCLE]
        [MAXVALUE value]
        [MINVALUE value]
        [CACHE value | NOCACHE];

Usage: sequence-name.NEXTVAL
        sequence-name.CURRVAL

DROP SEQUENCE sequence-name;

CREATE INDEX index-name
ON table-name (column-name[, column-name,...]);

DROP INDEX index-name;

CREATE SYNONYM synonym-name
        FOR table-name;

DROP SYNONYM synonym-name;

GRANT object-privilege [(columns)]
        ON object-name
        TO {userID | PUBLIC}
        [WITH GRANT OPTION];
```

```
REVOKE {privilege(s) | ALL}
       ON object-name
       FROM {userID | PUBLIC};
```

Operators

```
Numeric: + - * /
String: ||
Date: + -
Comparison: > < = >= <= <>
Logical: AND OR NOT
BETWEEN expression AND expression
NOT BETWEEN
IN (value-list)
NOT IN
IS NULL
IS NOT NULL
LIKE character-string with wildcard(s)
       wildcards: % _
NOT LIKE
```

Functions (Can Be Nested)

```
SYSDATE
UPPER(string expression)
LOWER(string expression)
INITCAP(string expression)
ROUND (numeric expression [, position] )
TRUNC (numeric expression [, position] )
ADD_MONTHS (date value, number of months)
NEXT_DAY (date value, day of week)
MONTHS_BETWEEN(later-date, earlier-date)
TO_CHAR (numeric expression, format model)
TO_CHAR (date expression, format model)
TO_DATE( string expression, format model)
NVL(first expression, second expression)
COUNT ( * )
COUNT ( [DISTINCT] column-name)
SUM(expression)
AVG(expression)
MIN(expression)
MAX(expression)
```

Operators for Subqueries with Multiple-row Results

```
IN
NOT IN
> ALL   < ALL   >= ALL   <= ALL
> ANY   < ANY   >= ANY   <= ANY
```

SQL Plus Commands

```
ACCEPT parameter-name PROMPT 'prompt string'
       precede parameter-name with & in SQL stmt
SET VERIFY {ON | OFF}
SET FEEDBACK {ON | OFF}
SET PAGESIZE integer-value
SET LINESIZE integer-value
```

```
SET NUMWIDTH integer-value
SET PAUSE {ON | OFF}
SHOW system-variable-name
TTITLE {'character string' | OFF}
        use | within character string for linefeed
COLUMN column-name HEADING 'character string'
FORMAT format JUSTIFY position
        use - at end of line to continue on next line
CLEAR COLUMNS
BREAK ON column [SKIP n],...
CLEAR BREAKS
SET SERVEROUTPUT {ON | OFF}
```

Data Dictionary Views

```
ALL_INDEXES
ALL_OBJECTS
ALL_SEQUENCES
ALL_SYNONYMS
ALL_TABLES
USER_COL_COMMENTS
USER_COL_PRIVS_MADE
USER_COL_PRIVS_RECD
USER_CONSTRAINTS
USER_INDEXES
USER_OBJECTS
USER_ROLE_PRIVS
USER_SEQUENCES
USER_SYNONYMS
USER_TABLES
USER_TAB_COLUMNS
USER_TAB_COMMENTS
USER_TAB_PRIVS_MADE
USER_TAB_PRIVS_RECD
USER_VIEWS
```

PL/SQL Blocks

```
DECLARE
        variable-name  variable-type;
        ...
BEGIN
        statements
[EXCEPTION
        WHEN exception-name THEN
                statement(s);
        [WHEN exception-name THEN
                statement(s);]
        ...
        [WHEN OTHERS THEN
                statement(s);]]
END;
```

Statements

```
Any SQL statement (SELECT must include an INTO clause)
Assignment:  variable := expression;
```

```
DBMS_OUTPUT.PUT_LINE (character-string);

IF condition THEN
        statement(s)
[ELSIF condition THEN
        statement(s)]
...
[ELSE
        statement(s)]
END IF;

WHILE condition LOOP
        statement(s);
END LOOP;

OPEN cursor-name;
LOOP
FETCH cursor-name INTO [variables | record-name];
        EXIT WHEN cursor-name%NOTFOUND;
```

Note—Include various statements to process one row of values here

```
END LOOP;
CLOSE  cursor-name;

FOR record-name IN cursor-name LOOP
```

Note—Include various statements to process one row of values here

```
END LOOP;

RAISE exception-name;

Predefined exceptions: TOO_MANY_ROWS, NO_DATA_FOUND,
        ZERO_DIVIDE, INVALID_CURSOR
```

Variable Types

```
VARCHAR2(max length)
CHAR(length)
NUMBER(max digits, decimal positions)
DATE
tablename.columnname%TYPE
tablename%ROWTYPE
```

Other Declarations

```
CURSOR cursor-name IS select-statement;
User-defined-exception-name EXCEPTION;
```

Appendix

The Two Databases Used in Examples

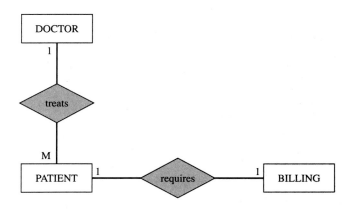

```
SQL> DESC doctor
 Name                                      Null?    Type
 ----------------------------------------- -------- -----------------------
 DOC_ID                                    NOT NULL NUMBER(3)
 DOC_NAME                                           VARCHAR2(9)
 DATEHIRED                                          DATE
 SALPERMON                                          NUMBER(12)
 AREA                                               VARCHAR2(20)
 SUPERVISOR_ID                                      NUMBER(3)
 CHGPERAPPT                                         NUMBER(3)
 ANNUAL_BONUS                                       NUMBER(5)

SQL> DESC patient
 Name                                      Null?    Type
 ----------------------------------------- -------- -----------------------
 PT_ID                                     NOT NULL NUMBER(3)
 PT_LNAME                                           VARCHAR2(15)
 PT_FNAME                                           VARCHAR2(15)
 PTDOB                                              DATE
 DOC_ID                                             NUMBER(3)
 NEXTAPPTDATE                                       DATE
 LASTAPPTDATE                                       DATE
```

```
SQL> DESC billing
Name                                      Null?     Type
---------------------------------------- -------- ----------------------------
PT_ID                                     NOT NULL NUMBER(3)
BALANCE                                            NUMBER(9)
DUEDATE                                            DATE
PHONE                                              VARCHAR2(8)
ADDR                                               VARCHAR2(20)
CITY                                               VARCHAR2(11)
ST                                                 CHAR(2)
ZIP                                                NUMBER(5)
PT_INS                                             VARCHAR2(11)
```

```
SQL> SELECT * FROM doctor;
```

DOC_ID	DOC_NAME	DATEHIRED	SALPERMON	AREA	SUPERVISOR_ID	CHGPERAPPT	ANNUAL_BONUS
432	Harrison	05-DEC-94	12000	Pediatrics	100	75	4500
509	Vester	09-JAN-02	8100	Pediatrics	432	40	
389	Lewis	21-JAN-96	10000	Pediatrics	432	40	2250
504	Cotner	16-JUN-98	11500	Neurology	289	85	7500
235	Smith	22-JUN-98	4550	Family Practice	100	25	2250
356	James	01-AUG-98	7950	Neurology	289	80	6500
558	James	02-MAY-95	9800	Orthopedics	876	85	7700
876	Robertson	02-MAR-95	10500	Orthopedics	100	90	8900
889	Thompson	18-MAR-97	6500	Rehab	100	65	3200
239	Pronger	18-DEC-99	3500	Rehab	889	40	
289	Borque	30-JUN-89	16500	Neurology	100	95	6500
100	Stevenson	30-JUN-79	23500	Director			

```
12 rows selected.
```

```
SQL> SELECT * FROM billing;
```

PT_ID	BALANCE	DUEDATE	PHONE	ADDR	CITY	ST	ZIP	PT_INS
168	15650	21-AUG-03	833-9569	128 W. Apple #4	Jonesboro	IL	62952	SIH
331	300	09-SEP-03	833-5587	3434 Mulberry St.	Anna	IL	62906	BCBS
313	0	01-JAN-04	893-9987	334 Tailgate Ln	COBDEN	IL	62920	Military
816	0	01-JAN-04	833-6654	8814 W. Apple	JONESBORO	IL	62952	SIH
314	100	31-MAR-03	457-6658	445 Oak St.	Carbondale	IL	62901	BCBS
264	35000	11-JAN-03	942-8065	8898 Bighill Drive	HERRIN	IL	62948	MediSupplA
103	4500	01-JUL-03	833-5547	298 Murphy School Rd	Anna	IL	62906	HealthCare
108	0	01-JAN-05	833-5542	334 Pansie Hill Rd.	JONESBORO	IL	62952	HealthCare
943	0	01-JAN-07	529-9963	456 E. Grand #14	Carbondale	IL	62901	Military
847	98000	31-JAN-02	549-8854	6543 W. Parkview Ln.	Carbondale	IL	62901	BCBS
504	0	01-JAN-03	549-6139	6657 N. Allen	Carbondale	IL	62901	QualityCare
809	450	19-JUL-03	687-8852	3345 Hwy 127 N.	Murphysboro	IL	62966	QualityCare
703	225	31-AUG-03	529-8332	909 N. Brown St.	Carbondale	IL	62901	HealthCare
696	79850	15-JUL-03	549-7231	5546 W. James	Carbondale	IL	62901	BCBS
966	98700	15-JUL-03	833-5375	9009 Taylor Ave.	Anna	IL	62906	BCBS
267	0	01-JAN-05	942-3321	6755 US Route 148	HERRIN	IL	62948	QualityCare
307	450	31-AUG-03	457-6967	234 N. Allen	Carbondale	IL	62901	HealthCare
719	0	01-JAN-04	549-7848	867 Henderson St.	Carbondale	IL	62901	HealthCare
439	500	31-AUG-03	833-5541	4456 N.Springer	Anna	IL	62906	QualityCare
315	1500	14-SEP-03	833-6272	404 Williford Rd.	JONESBORO	IL	62952	HealthCare

```
   163        0 01-JAN-04 833-2133 129 Fountain St.     Anna       IL  62906 HealthCare
   669   128450 15-JUL-03 833-6654 353 Tin Bender Rd.   Jonesboro  IL  62952 BCBS
```

22 rows selected.

```
SQL> SELECT * FROM patient;

    PT_ID PT_LNAME         PT_FNAME         PTDOB        DOC_ID NEXTAPPTD LASTAPPTD
---------- ---------------- ---------------- --------- ---------- --------- ---------
       168 James            Paul             14-MAR-97        432 01-JUL-03 01-JUN-03
       331 Anderson         Brian            31-MAR-48        235 01-JUL-03 01-JUN-03
       313 James            Scott            26-MAR-33        235 20-JUL-03 20-JUN-03
       816 Smith            Jason            12-DEC-99        509 15-NOV-03 15-MAY-03
       314 Porter           Susan            14-NOV-67        235 01-OCT-03 01-MAR-03
       315 Saillez          Debbie           09-SEP-55        235 01-JUL-03 01-JUN-03
       719 Rogers           Anthony          01-JAN-42        504 01-NOV-03 01-JAN-03
       264 Walters          Stephanie        26-JAN-45        504 12-DEC-03 12-DEC-02
       267 Westra           Lynn             12-JUL-57        235 02-FEB-04 02-FEB-03
       103 Poole            Jennifer         13-MAY-02        389 01-DEC-03 01-JUN-03
       108 Baily            Ryan             25-DEC-77        235 06-JUN-05 06-JUN-03
       943 Crow             Lewis            10-NOV-49        235 01-JUL-05 01-MAR-02
       847 Cochran          John             28-MAR-48        356 02-DEC-05 01-JAN-02
       163 Roach            Becky            08-SEP-75        235 01-DEC-05 01-JAN-02
       504 Jackson          John             08-NOV-43        235 21-JUL-03 10-NOV-02
       809 Kowalczyk        Paul             12-NOV-51        558 29-JUL-03 19-JUN-03
       703 Davis            Linda            17-JUL-02        509 21-JUL-03 22-MAY-03
       307 Jones            J.C.             17-JUL-02        509 21-JUL-03 22-MAY-03
       439 Wright           Chasity          23-APR-73        235
       696 Vanderchuck      Keith            08-AUG-68        504           15-JUN-03
       966 Mcginnis         Allen            03-MAY-59        504           15-JUN-03
       669 Sakic            Joe              16-SEP-76        504           15-JUN-03
```

22 rows selected.

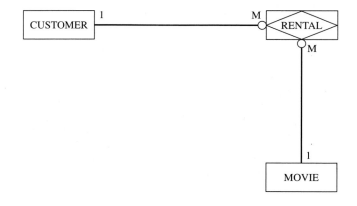

```
SQL> DESC movie
 Name                                                  Null?    Type
 ----------------------------------------------------- -------- -------------
 M_ID                                                  NOT NULL NUMBER(3)
 FEE                                                            NUMBER(3,2)
 TITLE                                                          VARCHAR2(20)
 CATEGORY                                                       VARCHAR2(10)
```

```
SQL> DESC customer
 Name                                               Null?    Type
 -------------------------------------------------- -------- -------------
 C_ID                                               NOT NULL NUMBER(3)
 PHONE                                                       VARCHAR2(8)
 LNAME                                                       VARCHAR2(10)
 FNAME                                                       VARCHAR2(10)
 CURR_BAL                                                    NUMBER(5,2)
 DUEDATE                                                     DATE

SQL> DESC rental
 Name                                               Null?    Type
 -------------------------------------------------- -------- -------------
 C_ID                                               NOT NULL NUMBER(3)
 M_ID                                               NOT NULL NUMBER(3)
 DATE_OUT                                                    DATE
 DUE_DATE                                                    DATE

SQL> SELECT * FROM movie;

      M_ID        FEE TITLE                 CATEGORY
---------- ---------- -------------------- ----------
       204       1.99 City of Angels        Drama
       216       2.99 Ocean's Eleven        Action
       233       2.99 Gone in 60 Seconds    Action
       236        .99 Monsters, Inc.        Kids
       237        .99 E.T.                  Kids
       249       1.99 U-571                 Action
       254       2.99 Road to Perdition     Drama
       255       2.99 Amelie                Foreign
       278       1.99 Monster's Ball        Drama
       287       2.99 A Knight's Tale
       289       1.99 The Royal Tenenbaums  Comedy
       304       2.99 Wild, Wild West       Comedy
       315       2.99 Himalaya              Foreign
       316        .99 Horse Whisperer       Drama
       320       1.99 A Beautiful Mind      Drama
       324       2.99 Field of Dreams       Drama
       325       2.99 Beautiful Life        Foreign
       337       1.99 Grease
       349       1.99 Cast Away             Drama
       354       2.99 O Brother
       355       1.99 Spiderman             Kids

21 rows selected.

            SQL> SELECT * FROM customer;

                C_ID PHONE    LNAME      FNAME      CURR_BAL DUEDATE
          ---------- -------- ---------- ---------- -------- ---------
                 388 549-6730 Woolard    Jessica
                 402 529-8420 St. James  Ellen          4.99 03-JUL-03
                 673 549-8400 Akers      Janet          9.97 23-JUN-03
                 579 549-1234 Poston     Blaine
                 799 549-6711 Ackers     John           1.99 01-JUL-03
```

```
767 453-8228 Ralston    Cheri           14.9 30-JUN-03
133 453-2271 Akers      Leita          20.18 02-JUL-03
239 549-1235 Macke      Greg
400 549-8440 Salyers    Loretta            5 06-JUL-03
701 549-8840 Williams   Tisha             20 28-JUN-03
```

10 rows selected.

SQL> SELECT * FROM rental;

```
      C_ID       M_ID DATE_OUT  DUE_DATE
---------- ---------- --------- ---------
       673        216 30-JUN-03 02-JUL-03
       673        249 30-JUN-03 01-JUL-03
       388        320 01-JUL-03 04-JUL-03
       400        354 29-JUN-03 30-JUN-03
       579        354 01-JUL-03 04-JUL-03
       673        304 29-JUN-03 01-JUL-03
       673        337 01-JUL-03 04-JUL-03
       388        216 30-JUN-03 02-JUL-03
       388        316 01-JUL-03 04-JUL-03
       388        236 01-JUL-03 04-JUL-03
       400        320 01-JUL-03 04-JUL-03
       400        255 29-JUN-03 01-JUL-03
       701        216 30-JUN-03 02-JUL-03
       701        278 29-JUN-03 01-JUL-03
       579        320 01-JUL-03 03-JUL-03
```

15 rows selected.

Index